Disaster Hits Home

Disaster Hits Home

New Policy
for Urban Housing Recovery

M A R Y   C O M E R I O

UNIVERSITY OF CALIFORNIA PRESS
Berkeley   *Los Angeles*   *London*

University of California Press
Berkeley and Los Angeles, California

University of California Press, Ltd.
London, England

© 1998 by
The Regents of the University of California

Library of Congress Cataloging-in-Publication Data

Comerio, Mary C.
    Disaster hits home : new policy for urban
housing recovery / Mary C. Comerio.
        p.   cm.
    Includes bibliographical references (p.   )
and index.
    ISBN 0-520-20780-7 (alk. paper)
        1. Disaster relief—United States.
    2. Housing policy—United States.
    3. Buildings—Natural disaster effects—United
States.   4. Earthquakes—United States.
    5. Hurricanes—United States.   6. Floods—
United States.   I. Title.
    HV555.U6C64   1998
    363.34'8'0973—dc21   98-6245
                                            CIP

Printed in the United States of America
9 8 7 6 5 4 3 2 1

The paper used in this publication meets
the minimum requirements of American
National Standards for Information Sciences—
Permanence of Paper for Printed Library
Materials, ANSI Z39.48-1984.

In Memory of Mario Augustus Comerio

Contents

Illustrations

TABLES

MAPS

Acknowledgments

The research for this book was begun with a Humanities Research Fellowship from the University of California at Berkeley. Three days after I received notification of the award, the Northridge earthquake struck the Los Angeles Basin. Needless to say, the book plan and timeline changed significantly. With grants from the National Science Foundation, the California Governor's Office of Emergency Services, and the James Irvine Foundation to study various aspects of the Northridge housing losses, and with funds from the California Policy Seminar to study earthquake recovery policy in California, I was able to develop detailed analyses of housing and recovery issues that contributed a great deal to the book.

Additional funding for illustration permissions and research assistance came from the University of California Committee on Research. The Center for Real Estate and Urban Economics in the Haas School of Business at the University of California supported summer work on completion of the manuscript. I am deeply grateful to the university for the time and the financial support for this book.

Many individuals, institutions, and agencies were extremely helpful to me in the course of my research. Professor Robin Spence, Director of the Martin Centre for Architectural and Urban Studies at the University of Cambridge, hosted me for a term as a visiting scholar. Robin Spence, Andrew Coburn, and Antonios Pomonis not only opened their archives on Mexico City and other earthquakes, they offered stimulating discussion and ideas throughout my stay.

Many others were extremely helpful in gathering data that were not easily accessible. Kazuyoshi Ohnishi of Kobe University provided and translated damage and census data for the Hyogo and Osaka Prefectures. Dave Morton, librarian at the Natural Hazards Research Center at the University of Colorado at Boulder, and Katie Fromberg, former librarian at the Earthquake Engineering Research Center, went above and beyond the call of duty to help me find obscure documents. Richard Eisner and Sarah Nathe at the California Governor's Office of Emergency Services; Richard Roth Jr. at the California Department of Insurance; Deborah Curtain, Director of Project CHART (Coordinated Hurricane Andrew Recovery Team); Charles Blowers, Chief of the Research Division for the Metropolitan Dade County Planning Department; and Raleigh Close of the Florida Department of Insurance answered countless questions and dug into their files for data and information. Catherine Bauman, Senior Planner for the city of San Francisco, and Charles Eadie, Senior Planner for the city of Watsonville, generously shared data they had collected in Kobe. It is impossible to mention all the names of the many staff at local, state, and federal government agencies who were helpful and kind in providing information and access to internal documents.

Similarly, I owe a debt of gratitude to Michael Stegman, Assistant Secretary of the U.S. Office of Housing and Urban Development; Laurence Zensinger at the Federal Emergency Management Agency; and Barbara Zeidman, former Deputy General Manager of the Los Angeles Housing Department, for their assistance and cooperation.

I owe a great deal to Susan Tubbesing and Marjorie Greene, Executive Director and Senior Planner at the Earthquake Engineering Research Institute. They provided me with many opportunities to integrate housing and recovery concerns with traditional earthquake engineering investigations. Luigia Binda at the Polytechnic of Milan and Gary Hart at the University of California at Los Angeles worked with me to organize two important exchanges between American and Italian engineers and architects. These interactions were crucial to my understanding of American policy in the global context.

Jack Moehle, Vitelmo Bertero, and James Kelley of the University of California Earthquake Engineering Research Center, and several practicing structural engineers, particularly Dan Shapiro, William Holmes, Chris Poland, Ron Hamburger, and Ron Eguchi, always made time for discussion and friendly arguments about design standards and building codes.

Several friends and colleagues helped me immeasurably. John Landis, Professor of City and Regional Planning and my coauthor on two studies of residential recovery after the Loma Prieta and Northridge earthquakes, regularly challenged conventional wisdom and asked hard questions that sent us back to the data files over and over. Francine Rabinovitz, Professor of Public Policy at the University of Southern California and a coauthor on a number of studies, helped me to understand the complex relationship between the regulators and the developers. Catherine Firpo, my research assistant, was simply wonderful. Manuel Castells, Sam Davis, John Ellwood, Kathleen James, Peter May, Stephen Tobriner, and Marc Trieb read various drafts and offered suggestions, encouragement, and support.

Last but not least, I owe special thanks to my family: Michael Teitz, Professor of City and Regional Planning at the University of California, taught me a great deal about research design. He listened to my concerns, he offered suggestions, and he was always insightful and helpful through out two years of what we often called the dinner seminar. Alexandra Teitz was levelheaded and lawyerly when I asked her advice, and Catherine Teitz learned to question the structural integrity of every building she entered. At the age of three, she demanded that her teachers at preschool tell her if the building had shear walls.

CHAPTER ONE

Thinking about Disasters and Housing

Large Asteroid May Hit Earth in Million Years or So. . . .
One consolation, an expert says, is that "we have some time
to prepare."

New York Times, 25 *April 1996*

Since 1989 there has been trouble in paradise: hurricanes in Florida and Hawaii and earthquakes, wildfires, drought, and flooding in California have devastated American households and transformed the formerly placid sunshine states into symbols of nature's destructive forces.

What people think about disasters depends on whether they have been in one. Most people think hurricanes, tornadoes, floods, and earthquakes are unfortunate events that happen to somebody else, somewhere else. What they see on CNN is what they know—mother nature is wreaking havoc, people have been killed, buildings have been damaged. Then it's over. No more news. End of story—except perhaps the occasional tidbits on appeals by the Red Cross for donations or news of a congressional appropriation of disaster relief funds.

For those people who happen to be the victims of disaster, the TV news bears little resemblance to reality, and the long process of rebuilding their lives is just beginning when the reporters and camera crews are going home. For victims, the disaster is more than uprooted trees, downed power lines, damaged homes, damaged businesses, and collapsed freeways: it is a state of shock that begins with the need to find alternatives to the things normally taken for granted—a place to live, a place to shop, a school for the children, a way to get to work, and so on—and continues with the need to find the money to rebuild and replace material losses.

For people who live in California, Florida, or the Carolinas, where the evidence of destruction from recent earthquakes and hurricanes is still visible (see figures 1 and 2), the potential for another disaster is immediate, yet difficult to fathom and easy to deny. Despite all the efforts at public education, people are not voluntarily improving their homes and commercial buildings. Instead, most citizens "come to grips with" the potential for a major earthquake or storm in their community by expressing outrage over the doubling and tripling of their home-owners' insurance premiums, and bemoaning the limitations on payments for earthquake or hurricane damage built into their polices. There is sometimes an equivalent degree of outrage among some who find their policies canceled because their insurer has decided to leave the state entirely.

But most citizens usually temper their anger by repeating what has become the disaster mantra: "Why pay for insurance? If it's that bad, FEMA will come and write us a check."

Yet the mechanisms traditionally used to finance disaster recovery are wholly inadequate to meet the needs of urban populations. The present system of such financing relies on private insurance to compensate the majority of the losses incurred by private individuals. The federal government's primary commitment in disaster recovery funding is to public infrastructure and public buildings. Government programs for supplementary assistance to citizens without insurance have been designed for regularly occurring, garden-variety events such as a tornado in Topeka or a flood in Yuba City—where it is unlikely that more than two or three thousand housing units will be damaged or the total cost of recovery for public and private sector losses will be more than $2 billion.

The present system of disaster recovery *was never* designed to provide as many as three hundred thousand home owners with insurance payments and/or government loans of forty thousand dollars each, and the present system is completely incapable of covering the costs of repairs in fifty thousand apartment units. Yet that is the scale of the loss experienced in Dade County, Florida, after Hurricane Andrew and in Los Angeles, California, after the Northridge earthquake, where $20 to $30 billion was paid to home owners and local governments in each event. The chance that such large payments will ever again be made to a single metropolitan area to finance disaster repairs is virtually nil. Neither the taxpayers nor the insurance industry will stand for it.

This book examines the impact that natural disasters have on housing in urban areas and challenges the conventional methods for evaluating loss and developing recovery programs. But why should low probability events like urban disasters be on anyone's policy agenda? Because America has become a nation of urban and suburban dwellers

Figure 1. Housing Damage, Hurricane Hugo. Hurricane damage to residential structures is caused by high wind and storm surge. (Peter R. Sparks)

Figure 2. Residential Earthquake Damage, Loma Prieta. Earthquake damage to multifamily structures is often caused by the collapse of a "soft" first story. (California Governor's Office of Emergency Services, Earthquake Program)

congregated in hazard-prone coastal regions: there is no doubt that the number of people who will suffer economic hardships as a result of disasters is increasing. For this reason I propose and develop new criteria for determining disaster policy.

WHAT CONSTITUTES A DISASTER?

When is a storm or an earthquake just a passing event? When does it become a federally declared disaster? How do we know if it is a big disaster or just a "regular" one? Not all the violent manifestations of nature—earthquakes, volcano eruptions, hurricanes, floods, tornadoes, wildfires—constitute disasters. Disasters result because individuals and societies build and develop on hazardous soils, on floodplains, or in other hazard-prone areas. An 8.2 magnitude earthquake in an unpopulated area will provide ample research data for geologists and seismologists, but it will not be considered a disaster. When an earthquake of similar magnitude occurs in a densely populated city, the results are catastrophic.

Nonetheless, people have always managed to coexist with natural hazards. All children in grammar school learn about the eruption of Mount Vesuvius and the lost city of Pompeii. They also learn that no matter how many times the volcano erupts, Neopolitans have rebuilt. The local population have never abandoned their homes for a safer environment. Instead, they accept the hazard as part of the life to which they were born. The great disasters in history are chronicled in what might be coarsely termed the "death and dollar indexes." These indexes typically list noteworthy disasters in chronological order or in order of magnitude, the number of people killed, or, in modern times, the dollar value of the losses. They are important in understanding why populations in the developed world, like those in developing counties, are now increasingly at risk.

In the disaster research community, it has been accepted that thousands of people in developing countries will die as a result of earthquakes, hurricanes, floods, and volcanic eruptions. These populations are vulnerable not only because their houses and buildings are poorly built but also because their vulnerability is increased by their poverty, state of health, food supply, and physical and social infrastructure (Anderson and Woodrow 1989, 10–11). By comparison, Americans, Europeans, and the Japanese (that is, inhabitants of the developed world) are considered to be less at risk from disasters because of the quality of their built environment and the sophistication of their infrastructure and support systems.

In recent years, however, the lives lost, the property damage, and the economic dislocation in disasters in the United States and Japan have called these sacrosanct assumptions into question, even though the quality of the built environment in the two countries remains among the best in the world. What has changed? The frequency of events has increased in recent years[1] and, more important, the population in areas vulnerable to natural hazards has increased exponentially. These two critical factors frame the problem addressed in this book: the costs of natural disasters are now too high for individuals and for society as a whole.

Natural hazards of all types affect the United States and other developed nations, but the primary focus of this book is on two types of events: earthquakes and hurricanes. As individual events, they affect more people in more sectors of the economy than any other type of disaster. As stated earlier, while earthquakes in unpopulated regions are not at issue, an earthquake anywhere along the densely developed coast of California will affect thousands. Similarly, hurricanes annually threaten Florida, the Gulf Coast, and much of the eastern seaboard, and these coastal areas are home to more than 50 percent of the American population (U.S. Census 1990).

By contrast, floods are dramatic and threatening events whose damage is largely concentrated in agricultural and transportation sectors. Although there are dozens of examples of vastly destructive floods in American history—the Johnstown, Pennsylvania, flood in 1889, which killed 2,200 people; the Ohio River flood in 1937, which inundated the city of Evansville, Indiana; the 1951 flooding in Kansas City; and repeated flood damage in cities along the Mississippi River—flooding has been largely a rural problem without extraordinary impact on large human settlements (Smith and Reed 1990). It was not until the great midwestern flood of 1993 that property damage from floods and storms soared into the millions of dollars and thousands of people were displaced from their homes. See figure 3. Still, in the 1993 flood, where damage covered thousands of square kilometers across nine states, housing losses represented only about 15 percent of the total loss value (Interagency Floodplain Management Review Committee 1994).

In 1997, massive winter storms and flooding forced the evacuation of the city of Grand Rapids, North Dakota. In California, rising rivers threatened levees throughout the Central Valley, the nation's largest and richest agricultural region. The 1997 storms also demonstrated the potential for a new kind of flood risk—urban development. With the growth of valley cities in the last decade, more than 750,000 residents live within

Figure 3. Flooded Mobile Homes near St. Louis, Missouri, 1993. The Princess Jodi mobile home park in St. Charles County was underwater after the midwestern floods. (Odell Mitchell Jr., *St. Louis Post Dispatch*)

the hundred-year-flood plain. The new development presumes to be protected from floods by the aging levees.

Tornadoes, another type of dramatic natural hazard, are typically formed over the plains states in the central and southern United States. The majority of them impact an area from the Texas panhandle north and east through Indiana, an area largely composed of farms and small towns, and the potential for massive urban damage is small. Wildfires, particularly in areas that meet an urban edge, can cause expensive losses, as was evident in California in the Oakland Hills fire in 1991 and the Malibu and Santa Barbara fires in 1993. Still, these typically affect a limited number of residential structures, and the threat can be mitigated through boundary separations, fire breaks, reduction of brush, limits on vegetation around buildings, and use of fire-retardant building materials.

Manmade disasters range from intentional to accidental, from the destruction of lives and property in war or through terrorism to explosions, fires, or chemical spills. Americans have been spared the physical losses suffered by other nations in wars and civil strife. The unpredictability of such events as the bombing of the World Trade Center in New York in

1994 and the Oklahoma City federal office building in 1995 makes it difficult to include such events in disaster recovery planning.

EARTHQUAKES

Scientists have attempted to collect information about earthquakes since the seventeenth century, but the real advances in science and in engineering design are very recent. Charles Richter first defined earthquake magnitude in 1935. The commonly known Richter scale has been improved in recent years with two similar techniques that measure either the surface wave or the moment magnitude. The surface wave method measures the surface waves generated by an earthquake. This is now the most common measurement because it has the best correlation to surface effects. The moment magnitude scale takes into account the rigidity of the rocks that rupture along the fault, the area of the rupture, and the amount of fault slip due to the rupture. This provides a representation of the amount of energy released in an earthquake and has a more precise meaning for scientists (RMS and FAA 1995).

In general, magnitude is used to describe the approximate strength of an earthquake. In each method, the scales are nonlinear, and a one-unit increase in magnitude represents approximately a thirtyfold increase in energy. A three-unit increase in magnitude, from 5 to 8, would render approximately a 30 x 30 x 30 increase in energy released (Lagorio 1990).

The ability to map earthquake risks and understand their potential hazards changed dramatically with the introduction of the theory of plate tectonics in 1967. This theory asserts that the upper crust of the earth is in constant motion as six major plates and several smaller, minor plates continuously slide over the earth's interior. See map 1. Earthquakes take place as pressure builds, when plates press against each other or one is forced under another.

Seismic risk is a function of (1) hazard, or ground-shaking potential and attendant fault ruptures, landslides, liquefaction, and other impacts; (2) exposure, in terms of public health and safety, depending on the type of buildings, roads, bridges, lifelines, and other structures in the area; (3) vulnerability, in terms of quality of construction; and (4) location, in terms of the number of buildings or the density of development in an area (Lagorio 1990). The urban areas within the "Ring of Fire," the edges of the Pacific Plate, represent the greatest risk in the world, not only because of the level of seismic activity there but also because of the density of development.

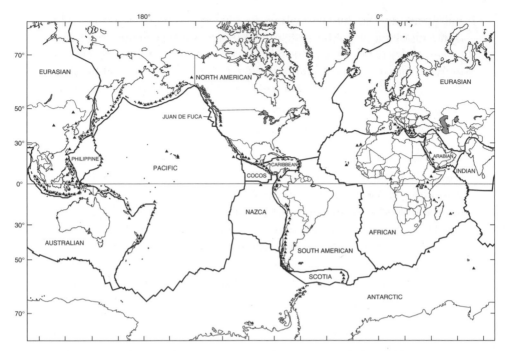

Map 1. World Map of Seismic Zones and Major Crustal Plates. The area surrounding the Pacific Plate is known as the "Ring of Fire." (U.S. Geological Survey)

HURRICANES

Annually, some eighty cyclones, or hurricanes, as they have come to be known in the Western Hemisphere (from the indigenous term "Hura Kan"—winds of the Gods), form over warm tropical waters during the summer months. All hurricanes are dangerous, but some are more so than others. The combination of storm surge and wind determine a hurricane's destructive power. To make comparisons easier, and to allow for consistency in forecasting, the National Oceanic and Atmospheric Association (NOAA) uses the five-point Saffir/Simpson Scale to estimate the property damage and flooding expected along with a hurricane. See map 2.

A category 1 hurricane, the weakest hurricane, has winds of 74 to 95 miles (118 to 152 km) per hour and a storm surge four to five feet (1.2 to 1.5 m) above normal.[2] In a category 1 hurricane there is no real damage to buildings other than unanchored mobile homes. A category 5 hurricane, the most intense hurricane, has winds greater than 155 miles (248

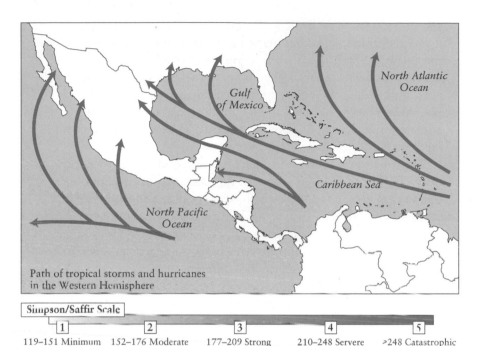

Path of tropical storms and hurricanes
in the Western Hemisphere

Simpson/Saffir Scale

1	2	3	4	5
119–151 Minimum	152–176 Moderate	177–209 Strong	210–248 Servere	>248 Catastrophic

Map 2. Path of Storms with Saffir/Simpson Scale. The five categories are
distinguished by wind speed (expressed here in kilometers per hour) and
damages. Tropical storms and hurricanes in the Western Hemisphere generally
start in the warm waters of the North Pacific Ocean and the Caribbean Sea.

km) per hour and a storm surge greater than eighteen feet (5.5 m) above
normal. In such a storm, one can expect complete roof failure on many
residential and industrial buildings, some complete building failures, and
major damage to the lower floors of all structures within five hundred
yards of the shoreline. Massive evacuations within eight to sixteen kilometers of the shoreline may be required (NOAA 1993).

THE FREQUENCY AND INTENSITY
OF DISASTERS IN THE UNITED STATES AND THE WORLD

After a series of major calamities at the turn of the century, American
urban dwellers have lived for nearly one hundred years without the experience of significant losses from natural or manmade disasters. In the
same time period, there have been 50 to 60 earthquakes around the globe
that have resulted in major loss of life. See table 1. Add to that the damage and loss of life from monsoons, hurricanes, floods, droughts, and

TABLE I
EARTHQUAKES RESULTING
IN MAJOR LOSS OF LIFE SINCE 1900

Year	Locality	Estimated Deaths
1905	Kangra, India	20,000
1908	Messina, Italy	75,000
1915	Avezzano, Italy	29,900
1920	Kansu, China	180,000
1923	Tokyo, Japan	143,000
1932	Kansu, China	70,000
1935	Quetta, Pakistan	60,000
1939	Chillan, Chile	30,000
1939	Erzincan, Turkey	23,000
1960	Agadir, Morocco	12,000
1962	Northwest Iran	10,000
1970	Northern Peru	38,000
1972	Managua, Nicaragua	12,000
1976	Guatemala City	23,000
1976	Tangshan, China	655,000
1985	Mexico City	7,000
1988	Soviet Armenia	25,000
1990	Manjil, Iran	40,000
1993	Maharashtra, India	8,000
1995	Kobe, Japan	6,000

SOURCES: G. L. Berlin 1980; chapter 3 of this book.

the ravages of war—in London alone, a half million housing units were destroyed and 4 million units were damaged in the bombing raids of World War II—that have occurred outside the United States and America's good fortune is evident.

In the western United States, excluding Alaska, there are on average about 18 major earthquakes per year, and more than 120 strong earthquakes per year. See table 2. However, nature does not follow such average patterns on an annual basis. For example, between 1836 and 1911 moderate earthquakes were common in Northern California, and shocks of magnitude 6.5 to 7 occurred every ten to fifteen years. However from 1911 until 1979, no temblors of even moderate magnitude occurred in Northern California (see figure 4) and only 4 moderate earthquakes occurred in Southern California. Since 1980, California has experienced 21 earthquakes greater than magnitude 5.5, of which 7 have been greater than 6.5. See table 3.

Although major hurricanes in the United States have been frequent,

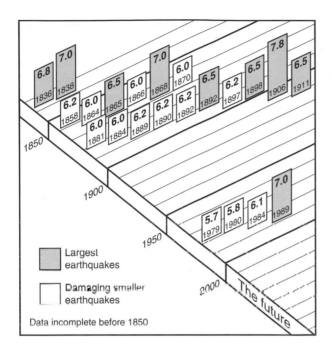

Figure 4. Pattern of Earthquakes in Northern California. After a sixty-eight-year lull, a new period of high earthquake activity began. (U.S. Geological Survey)

TABLE 2

FREQUENCY OF OCCURRENCE AND NUMBER
OF EARTHQUAKES IN UNITED STATES SINCE 1900

Descriptor	Magnitude	Average Annually
Great	8 and higher	1
Major	7–7.9	18
Strong	6–6.9	120
Moderate	5–5.9	800
Light	4–4.9	~ 6,200
Minor	3–3.9	~ 49,999
Very Minor	2–3	~ 1,000/day
Extremely Minor	1–2	~ 8,000/day

Magnitude	Western U.S.	Eastern U.S.	Alaska	Hawaii
8 and higher	1	0	7	0
7–7.9	18	0	84	1
6–6.9	129	1	411	15
5–5.9	611	41	1,886	36
4–4.9	3,171	335	8,362	315

SOURCE: USGS, as reported in *Western States Seismic Policy Council Newsletter* 1996.

TABLE 3

LARGE EARTHQUAKES IN CALIFORNIA, 1900–1994

Location	Date	Magnitude	Deaths	Property Damage ($ Millions)
Northridge	1994	6.8	57	$25,700
Big Bear	1992	6.6	0	$91
Landers	1992	7.5	1	included above
Cape Mendocino	1992	7.1	0	$48
Joshua Tree	1992	6.1	0	$34
Loma Prieta	1989	6.9	63	$7,400
Imperial County	1987	6.6	0	$2
Morgan Hill	1984	6.2	0	$10
Coalinga	1983	6.4	0	$31
Eureka	1980	7.0	0	$2
Owens Valley	1980	6.2	0	$2
San Fernando	1971	6.4	58	$511
Eureka	1954	6.6	1	$2
Kern County	1952	7.7	12	$50
El Centro	1940	7.1	9	$6
Long Beach	1933	6.3	115	$40
Santa Barbara	1927	7.0	unknown	unknown
Santa Barbara	1925	6.3	12–14	$6
San Francisco	1906	8.3	3,000	$400

SOURCE: California Seismic Safety Commission, internal document, 1996.

they have not been particularly destructive over the course of the century until recently. During the period between 1900 and 1992, sixty-one hurricanes (categories 3, 4, and 5) made landfall somewhere along the U.S. Gulf or Atlantic Coasts. While that is an average of two major hurricanes every three years, only those since Hurricane Camille in 1969 have caused property damage exceeding $1 billion dollars at the time of the hurricane (NOAA 1993). See table 4.

In the United States, there are on average thirty disaster events per year that cause short-term problems in various parts of the country (Sylves 1995). Such events are the garden-variety disasters in which federal assistance is requested by and provided to victims of localized floods, tornadoes, and winter storms, as well as earthquakes and hurricanes affecting rural areas—the events in which state and federal emergency management professionals do their jobs according to the standard procedures outlined in disaster relief legislation. These are not the catastrophic disasters that capture media attention and politicize the process of disaster relief, but these events, and the federal procedures developed to respond to them, have formed the basis for policy. Unfortunately,

TABLE 4

TOP TEN DEADLIEST, COSTLIEST HURRICANES, 1900–1994

Deadliest	Year	Category	Deaths
Galveston, Tex.	1900	4	6,000
Lake Okeechobee, Fla.	1928	4	1,836
Florida Keys/S. Tex.	1919	4	600
New England	1938	3	600
Florida Keys	1935	5	408
Audry, La., N. Tex.	1957	4	390
Northeast U.S.	1944	3	390
Grand Isle, La.	1909	4	350
New Orleans, La.	1915	4	275
Galveston, Tex.	1915	4	275

Costliest	Year	Category	Damage ($ Millions)
Andrew: S. Dade Co., Fla.	1992	4	$22,600
Hugo: S.C.	1989	4	$7,000
Frederick: Ala./Miss.	1979	3	$2,300
Agnes: N.E. U.S.	1972	1	$2,100
Alicia: N. Tex.	1983	3	$2,000
Bob: N. Carolina, N.E. U.S.	1991	2	$1,500
Juan: La.	1985	1	$1,500
Camille: Miss., Ala.	1969	5	$1,420
Betsy: S.E. Fla.	1965	3	$1,420
Elena: Miss., Ala., Fla.	1985	3	$1,250

SOURCE: NOAA 1993.

policies that work reasonably well to provide assistance in most ordinary disaster circumstances often create more problems than they solve in catastrophic urban disasters.

FIVE YEARS OF CATASTROPHE

During the fall of 1989, within a month of each other, Hurricane Hugo devastated the South Carolina coast near Charleston and the Loma Prieta earthquake shocked the San Francisco Bay Area. Hugo caused $6.4 billion in damages, nearly half of which reflected damage to residential structures. Nine thousand homes were destroyed, 26,000 were severely damaged, and another 75,000 had some minor damage. Loma Prieta damage was valued at $7.4 billion, of which 45 percent was attributed to private property. Half of that was residential, with about 11,500 units destroyed or severely damaged and 31,000 units sustaining minor damage.

The federal government was stunned by the scale and circumstances of these back-to-back disasters. Simply expanding existing agency missions would not address the problems that emerged. These were the most costly disasters in U.S. history and they were urban. Damages were concentrated in privately owned buildings, largely nonengineered, lightweight wood-frame residential structures. In South Carolina, the combination of private insurance, National Flood Insurance, Small Business Administration (SBA) loans, and Federal Emergency Management Agency (FEMA) grants were sufficient to allow the state to claim 90 percent recovery within one year. However, many of the postdisaster evaluations suggest that the homes of the rural poor and most multifamily structures were largely overlooked, unassisted, and unrepaired. Moreover, engineering and policy reviews raised questions as to why governments and insurance companies allowed low-quality construction with insufficient wind resistance to be built in high-hazard coastal areas (Sparks 1991; Miller 1990).

In California, more than 60 percent of the housing units lost as a result of the Loma Prieta earthquake were in multifamily structures, and overwhelmingly these units were occupied by low-income renters. One year after the event, the single-family homes were largely repaired but no owners of multifamily dwellings had begun construction (Comerio et al. 1994). The frustrations with the uneven treatment of poor and minority victims and the lack of any programs for the repair of multifamily housing led the California Governor's Office of Emergency Services and the National Center for Earthquake Engineering to host a Symposium on Policy Issues in the Provision of Post-Earthquake Shelter and Housing, in October 1992, which coincidentally took place two months after Hurricane Andrew—at the time the latest, most expensive disaster in U.S. history.

Thus, while trying to understand the housing and recovery issues of 1989, the federal government was overwhelmed by another catastrophic urban disaster where the physical damages cost $23 billion, of which 70 percent represented residential structures and contents. Nearly 50,000 housing units were destroyed and, overall, a total of 136,000 units was damaged. Then, in the spring and summer of 1993, nine midwestern states were inundated by a five hundred–year flood on the Mississippi River. The total cost of damage ranged between $15 and $20 billion, and another 50,000 homes were impacted. Six months later, the Northridge earthquake rivaled Hurricane Andrew for the top spot as the costliest disaster in U.S. history, with damages amounting to $25 billion. Once again, half the damage was in residential structures: 60,000 units were destroyed or severely damaged and more than 300,000 had some minor damage. In this disaster 85 percent of the inspected damages were in multifamily structures.

In a five-year period, between 1989 and 1994, five U.S. disasters caused $75 billion in damages, half of which was in residential structures: 200,000 housing units were destroyed or severely damaged, and another 600,000 were damaged and in need of repair. That total number is roughly equivalent to the total number of housing units in the city of Houston or metropolitan Seattle. It is also more than half the number of new housing starts in the United States in a single year.

WHY HOUSING IS CRITICAL

This book focuses on damage caused to housing in earthquakes and hurricanes and on the ways in which individuals and communities are able to recover from those losses. Housing makes up the greatest portion of the building stock in any community. Although we do not have census counts of office, commercial, and industrial buildings as we do for housing, urban planners estimate that housing constitutes about 60 to 70 percent of the buildings in the built environment. From census data we know that there are approximately 112 million housing units in the United States, the majority of which (75 percent) are concentrated in urbanized areas. Florida and California, two highly populous, highly urbanized states at greatest risk from earthquakes and hurricanes, have 17 percent of the nation's housing (U.S. Census 1990).

The American dream is one of home ownership, and American policy from federal tax laws to local land-use planning has always supported that ideal. In fact, single-family homes account for 64 percent of the total housing stock, though not every home is occupied by an owner. Similarly, not every multifamily unit is occupied by a renter. With the invention and promotion of condominiums in the 1970s, new multifamily buildings were constructed for individual ownership of the units, and many existing rental apartment buildings have been converted to condominium ownership. At the same time, many single-family homes are available for rental. Thus, Americans have a housing stock in which about 60 percent of the units are single-family homes, but only slightly more than half of the total units are owner occupied. See table 5.

TABLE 5

CHARACTERISTICS OF HOUSING UNITS
IN HAZARDOUS REGIONS

	United States	East Coast	California	Florida
Total Housing Units	102,200,000	33,400,000	11,200,000	6,100,000
% Single Family	64	61	61	55%
% Owner Occupied	58	57	51	57%

SOURCE: U.S. Census 1990.

Understanding the nature of the housing stock and the potential for housing loss is central to understanding the impact that disasters have on people's lives and on their ability to personally and financially recover. The collapse of the Northridge Meadows apartment complex in Los Angeles in the 1994 Northridge earthquake, which killed sixteen people, made national news headlines. The failure of this relatively modern wood-frame building was significant because it contradicted the popularly held belief that American wood-frame structures are relatively safe in earthquakes. In fact, the damage to Northridge Meadows and other modern wood-frame residential and commercial structures exposed a historic lack of attention to seismic design issues for nonengineered structures in California's building codes (EERI 1995, 443–52; EERI 1996, 125–76; Russell 1994; Comerio 1995).

The American system of wood-frame construction is still one of the safest in the world, but the amount of damage to housing and commercial structures in Los Angeles raised questions about the efficacy of the whole system of building construction (from design standards to construction quality) that allowed so much damage. Building standards are not simply created by architects, engineers, and building officials. The building industry is largely controlled by development and real estate interests who strive to keep costs down. When codes are written, the demands of various interest groups are met, and the building code is a compromise. The standards of best practice are tempered by market forces.

Defining "acceptable" levels of damage from disasters that may or may not occur over the life of a building is one part of the complexity inherent in the regulatory process. In order to keep front-end costs down, modern codes allow for buildings to crack and sustain other types of damage from wind and earthquake forces. Architects and engineers understand that codes are minimum standards designed to protect life, not to guarantee the performance of a building under unusual loading. Building owners and the general public, by contrast, perceive codes as the penultimate measure of safety. The reasonable compromise that allowed nonstructural, non-life-threatening damage as acceptable in the event of strong earthquakes and hurricanes seemed much less reasonable or acceptable when owners of damaged buildings started to add up the costs incurred in recent disasters.

Investment in housing is a huge percentage of the U.S. economy. The mortgage debt on residential property represents 85 percent of the national debt outstanding on all property types. And owner-occupied real estate constitutes 30 percent of the national wealth, more than one and one half times corporate equity (Council of Economic Advisors 1995, 362, 404). For individuals and families, the purchase of a home represents the single largest investment they will ever make, and the single largest asset they will ever hold in their lives. People will spend hours in traffic driving to and from work in order to live in a house they can afford. They will turn down high-paying, high-status jobs if the housing in the area does not suit their families' needs. Most of a family's major financial decisions are tied to home ownership for years after the initial purchase. Home equity loans allow people the use of their asset to finance everything from cars to vacations to college tuition.

For the investors in rental housing, ownership is a business with a high initial investment, expenses, debt service, and, they anticipate, a reasonable profit. Rental housing is often perceived as something for the young or for those too poor to purchase a home, although, in fact, rental housing serves almost half the nation's households, providing for a variety of needs in the market for all ages and all income groups. Rental housing is a stable and important sector of the housing marketplace.

In short, housing is important not only as a key sector in the nation's financial infrastructure but also in the social infrastructure of cities. Prospective residents choose houses and neighborhoods not only by price but also by the quality of schools; proximity to jobs; and availability of transportation, services (such as day care and health care), parks, shops, and other social amenities. Owners and renters alike are attached to their neighborhood. At a personal level, they are familiar and comfortable with the grocers and dry cleaners and other neighbors in the community. At a functional level, their location in the region serves their financial and personal needs.

Although grossly oversimplified, this description of housing as a key sector in the built environment and a complex and highly stratified market is intended to underscore the relationship between disasters and hous-

ing markets. How Americans finance, build, own, and insure housing influences the type of losses caused by disasters as well as their capacity to
recovery, socially and financially, from disasters.

WHAT HAPPENS AFTER A DISASTER?

In the event of a major disaster, what happens afterward follows a fairly
predictable path. The first stage is the emergency response. Fires are put
out. Searches are conducted for the injured and the dead. Victims are
rescued; triage operations are set up in hospitals to attend to the injured.
Those without food or shelter are directed to predetermined public buildings that have been designated as shelters, but many fend for themselves
in backyards and parks. Victims and emergency service providers alike
try to get some information on the extent of the damage. The process
may be slow if communications are down, power is out, and road networks are interrupted. At the same time, teams of volunteers, government officials, and technical experts pour into the area to assess the damage and organize the relief efforts.

As the crises of the immediate postdisaster period are brought under
control, the two most pressing needs are (1) to restore power and lifeline services, clear roads of debris, and reroute traffic until infrastructure
repairs can be made; and (2) to move displaced victims out of the shelters and tent camps and into some form of temporary housing. The first
activity is largely within the control of government agencies and utility
companies; the second involves a complex process of interactions among
volunteers, victims, and government officials.

In order to determine the extent of the damage to the housing stock,
city building officials must inspect the damaged buildings to determine
which units are unsafe for occupancy and which are habitable. This preliminary estimate of damage is then used by a variety of charities, social
service agencies, and federal government disaster management officials
to determine whether there is sufficient alternative housing available in
existing vacant apartments, or whether they will need to place victims
in hotels and mobile homes. Similarly, the inspection data are used to
encourage those in shelters or tent camps to go back to their homes if
the damage is only cosmetic.

The management of this complex but relatively logical process is done
military style, with a hierarchy of issues and a hierarchy of command.
Unfortunately, disasters tend to be more like terrorism than conventional
warfare; that is, chaos and confusion are high, and there are no rules of

engagement to govern individual behavior. Victims are in shock and need direction; volunteers and emergency professionals work eighteen-hour days, madly trying to simultaneously understand the situation and provide assistance. While the first week after any large disaster is utter chaos, in recent years the sense of urgency has been compounded by the advent of a new player on the scene—the TV news camera.

Disasters have become big-time news, filling living rooms with images of nature at its most dramatic, flattened or falling buildings, collapsed roadways, and, of course, a relentless stream of images of victims in shock and tears. Then, when the pathos of human suffering becomes stale, reporters begin interviewing victims who demand assistance and blame the government for not helping them fast enough. This is the "CNN-ization" of disasters. It personalizes disasters and leads to their politicization, as well as to incredible pressures on emergency responders, volunteers, and government officials to act. And the relentless presence of the cameras often leads to what has been called "the camcorder policy process" (NAPA 1993, 18). Decisions on recovery aid and funds for temporary housing for victims are made without real information about the true nature of the damages (and clearly without information on the market conditions of housing in the area) in order to satisfy the need to appear to be doing something.

Whatever the local circumstances, government agencies pull the existing aid programs off the shelf and begin disbursing funds for home repairs and personal losses, while simultaneously disbursing funds for temporary housing and trying to get an accurate count of the number of buildings and housing units actually damaged. In practice, what this means is that assistance programs are generally based on what happened in the last disaster, not on the unique conditions of the damage, the market, or the building stock in the current crisis.

In the first two weeks after a disaster, thousands of decisions are made by exhausted volunteers and government workers under pressure to do all they can. At the same time, thousands of promises are made by politicians in front of TV cameras. Victims who have lost everything, and victims who have lost a few of grandma's dishes, all expect to be made whole, and many in the latter category secretly hope to do better. After the first week, the cameras leave, and the process of finding temporary housing for homeless victims is completely muddled with the settling of insurance claims and the filing of applications for government loans and grants.

Nobody actually knows how much damage is really out there, how many people are really homeless, or how much money is really needed, but the process moves forward until two years later when insurers are shocked by the number of claims they have paid, and even Democrats are shocked by the amount of government spending required for disaster assistance. After the series of recent disasters between 1989 and 1994, governments and insurers have agreed that the cost of natural disasters is just too high. Each wants to find a way to limit its exposure, which means that government would like private insurance to shoulder more of the cost of disaster recovery, and the insurance industry would like government to protect it from catastrophic losses.

In fact, neither the government nor the insurance industry has a clear grasp of whether the amount of funds expended in any disaster has been appropriate to the damage sustained. Since there is no accurate review of damages in the first place, there is nothing to measure costs against. Instead, the standard procedure is to sum up insurance claims and government expenditures and call this sum the amount of damage. Then, the sum of expenditures becomes the calibration for estimating the potential damage from the next disaster. In view of this, it is not surprising that recovery costs continue to rise, and that insurers increasingly find it easier to leave a market than to attempt to raise premiums to cover their potential risks.

The problems of insurance availability and the increased cost of disaster recovery are real, but the source of the problem has not been fully identified. It is true that greater urban development in hazard zones means greater exposure. It is not true that past expenditures are accurate predictors of future losses—unless one assumes that all the bad management and bad decision making in past disasters will inevitably be carried forward.

CHALLENGING THE CONVENTIONAL WISDOM
FOR MEASURING LOSS AND DISPENSING RELIEF

Aside from the scientific measures of earthquake movement or hurricane wind speeds, the most common measure of disaster intensity is the death toll. Historically, the cost in lives was a true measure of a disaster's impact on a community. This measure is still accurate in rural areas and developing countries, where building loss does not represent a significant investment. However, in cities and in developed countries the value of the building and infrastructure loss is an important measure of the impact of a disaster. Unfortunately, what ought to be a straightforward count of people killed and buildings damaged never is. In the chaos and confusion following a major disaster, bodies may not be found, missing persons may not be accounted for, and ballpark estimates of damage are never checked for accuracy. In addition to the technical difficulties in accurately representing disaster losses, local businesses and governments may not want to acknowledge the full extent of the loss.

For these reasons, accurate representations of disaster loss are difficult under the best of circumstances, and they are subject to politics of information. Housing losses in four recent American disasters and in two cities outside the United States are discussed in detail in chapters 2 and 3. As we will see, what is striking in each of these case studies is the discrepancy between the estimated number of damaged housing units and the numbers of households seeking housing assistance and/or insurance payments for housing repairs. In each of the American cases, the number of single-family homes receiving either public recovery assistance or private insurance settlements is at least three times greater than the estimated number of losses. Further, the lion's share of all recovery money is targeted to single-family homes, even when the losses are predominantly in multifamily structures.

This means that neither the initial estimate of damaged housing units, nor the final tally of public and private recovery spending, is accurate, because of what they do not include. At the front end, damage estimates tend to focus on the most serious damage, excluding a significant portion of the minor damage, such as cracks in walls or driveways, broken windows, water-soaked carpets, and other nonstructural damage. But because home owners are likely to carry disaster insurance and/or qualify for government programs, when it comes to collecting on insurance or gaining access to government low-interest loans they are likely to make claims for damage, no matter how small. Owners of multifamily buildings with major and minor damage are less likely to have insurance or qualify for government assistance. These owners rely primarily on private financing for repairs, and their costs never appear in the "value of loss" estimates based on insurance claims.

California and Florida have succumbed to pressures for state government participation in disaster insurance for home owners. At the same time, government programs, which have provided assistance to record numbers of disaster victims in recent years, want to reduce costs. But neither the insurance industry nor the government fully understands how to project future losses, because the estimating models are based on inaccurate damage estimates and unrepresentative disaster recovery costs.

Reports on disaster losses are typically produced by engineering researchers interested in specific kinds of building or infrastructure fail-

ures. These reports contain examples of structural losses (e.g., roof failures in wood structures caused by hurricane-force winds or the collapse
of the soft first stories of structures in earthquakes), but they do not contain statistics on building loss indicating use, age, or construction type.
Thus, despite the apparent sophistication of loss estimation models based
on the Geographic Information System (GIS), these provide only a crude
picture of losses in a region, not a complete estimate of the total value
of the losses.

To improve government disaster assistance policy and private disaster insurance, the first task is to reevaluate the measurement of housing
loss. A more accurate method would include a variety of measures: detailed information on the types of housing damaged; the portion of damaged units that are uninhabitable; the concentration of damage; the value
of the loss; the social and economic circumstances of victims; as well as
local housing market characteristics. Together, these factors provide better information on the short- and long-term needs of disaster victims,
specifically the availability of alternative shelter and access to capital for
rebuilding.

WHAT OUGHT TO HAPPEN AFTER DISASTERS

Despite the chaos, despite the confusion, it is imperative that emergency
and relief activities be complete before decisions about recovery assistance are made. There is no question that the federal government has a
role in managing and funding emergency response and relief efforts in
catastrophic disasters. No taxpayer would begrudge help to another community for rescuing victims trapped in buildings or cars. No taxpayer
would begrudge the help of a few months' or even a year's worth of temporary housing assistance to victims whose homes were destroyed.

When it comes to recovery—that is, when it comes to providing financing for the repair of public infrastructure—it is imperative to move
quickly. But when it comes to damaged private houses, there is no reason to begin doling out public moneys three days or a week after the
event. The actors in dispensing public funds for recovery assistance include some of the federal agencies involved in relief operations, as well
as local housing officials, who are already active participants in the temporary-housing assistance process. Others, like the SBA, are not part of
the emergency process. All of these government entities, along with insurance companies and banks, depend on having information on the num-

ber and types of units damaged before they assess the scope of the problem and estimate the need for funding.

If recovery lenders could wait a month or two, owners would have the time to assess their actual damages, insurers and lenders would have time to better understand the extent of their exposure, and government could evaluate whether additional federal assistance is really necessary. This assumes there would be some process whereby private and public recovery lenders share information on claims inquiries and damage, and it assumes that policies would be in place that establish eligibility for both insurance and government lending.

WHY RECOVERY IS CRITICAL

The frequency and intensity of disasters since 1989 reopens the question of how society organizes disaster response and pays for recovery assistance. We cannot continue under the present model. Insurers are no longer willing to provide affordable coverage for full replacement value on every house in areas of high risk. They would rather leave the market entirely. At the same time, government cannot take on the role of a full-service disaster-recovery lender. Further growth of government spending in disaster recovery raises the issue of whether there should be any public assistance for private losses.

The federal government plays an important role in handling natural disasters, providing early warning for storms and floods when possible, emergency assistance, and resources to help in the long-term recovery, particularly for public infrastructure. But the government is only one of a complex set of institutions that the nation utilizes for dealing with natural disasters. Individuals and businesses use commercial insurance and self-insurance to protect against financial losses, and they can take advantage of damage prevention technology to reduce the potential for damage. State and local governments play a critical role through land use controls and the enforcement of building codes, as well as through regulation of insurance markets. State and local governments are also the first on the line in postdisaster response and relief activities. In providing funds for recovery, the government, insurance, and financial sectors are highly interdependent, and they need to recognize the changing nature of their relationship.

Together, insurance and government have paid out billions in disaster recovery assistance, but neither fully recognizes the importance of more careful evaluations of past claims and the importance of mitigation in reducing future costs. Mitigation has been given lip service as the national strategy for reduction of disaster losses, but no substantial policies have been put forward to tie mitigation to the cost and availability of insurance or the availability of public assistance for disaster recovery.

At the same time, all evidence indicates that insurance markets are not functioning well. Particularly in the area of home-owners' insurance, losses by primary insurers and reinsurers have led insurers to raise premiums, restrict coverage (e.g., to exclude wind damage from home-owners' policies along the Florida and Texas coasts), or pull out of markets by refusing to write new policies or renew existing policies. In California and Florida, insurance covering earthquake or hurricane damage is only available by newly established state-operated risk pools providing very limited coverage.

The current problems of insurance availability and affordability have occurred because insurance companies have consistently underestimated risk, in part because there have been so few major disasters in the past forty years, and in part because insurers assumed that the risk was spread among a small number of consumers purchasing such coverage. In addition, the traditional measures of disaster losses have consistently underrepresented the true cost of repairs.

CRITERIA FOR A GOOD HOUSING RECOVERY POLICY

Obviously, many factors contribute to a community's capacity to successfully rebuild after a disaster—political and economic conditions, the nature of the state's role, the regulatory system, and the disaster management system (Greene and Pantelic 1991)—but the most important factor is the system of finance for housing repairs. One approach to recovery is for a government to take on the entire program of rebuilding. This is rarely done, however, except in cases of massive devastation, such as in the city of Tangshan, China, after it was leveled by an earthquake.

In developing countries, various international aid organizations assist the government with financing and technical assistance to build replacement housing when a particular area has been hard hit. This somewhat paternalistic model, developed and applied after a number of disasters in the 1970s, assumes that individual victims are too poor and too devastated to rebuild on their own. For example, international relief organizations financed and oversaw the construction of new housing in downtown Managua after a devastating earthquake, replacing some 40 percent of the city's housing stock. The Italian government committed funding and expertise to rebuilding towns in the Friuli region in the north and the Campania-Basilicata region in the south when scores of towns were destroyed by a series of earthquakes.

Although well intentioned, the funds were in many cases misappropriated, if not stolen, and the housing built was often inappropriate to the climate, social, and economic conditions in the affected community. In response to criticism, the "infusion of aid" model was modified in the 1980s to mix the provision of replacement housing by outside contractors with locally managed self-help building programs, as aid organizations recognized that large-scale interventions often caused other difficulties.

In the United States and other developed countries, where standards of living and personal wealth are higher, no one would expect an outside entity to rebuild the homes of disaster victims. Home owners and businesses are expected to insure their investments against catastrophic losses or borrow from banks to finance property repairs. Those without access to other resources can look to the American Red Cross and other charities, which were formed to provide help in such cases. In the event of a major disaster, the federal government is expected to furnish an infusion of capital to assist in the repair of public infrastructure. Over time, however, the government has taken on the additional role of providing supplementary assistance to citizens for emergency relief and home repairs. Such relief efforts were instituted in the 1930s, when a series of floods devastated Depression-weary citizens and overwhelmed the capacity of the Red Cross and other charities to provide for the victims. Public assistance programs for private losses were formalized in the 1950s and expanded after two devastating disasters, the 1964 Alaska earthquake and Hurricane Camille in 1969.

Because recovery from disasters presumes the existence of financing for building reconstruction, the study of recovery has tended to focus on the mechanics of planning and public works necessary with any large volume of construction. Today, the focus of any study on disaster recovery is bound to include the problems of funding the construction. After numerous natural disasters in the 1980s, as well as refugee problems created by civil strife, the international Red Cross and other relief organizations began to have difficulty raising funds from a donation-weary public. In the same period, United Nations aid organizations were also spread thin as they attempted to cope with natural and manmade disasters. In developed nations, the enormous cost of several recent disasters has brought changes in the availability, and doubts about the future viability, of disaster insurance. The current limitations on the availability of aid and insurance create new, long-term financial risks for citizens and governments in disaster-prone regions.

One approach to disaster recovery would be to simply let the marketplace sort out the winners and losers after a disaster, focusing government and charitable aid only on the emergency period. Individuals would then make decisions to stay in or leave an area, to rebuild housing or not, based on their jobs and their personal financial circumstances. After a disaster, a region might grow with new investment or shrink if people and businesses decided to relocate rather than rebuild. In this circumstance, a government might decide to intervene in financing rebuilding efforts or not, depending on the impacts to particular market sectors or the economic significance of the region.

Another approach would be to use insurance or government programs to provide very limited assistance to victims, for building materials, tools, or the replacement of personal possessions. This approach accepts the notion that in disasters private losses are too expensive and too unpredictable to be fully covered by insurance or government programs, but that limited assistance will help speed individual actions within the market.

If such hard-hearted market-driven models are unacceptable in a society, then private or public disaster recovery requires a reliable source of capital to finance building repairs. In order to guarantee that financing will be available in future disasters, the policies and programs developed in the twentieth century will need to be redesigned to accommodate the new scale of risk in urban centers.

How do we judge the success of any disaster recovery process and how do we set criteria for evaluating a financing program? The success of any recovery effort should be judged by its ability to enable a community to temporarily rehouse disaster victims while moving quickly on repairs and reconstruction. Five criteria define the process:

1. Losses must be manageable; that is, the volume of damage should be limited by predisaster hazard mitigation.

2. Rebuilding and/or repairs must take place within two years.

3. Financing must be available for all economic sectors and housing types.

4. Public or private program funds must not exceed the cost of damage.

5. Public and private program funds must complement, rather than substitute for or duplicate, each other.

To meet these ideals probably requires that multiple (i.e., redundant) systems of public assistance and private insurance are in place, that predisaster mitigation is effective, and that the patterns of damage in a particular event influence the patterns of recovery assistance made available.

A good disaster recovery program starts with a serious commitment to reducing future damage through preparedness and mitigation. Lowering the cost of recovery by lessening the potential for damage is the single most effective disaster recovery policy. Improved mitigation benefits insurance companies through lower payouts, taxpayers through lower program costs, and renters and home owners through reduced damage.

A good financing program for repair of disaster damage would assess the overall impact and get the funds into use within two years. Delays have physical and economic consequences. If a house or apartment building is damaged to the point that it is uninhabitable, the longer it sits unrepaired the more those repairs are going to cost. There will be further damage and deterioration from a combination of vandalism, crime, rodents, and weather. Moreover, inflation as well as the lost income from vacancy will add to the increase in repair costs. If properties are habitable, minor damage claims should still be settled quickly, to avoid inflationary costs, even if the owners want to delay the repairs.

To create an expedient means of disbursing recovery funds to owners of both single-family homes and multifamily structures requires that some hard work be done before another urban disaster strikes. In recent disasters, the majority of insurance payments and government grants and loans have benefited owners of single-family homes with minor damage. To insure that the spatial distribution of assistance matches the spatial distribution of damage, some form of disaster insurance must be available to all housing sectors and be realistically priced. At the same time, before providing such coverage both insurance companies and government programs ought to be asking what that property owner has done to lessen the potential for damage.

Whether public or private, precious rebuilding funds should not be wasted. Insurance claims and government grants and loans provided during past disasters need to be reviewed to distinguish the actual cost of repairs from refinishing and redecorating, and from the replacement of contents and personal possessions, which may or may not have been impacted by the disaster. A functioning disaster recovery program may not be able to replace carpets and televisions in every damaged housing unit, but it should be able to make those units habitable.

Finally, public disaster recovery programs should be targeted to two key areas. First, these programs should continue to take responsibility for the reconstruction of the public infrastructure, such as roads, schools, hospitals, government buildings, and public utilities. Second, they should provide reconstruction funding for victims who, by virtue of low incomes or some form of market failure, cannot afford to purchase private insurance. For example, owners of housing affordable to low- and moderate-income groups may not be able to purchase insurance because they cannot cover its cost through higher rents. Home owners, condominium owners, or market-rate apartment owners with access to insurance should not receive government assistance for disaster repairs.

Overall, an ideal disaster-rebuilding policy must minimize the potential for damage through serious and effective mitigation programs and, when damage occurs, link property owners to reliable sources of recovery capital. Every technical report on damage to housing in earthquakes and hurricanes makes it clear that much of the damage could have been avoided through mitigation and preparation. Nonetheless, preparedness officials have not been able to educate the public, and policymakers have not been able to legislate action. Motivating a substantial number of home owners and apartment owners is likely to require a direct financial incentive in the form of a state or federal tax credit—itself a powerful incentive for mitigation, but one that needs to be coupled with a clear message that no further federal assistance will be available for disaster repairs to those with access to insurance. Thus, the primary goal of postdisaster public policy should be to increase the utilization of private insurance. The more that insurers can do to fairly insure home owners, renters, and apartment and commercial-building owners, the better, since only the private insurance industry has access to the volume of capital required to finance postdisaster repairs and reconstruction.

Any new policy regulating government assistance or private insurance must address the true cost of urban housing recovery. This book is structured to build the case for a new approach to disaster policy. Chapter 2 reviews the methods used to measure and define disaster losses and the problems inherent in accurately representing those losses. The chapter includes four detailed case studies of housing impacts resulting from Hurricanes Hugo and Andrew and the Loma Prieta and Northridge earthquakes. The level of damage and the cost of repairs following these four disasters have changed our understanding of disaster losses and called into question our ability to finance repairs.

Chapter 3 evaluates various approaches to recovery and describes recovery experiences after earthquakes in Mexico City and Kobe, Japan. These two disasters in major urban centers have much in common with American urban disasters, but Mexico and Japan each employed a very different approach to the financing of disaster recovery.

Chapter 4 develops a catastrophe index—that is, a model for determining when a natural disaster has created a housing crisis—and presents an alternative method for measuring housing loss and evaluating recovery, based on the four cases studies reviewed in chapter 2. In addition, the Mexico City and Kobe experiences are compared to a scenario for a magnitude 7.0 earthquake on the Hayward fault in the San Francisco Bay Area, in order to illustrate the impact of a future disaster without adequate recovery resources.

Chapter 5 looks at the evolution of U.S. disaster assistance policies, and the problems that arise in large-scale urban-centered disasters. The expansion of federal programs in response to media attention focused on recent disasters has created a heightened sense of expectation on the part of the public. At the same time, insurers have fled the Florida and California markets, forcing the states to create programs to underwrite disaster insurance. The result is a situation of extreme vulnerability for cities on the East and West Coasts, which have been left with no rea sonable strategy to finance future losses.

Chapter 6 rethinks the disaster recovery problem, compares market and planning solutions, and proposes a strategy for flexible, fast, and fair recovery financing. Based on the five criteria enumerated above, the chapter and the book argue for a strategy of shared responsibility with government incentives for mitigation, private insurance for private ownership, and limited, specially targeted public assistance for low-income populations. Ultimately, the book argues that strategies to protect the housing stock from potentially devastating disaster damage, and a healthy and functioning insurance industry with policies in place to quickly finance disaster-related repairs, are critical to maintaining the viability and economic vitality of American cities on the East, West, and Gulf Coasts.

CHAPTER TWO

Measuring Housing Loss and Recovery in Recent American Disasters

We have been using 56 [as the official casualty count] but
I see the federal report uses 57, so I guess that is what we
should use . . . [pause]. . . . I know damn well FEMA paid
for more than 300 funerals.

An exasperated state employee
after the Northridge earthquake

In 1989, within one month of each other, the twin disasters Hurricane
Hugo and the Loma Prieta earthquake destroyed nearly twenty-nine
thousand housing units and damaged three times that many more in
urban and rural areas on the South Carolina coast and in the San
Francisco Bay Area. Estimated losses totaled $6 billion for Hugo and
$7 billion for Loma Prieta. Then, in 1992, Hurricane Andrew dam-
aged more than one hundred thousand units in south Dade County,
Florida, and economic losses tallied to $25 billion. Two years later, the
Northridge earthquake centered in Los Angeles, California, caused
similar amounts of housing damage and economic losses.

The scale of the losses in each of the four disasters, which will be examined in detail in this chapter, captured national attention and reshaped
local and national emergency response procedures. In order to clarify the
real impact of the losses and the potential for recovery with or without
public assistance, each case study will review the extent of damage, and
the concentration of damage in specific geographic areas and portions
of the housing stock, as well as market conditions and the financial characteristics of affected properties.

THE PROBLEM OF MEASURING LOSS

LIVES LOST

In all disasters, losses are measured in terms of lives lost, buildings and infrastructure affected, and the dollar value of economic losses resulting from the actual damage, as well as secondary losses such as business interruption or jobs displaced. Of the three measures, the number of deaths ought to be the most obvious and straightforward, except for the quibbling over the individual whose heart attack may or may not have been brought on by the disaster experience. In fact, counting casualties after a disaster is fraught with technical and political problems. Have all the casualties been found? Did the disaster cause a death? Will officials be held responsible for inadequate safety standards? Will businesses and financial institutions reinvest in the region? These and other uncertainties lead to disagreements in the estimation and publication of official casualty counts.

This problem is exemplified in the controversy caused by a recent book on the 1906 earthquake and fire in San Francisco. See figure 5. In *Denial of Disaster,* the authors use archival records and eyewitness accounts to suggest that the actual number of casualties caused by the earthquake was 3,000, instead of the 498 officially reported dead. The author contends that the cover-up was intentional to limit the shock to East Coast insurance companies and bankers and to ensure that funds and settlers would continue to flow west (Hansen and Condon 1989).

The casualty count has been called into question in some recent large disasters as well. In one case, the great Tangshan earthquake in China in 1976, the whole city was virtually leveled, and a true count of lives lost will never be known. Although official estimates put the number of casualties at 250,000 (Chen et al. 1988), many experts who surveyed the loss put the number substantially higher—650,000 is often quoted (Arnold and Lagorio 1987; Arnold 1990). Similarly, in the former Soviet Armenia the 1988 earthquake destroyed 80 percent of Leninakan and large portions of the town of Spitak, and it leveled many villages. Reported numbers range from 58 to 360 villages destroyed, and while the official death count is 20,000, the number may well be higher (Novosti 1989; Rost 1990; Ghahraman and Yegian 1993; Kosowatz 1990). Given that these large-scale disasters occurred in relatively remote areas, the discrepancies in estimations of casualties are not surprising.

However, there have been circumstances in urban areas where dis-

Figure 5. Fire and Earthquake Damage, San Francisco, 1906. The fire following the earthquake burned more than five hundred city blocks. (California
Governor's Office of Emergency Services, Earthquake Program)

crepancies between official and unofficial counts of lives lost cannot be
easily explained as technical difficulties. In the 1985 Mexico City earthquake, the damage to mid-rise and low-rise buildings was extensive in
the old center of the city. See figure 6. Official government reports suggest that damage was concentrated in three of the federal district's sixteen wards, with some fifty-seven hundred buildings destroyed or damaged and 7,000 people dead (Garcia-Perez 1986; Anaya-Santoyo 1986;
Armillas-Gil 1986). Newspaper accounts from Mexico City contradicted
these official numbers. Even one year after the event, reporters were estimating the number of housing units lost at more than double the official estimate and the number of deaths as high as 30,000 (Burt 1986;
Gaddis 1986; Kultenbrouwer 1986).

How can such large discrepancies exist in an urban area with government officials and outside agencies capable of verifying the numbers of
lives lost and buildings damaged? In the specific case of Mexico City, which
is discussed in the next chapter, the loss of two major hospitals and the
large number of building collapses made loss and casualty estimates
chaotic and difficult. The scale of the disaster was not solely responsible
for the counting problem, however. In the midst of an oil crisis and other

Figure 6. Damage to High-
Rise Residential Building,
Mexico City, 1985. Residents
of Tlatelolco and other large
public housing projects were
displaced by the massive
damage. (California Governor's Office of Emergency
Services, Earthquake
Program)

economic difficulties, Mexican officials were eager to downplay the impact of the earthquake on the capital city.

BUILDINGS DAMAGED

Although counting the number of damaged buildings in any given area
also appears to be a simple exercise, in actual postdisaster circumstances,
difficulties emerge. For example, a powerful hurricane may level an entire community, as Hurricane Andrew did to the southernmost communities of Dade County near the Homestead Air Force Base. In order to
count the damaged buildings, local officials had to reconstruct a picture
of what was there before, from maps, building permits, tax rolls, utility
records, and other documents. Of course, this had to be done at the same
time that government officials were coordinating emergency services and
relief efforts. At best, the local jurisdiction could estimate the number
and types of buildings destroyed, based on tax rolls compared with those
of similar blocks with similar uses and densities.

Moreover, in all disasters, big and small, what gets counted as "damage" depends on who is counting and for what purpose. Typically, there are two types of postdisaster inspections in American disaster events. First a "windshield survey" of the areas impacted is done in the first twenty-four hours after the event. With this method state and local officials assess the damage and decide whether to ask for a federal disaster declaration. After the Northridge earthquake in 1994, the California Governor's Office of Emergency Services used a computer simulation program, designed to estimate losses based on measured ground motion, to obtain an instant assessment of the damage. At the time of the earthquake, the simulation program (based on Geographic Information System software technology) was under development by EQE International, and the Northridge earthquake was the first disaster in California in which losses were estimated and mapped by computer and field-checked by inspectors as part of the first reconnaissance damage assessment (Comerio, Landis, and Firpo 1996; Eguchi et al. 1996). Also within the first twenty-four hours, the American Red Cross conducts its own damage assessment in order to estimate the potential number of victims in need of food and sheltering.

In most urbanized areas, local jurisdictions organize a safety assessment within the first few days after the event. Typically, these are arranged by local building departments using their own staffs of inspectors and engineers as well as volunteer engineers and architects provided by state professional associations. The inspections, which are separate from the immediate disaster response of putting out fires and rescuing injured victims, are part of the first wave of disaster response and are completed quickly, within a week of the disaster. They serve two purposes: First, inspectors identify hazardous situations that could be a threat to health and safety. Second, they use the inspection data to provide a more complete damage assessment that becomes part of the appeal for state or federal assistance. During postdisaster inspections in most parts of the United States, inspectors classify buildings as having major or minor damage. Sometimes a more fine-grained system distinguishes destroyed from heavily damaged structures, and structural from cosmetic damage, but the categories are still only a crude measure of the actual physical or financial impact. In California, every jurisdiction uses a tagging system developed by the Applied Technology Council, a nonprofit consortium of academic and practicing engineers.

Buildings heavily damaged and/or clearly hazardous are posted with a red tag, meaning no entry is permitted. Buildings that have sustained some structural damage and may be hazardous are posted with yellow tags. Such buildings may be entered only with permission of the local building official and only for a limited period—usually fifteen minutes to retrieve personal possessions. Buildings inspected and found to have nonstructural damage are typically tagged green to identify the fact that they have been inspected and are safe to enter. Green-tagged buildings may in fact be undamaged but tagged to show they have been inspected.

Because the inspections are done hurriedly, often by volunteers not necessarily from the local area, there is bound to be inconsistency in the reporting of damage. In addition, different jurisdictions may give their inspectors different instructions. For example, after the Northridge earthquake, inspectors for the city of Los Angeles proactively performed at least cursory inspections of all buildings within certain heavily damaged areas of the city—such as Northridge and Sherman Oaks—and of all known public buildings, schools, and hospitals within the city. Additional proactive inspections were conducted in areas where there was a prevalence of construction types known for their susceptibility to earthquakes. At the same time, the officials of the Department of Building and Safety performed thousands of "reactive" inspections in response to specific requests by, or damage reports from, building owners and tenants. By comparison, inspectors working in the city of Santa Monica focused primarily on buildings for which they had received requests for inspection, and on public and educational facilities. Sometimes the various cities and unincorporated areas of the county used different forms to record building damage information, and sometimes inspectors only partially completed the information on the inspection forms.

In some cases, building owners preferred to keep their buildings off the city's list of damaged buildings and may have failed to request an inspection or even steered inspectors away. In other cases, the earthquake damage was not apparent in the immediate aftermath of the event, so no request for inspection was made. In general, differences in inspection policy, combined with the self-exemptions, affect the ability to accurately represent the actual total number of buildings damaged, although the counting problem is usually limited to buildings with minor damage. Buildings with structural damage—that is, the red- and yellow-tagged buildings—are relatively easy to find, but sometimes much of the minor damage is difficult to see from the street.

The inspection records are extremely useful in the first weeks immediately after a disaster because they provide an initial indication of the scale of the disaster in physical terms, which in turn helps in estimating the magnitude of the economic losses, and helps local governments to formulate requests for federal assistance and begin recovery planning. These records become much less useful after two or three months because they lack the detailed information essential to recovery planning. How extensive is the damage? Is the building really uninhabitable? What is the estimated cost of repairs? The quick hazard assessment done in the first days after the disaster cannot answer these questions.

The inspection report on damaged structures provides the number of damaged buildings by tag type, but the information is insufficient for estimating the value or severity of the loss. For example, a house that has collapsed after sliding more than thirty meters down a hillside and a house with a cracked brick chimney are both red tagged. The first house has been destroyed, while the second is perfectly habitable once the chimney is removed. Similarly, a green-tagged house may have a crack in the driveway, or it may be missing all the stucco on one elevation. Here again, the house in the first case is habitable, while the second is not. Furthermore, the cost of repairs for a red-tagged house can easily range between a few thousand dollars and a few hundred thousand.

ESTIMATING THE ECONOMIC IMPACT

The disaster price tag is often estimated within the first few weeks after the event and adjusted over the first year or two as detailed data begin to emerge. The estimate and subsequent adjustments are based on the two major sources of recovery capital: federal agencies and insurance. At the same time that various federal agencies (e.g., FEMA, the Department of Transportation, Department of Housing and Urban Development, Small Business Administration, Department of Agriculture) estimate the costs of their expected loans and assistance programs, insurers are following similar procedures. While there is a great political push for early estimates of losses, there is little incentive to produce final loss figures. To continue the Northridge example, initial government estimates of the private building losses totaled approximately $1.5 billion and were used widely in recovery planning. Three months after the event, insurers estimated their losses at $2.5 billion, but two and a half years after the event, total insured losses amounted to nearly $12.5 billion (Eguchi et al. 1996), and public expenditures were similar.

The programmatic reasons that final and accurate loss estimates are difficult to obtain include the lengthy, cumbersome administrative processes in funding repairs (and/or mitigation procedures) for public buildings, and the delays in resolution of disputed insurance claims. In addition, there is rarely an attempt to distinguish between the "estimated value" of damage and the cost to complete repairs. Compare the situation of a damaged building to that of an automobile damaged in an accident. If the cost of repairs is greater than the value of the car, insurance pays no more than the depreciated value of the vehicle. By contrast, insurance pays to replace an older structure with new materials and finishes. Ultimately, the sheer number of individual cases makes an overall assessment of disaster loss difficult to obtain.

Separate from the technical difficulties, politicians and private interest groups play a significant role in the dissemination of information and disinformation on disaster losses (Comerio, Landis, and Firpo 1996; Eguchi et al. 1996; U.S. Congress 1995). Politicians will advertise or hide particular appropriations depending on political conditions. The insurance industry may exaggerate losses to obtain political or financial concessions, as may cities or individuals.

SUMMARY

The painful truth is we are not very good at initial estimation and despite having the luxury in the long-term post-disaster period to carefully assess our losses, we are not very good at achieving a final loss figure either.

R. T. Eguchi, J. D. Goltz, C. E. Taylor, S. E. Chang, P. Flores,
L. A. Johnson, H. A. Seligson, and N. C. Blais 1996

If it is difficult to accurately assess the damages in any disaster (in terms of numbers of buildings or housing units affected and severity of damage in individual buildings), it is doubly difficult to compare damage across disasters, except in the most simplistic terms. While the number of buildings destroyed or severely damaged may be reasonably comparable in a variety of disasters and a variety of urban and rural contexts, there is still the question of what was counted. In a developing country, we accept that there is no simple way of assessing the number of squatters' dwellings damaged in a given disaster, but the same problem exists in the U.S. How do we count nontraditional housing units in residential hotels and migrant camps, or illegal second units in the garages of American suburban homes?

The problem is further compounded in the method of separating major from minor damage. Engineers and building inspectors usually define major damage as structural damage because the existence of structural damage implies that the building is unsafe and therefore uninhabitable.

If all the stucco and plaster fall off a wood-frame house or apartment building, however, the building is likely to be uninhabitable, even if the structural system is undamaged. Another common definition of major damage is the 30 percent rule: that is, a building with more than 30 percent damage is classified as having major damage. Unfortunately, it is often difficult to draw the line between 29 percent and 30 percent damage.

In short, it is important to approach the standard measures of loss—particularly those for buildings—with some degree of caution. Most often, what becomes the official tally of building losses is based on initial hazard assessments conducted in the first days of the disaster. The numbers are exaggerated by local officials in their appeals for national or international assistance. The same numbers are downplayed by those same officials when they are trying to reassure the business and financial communities that the situation is stable and under control. Those very same numbers are quoted by researchers in papers and books and thus become part of the permanent historical record. They are used in allocating public funding, in assessing future hazards, in setting insurance rates, and in creating future disaster policy. They are very important, but they are not very accurate.

AN ALTERNATIVE STRUCTURE
FOR EVALUATING HOUSING LOSSES

Despite the cautions regarding limitations of postdisaster hazard assessment inventories, it is unlikely that heavily damaged buildings (red- and yellow-tagged structures, in the California parlance) would be grossly misrepresented, simply because significant structural damage is fairly obvious. The greatest uncertainty is likely to focus on buildings with minor damage, because inspections may be incomplete or damage may not be immediately visible. For these reasons, counting damaged buildings is not enough, not only because counts are inaccurate but also because the information is insufficient. In order to comprehend the full extent of disaster losses, it is important to use a number of alternative measures. These include:

1. Measurement of the amount of housing damage relative to the other building and nonbuilding damage;

2. Differentiation of damage to single- and multifamily dwellings;

3. Segregation of housing damage by degree of habitability;

4. Estimation of economic value of the losses and the cost to rebuild;

5. Description of the concentration of the residential losses; and

6. Evaluation of housing damage relative to local conditions.

Together these measures can permit a more comprehensive understanding of the losses in any given disaster and can form the basis for developing relief and recovery strategies.

HOUSING DAMAGE RELATIVE TO OVERALL DAMAGE

In any community, housing represents 60 to 70 percent of the total building stock, and it is likely to sustain a significant portion of the damage in any disaster, unless the event occurs in a sparsely populated rural area. In the great midwestern flood of 1993, forty to fifty thousand houses were damaged, but these were spread over a nine-state area and the impact was relatively small when compared to the industrial and agricultural losses. In most urban disasters, it is useful to compare loss of homes with loss of commercial buildings, public buildings, and infrastructure in order to evaluate the full impact of the damage.

In a situation where freeways and bridges are heavily damaged, there may be long-term impacts in the business sector, even if relatively small numbers of commercial buildings were affected, because employees will have difficulty commuting to work and shoppers may avoid certain shopping areas. This was the case in the San Francisco Bay Area after Loma Prieta. The Bay Bridge was closed for thirty days and downtown San Francisco had no Christmas season in 1989. Many freeways were closed for years; two important ones remained unfinished as of this writing, nine years after the earthquake, permanently altering commute patterns and frustrating residents. Alternately, large housing losses in a community with little commercial loss and minimal infrastructure damage permits victims to at least keep their jobs and be able to focus on housing recovery, as was the case in the Northridge earthquake. When both housing and commercial sectors are heavily damaged, as in the loss of the Homestead Air Force Base during Hurricane Andrew, the real loss of both population and a tax base makes recovery issues quite different.

Such comparisons take on a different hue in the international context, where the economic value of houses in developing countries is quite low and the construction is typically done by the occupant. Fred Cuny, an expert on international disaster recovery, argues that in these cases jobs are critical to recovery, and housing is secondary (1983). This argument holds for much of the disaster experience from Latin America to the Middle East but is certainly not the case in the two most recent, significant urban earthquakes, in Mexico City in 1985 and Kobe, Japan, in 1995. In these urban disasters, the relationship between residential, commercial, public building, and infrastructure damage was much more akin to circumstances in the United States than in other countries.

DIFFERENTIATING DAMAGE ACCORDING TO HOUSING TYPE

Another component of comparative loss evaluation is the need to distinguish between the loss of single-family homes and multifamily apartments and condominiums. In the Mexico City, Loma Prieta, Northridge, and Kobe earthquakes, a very high proportion of housing loss was in multifamily buildings, as compared to Hurricanes Andrew and Hugo, where losses were concentrated in single-family structures. See figures 7 and 8. Why does the distinction matter?

For most American home owners, their home is the single largest investment they will ever make. Their capacity to recover is tied to their capacity to recoup the value lost in the disaster. Single-family homes are bought, sold, built, and—after a disaster—rebuilt on the basis of three sets of attributes: the building itself (i.e., the space, the lot, the features, or the design); the location (i.e., the neighborhood, quality of schools, and proximity to work, shopping, or other activities); and the potential to generate wealth (through property appreciation and tax savings). Thus, the choice and the ability to recover after a disaster loss depend on personal and financial concerns. Do the owners want to stay in the community, given their ages, job situations, loss of services, access to transit, and so on, and can they afford to rebuild?

The situation is quite different for renters. Renters may prefer the flexibility of rental units or they may not have the capacity to invest in housing. Their choices are limited by what they can afford to rent and what is available in particular locations. Thus, if a substantial portion of the rental stock in a particular market is eliminated, renters may not have access to housing unless they leave the community. This was true after both the Mexico City and Loma Prieta earthquakes, when concentrations of older, poorly maintained buildings in low-rent areas were lost. This was also true in Kobe and in Dade County, Florida, where large numbers of both owners and renters lost housing. In each case, there were no equivalent units available to rent within a forty-kilometer radius.

While renters have only two concerns in choosing rental housing—

Figure 7. Repairs Under Way after Loma Prieta Earthquake. Houses in the Marina district of San Francisco required extensive restoration. (California Governor's Office of Emergency Services, Earthquake Program)

Figure 8. Damaged Multifamily Structure, Los Angeles. Soft first-story apartments were heavily damaged in the Northridge earthquake. (California Governor's Office of Emergency Services, Earthquake Program)

shelter and location—owners of rental property care about shelter and location only as it impacts a particular property's profit potential. Thus, the likelihood that an apartment owner will rebuild a damaged building depends primarily on his or her ability to raise rents without losing tenants. In this case, the ability to finance the investment in rebuilt or replacement housing has little to do with the social need for housing after a disaster and more to do with investment and business decisions for the landlord (Comerio, Landis, and Rofé 1994).

The situation is even more complex with condominiums because individual owners invest in shelter in the same manner as home owners, but what they own is a legally defined portion of space within the walls of a larger building. It is very difficult for one owner to make personal and financial choices about repairing or rebuilding his or her home when that home is inextricably linked to the homes of fifty others whose opinions and financial circumstances are different.

Thus, long- and short-term recovery issues are a function of the type of housing affected in a disaster, and the measure of the types of units lost will shape postdisaster planning.

HABITABILITY

Another mechanism for assessing the damage, and the long- and short-term recovery issues, is to divide the list of damaged units into categories that represent the habitability of the unit and the degree of damage. In hurricanes or fires, it is fairly easy to differentiate destroyed buildings from those that have partial damage, but with earthquakes it is often daunting to determine the distinction.

After the Northridge earthquake, the Los Angeles Housing Department reorganized the inspected damage database, replacing the count of red, yellow, and green tags with the labels *Vacated, At Risk,* and *Minor Damage. Vacated* represented all the permanently uninhabitable units in need of rebuilding or substantial repair. *At Risk* represented single-family homes with damage estimated at ten thousand dollars or more and multifamily structures with estimated damage of five thousand dollars or more per unit. Such units might or might not be habitable, depending on the damage conditions and the owners' and/or tenants' financial circumstances.

At risk was used to define a category of damage that suggests fairly substantial and expensive damage and that, because of the high cost to repair, could lead to the loss of those units from the housing stock (because owners might "walk away" from their damaged house or apartment building, allowing the bank to foreclose, rather than invest in the repairs necessary). Although these damage value estimates are based on the inspector's judgment after a cursory review of the damage, they do allow the local government an insight into the scale of the damage and the potential for abandonment and foreclosure. At the same time, the measure allows for the near-term assessment of temporary housing needs because it helps to clarify the real numbers of units that are uninhabitable and/or undesirable.

VALUE OF LOSSES AND THE COST TO REBUILD

In planning for recovery, the most important measure of disaster losses is the most difficult to estimate accurately. Northridge was the first American disaster in which inspectors attempted to place a value on the damage they saw. Their collective estimate turned out to be about ten times smaller than the actual amount expended within two years following the event. The problem was not with their judgment. From a construction or engineering point of view, the damage was frequently slight—for example, cracked plaster or interior wallboard—but insurance industry estimation formulas caused the cost of replacement materials and redecorating to skyrocket. Furthermore, original estimates were limited by what was and was not inspected. After Hurricane Andrew, planners had an easier time estimating the losses. Because so many single-family homes were completely destroyed, the local officials could use property tax valuations and real estate appraisals to accurately represent the value of structures lost. After the Northridge earthquake, the cost of repairs was complicated by the discrepancy between the cost of patching a crack and the additional cost of replacing finishes on undamaged, adjacent walls.

The "value" estimate is important in two respects. When combined with other measures of housing loss, it provides an insight into what portion of the losses is insured versus uninsured, as well as an indication of the length of time that may be needed for recovery. If there is a high percentage of single-family-home losses with high loss values, it could indicate that insurance will play a big part in the recovery; if, however, the losses are concentrated in multifamily buildings, this indicates a potential lack of insurance and a need for government intervention. At the same time, average- or low-value losses indicate that habitability may not be an issue, whereas high-value losses may indicate a long-term need for alternative housing because the reconstruction period will be slowed by engineering assessments and financing concerns.

CONCENTRATION OF LOSSES

Another component in the assessment of damage is the relative intensity of damage in a given area. In the 1992 Hurricane Iniki, 5,000 housing units on the island of Kauai were damaged. While this is not a particularly high number of units, it represented 90 percent of the housing on the island (EQE International 1992; NAHB Research Center 1993) and clearly indicated the need for a quick infusion of recovery aid or the development of alternative shelter plans. Similarly, in urban disasters, housing loss can be estimated in terms of the concentration of damage at the neighborhood or community level, and in terms of the percentage of the housing stock impacted in the city, county, or other appropriate jurisdictional level. After Hurricane Andrew, Dade County divided the hardest hit area, south of Kendall Drive, into four bands and assessed the impact to housing and population within each of these areas (Metropolitan Dade County Planning Department 1992).

After the Northridge earthquake, the city of Los Angeles understood that 90 percent of the damage was concentrated in the San Fernando Valley. The valley, with more than 450,000 housing units in 250 census tracts, is bigger than most American cities. Thus, to better understand the damage, the city identified 38 census tracts with more than 100 vacated units, and grouped these into fifteen neighborhoods with high concentrations of damage. These neighborhoods came to be known as "Ghost Towns," where the loss of housing units amounted to 60 to 90 percent of the available housing in the neighborhood (Los Angeles Housing Department 1995; Comerio 1995).

Damage concentration is important in assessing the need for alternative temporary housing. In a small town with high concentrations of damage or in an urban area where a particular market segment may be adversely impacted, there may not be long-term alternatives to Red Cross shelters. This was the case in Watsonville, a small farmworker community with a high percentage of housing units damaged by the Loma Prieta earthquake. The Federal Emergency Management Agency agreed to supply trailers after the local community demonstrated the lack of affordable housing within the immediate vicinity.

Moreover, measurement of damage concentration is particularly useful in targeting and prioritizing recovery-funding programs. Los Angeles targeted the Ghost Towns when the city applied to the U.S. Department of Housing and Urban Development (HUD) for supplemental appropriations of nondisaster housing programs. When funding was received, the city directed the loan programs to owners in the Ghost Town neighborhoods in order to speed the recovery in these neighborhoods and prevent looting and blight as well as further decline in the surrounding communities.

HOUSING DAMAGE RELATIVE TO LOCAL CONDITIONS

As a component of housing damage assessment, comparison of the social and economic conditions in the damaged areas to those in the surrounding community is critical to both relief and recovery planning. When Red Cross officials do an initial reconnaissance of disaster damage, they typically assume that 30 percent of people in damaged housing units will come to them for food and emergency shelter. In any specific disaster, the estimate is tempered by the general economic conditions of the impacted area. They expect fewer people in a wealthy area, where disaster victims may automatically check themselves into hotels. They increase their shelter estimates in impoverished areas where it is clear that the local population is unable to provide their own alternative shelter.

The Red Cross model can be made more sophisticated to estimate longer-term relief and recovery needs. For example, low vacancy rates in rental housing will certainly indicate the lack of alternative temporary housing and the need for trailers or other special provisions. A number of simple census data measures, such as ethnicity and average age, income, and household size, together with basic housing statistics such as vacancy rates, home values, and rental costs by unit type, are extremely helpful in understanding the victims and their housing problems. The ratio of typical housing costs in the area to average incomes could help to estimate the degree of difficulty individuals and families may have in finding alternative housing in the short term and provide some indicators of the financial circumstances of building owners.

SUMMARY

Together, these six measures of housing loss can help local communities to fully understand the scope of the housing problem after a disaster, and they are crucial to formulating effective relief and recovery programs. The case studies that follow examine these measures of housing loss to provide a more accurate and realistic picture of the nature of the loss beyond the number of units destroyed or damaged, and are summed up by a review of how the use of such data contributed to the recovery process.

CASE STUDIES OF URBAN DISASTERS

In 1900, a category 4 hurricane took six thousand lives in Galveston, Texas (NOAA 1993). In 1906, the 8.2 magnitude earthquake that struck San Francisco took three thousand lives (Hansen and Condon 1989). Since that time, Americans have been spared disasters that exact a large toll in human lives, and large, costly disasters have been few and far between. Between 1906 and 1989, only three earthquakes stand out in terms of their impact on people and property: 1933 in Long Beach, California; 1964 in Anchorage, Alaska; and 1971 in San Fernando, California. While there have been numerous storms and hurricanes that have caused costly damage along the eastern seaboard, only one, Hurricane Camille in 1969, is notable for both its intensity and its economic impact.

The era of low-impact disasters ended in 1989, when Hurricane Hugo was followed one month later by the Loma Prieta earthquake. In 1991, California was hit again, by the Oakland Hills firestorm. In 1992, Hurricane Andrew became the costliest hurricane in U.S. history. In 1993, there was a five hundred–year flood on the Mississippi River. In 1994, the Northridge earthquake struck Los Angeles, surpassing Hurricane Andrew in the category of costliest disaster. In the same year, the Northridge earthquake was followed by more wildfires and intense floods in California. Then, on the anniversary of the Northridge earthquake in 1995, the world was shocked by the devastation caused by an earthquake in Kobe, Japan.

Outstanding among all the recent disasters is the number of housing units lost or seriously damaged. For the first time, American housing losses have been comparable to losses experienced in disasters in developing countries. The losses have astonished many who thought that lightweight wood-frame construction and American building codes combined to make American housing safe and invulnerable. The losses tested federal and state disaster response agencies, who were clearly unprepared for the scale of the losses.

Before evaluating the factors that contribute to loss and recovery, it will be valuable to look in some detail at what actually happened during and after the four most significant housing disasters: Hugo, Loma Prieta, Andrew, and Northridge. The losses in each will be described in terms of the six measures outlined above. In addition, the relief and recovery efforts will be analyzed and compared in order to better determine what works and what is cost effective in the process of repairing and reorganizing people's homes and lives.

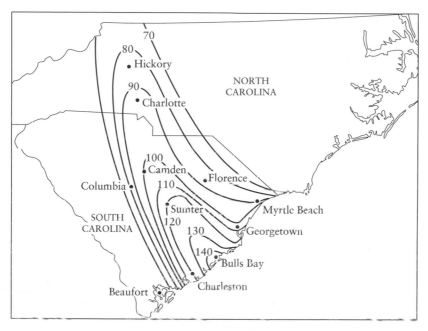

Map 3. Hurricane Hugo Impact Area. The concentric arcs show probable maximum gust speeds (mph). The hurricane slammed the coast of South Carolina at Sullivan's Island, northwest of Charleston. (Peter R. Sparks)

HURRICANE HUGO

On September 21, 1989, Hurricane Hugo left a path of destruction from the island of Guadeloupe in the Caribbean to the state of Virginia. The damage was greater than that of any North American hurricane in history. On the Saffir/Simpson Scale, the storm increased from a category 2 to a category 4 hurricane just before landfall (Saffir 1991). It was the eleventh most intense hurricane to hit the United States since 1900 (NOAA 1993). With winds of more than one hundred miles (160 km) per hour, the hurricane made landfall about sixty-five kilometers northwest of Charleston, South Carolina, just after midnight. In its first few minutes ashore, Hugo severely damaged many coastal communities and completely destroyed the town of McClellanville. In a matter of hours, the hurricane had cut a fifty-kilometer swath of destruction through the eastern half of the state, before dissipating in the Appalachian Mountains of North Carolina. See map 3.

Because the storm failed to weaken as it moved inland, twenty-four of South Carolina's forty-six counties were declared federal disaster areas.

Most of the wind damage, however, was concentrated in the coastal or near coastal counties of Charleston, Dorchester, Berkeley, Georgetown, and Horry. In this region, the population is concentrated in the Charleston metropolitan area and along the northern coast in an area known as the Grand Strand, between Georgetown and North Myrtle Beach (Sparks 1991).

HOUSING DAMAGE RELATIVE TO OVERALL DAMAGE

More than 250,000 people were evacuated prior to the storm's landfall. This effective evacuation effort prevented significant loss of life. The storm resulted in forty-nine deaths, though property loss was extensive. In a study for the governor's office conducted one year after the event, researchers placed the cost of overall physical damage by the storm at $6.4 billion. This figure included losses sustained by residences, commercial and industrial businesses, automobiles, utilities, the Port Authority, forests, agriculture, and military installations and other government structures. Residences suffered the greatest damage (see figures 9, 10, 11, and 12), followed by forests (Fontaine Company 1991). In fact, residential losses comprised almost half of the $6.4 billion in damages. See table 6.

Figure 9. Beach House, Garden City, South Carolina. Beachfront properties were damaged by a combination of erosion, floodwaters, and wind. (Peter R. Sparks)

Figure 10. Houses, 57th Avenue, Isle of Palms. The house on the right suffered considerably less damage than the one on the left because it had been elevated to protect it against storm surge. (Peter R. Sparks)

Figure 11. Sea Cabin Condominiums, Isle of Palms. Wind pulled the roof and walls from this and other large condominium structures. (Peter R. Sparks)

Figure 12. Ocean Club Condominiums, Isle of Palms. Inadequate codes and poor-quality construction contributed to the extensive damage to vacation developments. (Peter R. Sparks)

TABLE 6

ESTIMATES OF NET
DAMAGES FROM HURRICANE HUGO

Category	Damages ($ Millions)	Percentage
Residences	$2,960	46%
Forests	$1,181	18%
Commercial/Industrial	$1,029	16%
Agricultural Structures	$294	05%
Charleston Naval Base	$250	04%
Autos, Misc.	$215	03%
Utilities	$197	03%
Other Government	$142	02%
Agricultural Crops	$87	01%
Shaw Air Force Base	$50	01%
Ports Authority	$17	01%
Total	$6,422	100%

SOURCE: South Carolina Budget and Control Board, as reported in Fontaine Company 1991.

Considering the size of the storm and the relatively small number of people in the areas hardest hit, the property damage is surprising. However, the special characteristics of the storm help to explain the damage: the brunt of the wind and storm surge was borne by beachfront communities in a state without a statewide building code; and much of the inland impact area was heavily forested, resulting in secondary damage from falling trees (Monday 1992).

HOUSING TYPES DAMAGED

The devastation from Hugo may be most remembered by the damage to people's homes. Yet the impression is hard to back up with accurate data. Initial estimates made by the Red Cross in the aftermath of the storm were adapted and used by state and local governments in relief efforts as well as in analytic reviews of recovery efforts (Berkeley, Charleston, and Dorchester Council of Governments 1990; 1990a; Fontaine Company 1991; Miller 1990; Monday 1992a).

According to the Red Cross survey, more than 111,000 housing units were damaged by the storm. Based on the total number of occupied housing units in the twenty-four-county area, approximately 40 percent of all occupied homes were damaged by the storm. Single-family homes bore nearly three-quarters of the damage, with almost 80,000 homes sustaining some damage. However, only one-quarter of the total damage to single-family homes was severe. By comparison, damage to mobile homes in the disaster counties was almost total. Ninety percent of all mobile homes were damaged, with more than half of those affected destroyed or severely damaged (Fontaine Company 1991). See table 7.

TABLE 7
NUMBER OF RESIDENCES
DESTROYED OR DAMAGED, HURRICANE HUGO

	Destroyed	Major Damage	Minor Damage	Total	Percentage
Single Family	3,783	18,146	57,698	79,627	71%
Apartments/Condos	313	2,647	8,948	11,908	11%
Mobile Homes	5,200	5,976	9,063	20,239	18%
Total	9,296	26,769	75,709	111,774	100%

SOURCE: South Carolina Budget and Control Board, as reported in Fontaine Company 1991.

HABITABILITY

In order to understand the nature of damage to residential buildings, it is useful to consider how wind acts on buildings, which Peter Sparks explains in a special issue of the *Journal of Coastal Research* (1991, 17) dedicated to the impact of Hurricane Hugo:

> As wind flows around a building it induces positive (inward) pressures on the windward face and negative (outward) pressures on the leeward face. The side walls are generally subjected to negative pressures which can be very intense near the windward corners of the building. A similar situation occurs with flat roofs and on gable roofs when the wind is blowing parallel to the roof edge. . . . The creation of an opening in a windward wall creates a positive internal pressure which can add to the negative external pressure in producing an uplift on the roof.
>
> The intense negative pressures occur over quite small areas. Their effects are seen in the removal of roofing materials near the edges of the roofs and cladding materials near the corners of walls. . . . Major structural damage is often initiated by the loss of the roof structure, precipitated by increased internal pressure due to window damage. . . . A second form of failure [results from wind-induced] bending action [that] can sometimes overturn a structure or separate stories.

In Hurricane Hugo, buildings were declared destroyed when more than two-thirds of the building components making up the structure needed to be replaced in order for the structure to be habitable, functional, and sound. See figures 13, 14, and 15. Judgments about partially damaged homes were subject to some variation, but serious damage to roofs, load-bearing systems, or foundations determined the difference between the categories of major and minor damage (Miller 1990).

Structural failures in homes resulted from a combination of lost roofs from wind effects on poor construction, and surge effects on elevated block piers and foundations. Many one- and two-family dwellings lost roofing shingles, and in these cases the result of what was a minor wind failure caused the dollar value of damage to the interiors of the buildings to soar. It has been estimated that the resulting rain damage magnified the initial damage by a factor of ten to thirty times that of the damage to the roofs themselves (Miller 1990; Monday 1992; Sparks 1991). While only *one-quarter* of the total damage to residential structures was severe and concentrated in coastal counties, the rain damage forced many residents to seek alternative shelter at least in the short term and made the cleanup costly.

Manufactured buildings may represent one-half of the residential structures purchased in South Carolina, and they are particularly susceptible

Figure 13. Beach House, Folly Beach. Roofs constructed without hurricane clips were stripped by the high winds. (Peter R. Sparks)

Figure 14. Wild Dunes Condominiums. Wind pulled the roof from this and other poorly constructed condominiums. (Peter R. Sparks)

Figure 15. Aerial View of Damage to Moderate-Income Housing. Poorly built inland housing suffered damage similar to that of beachfront properties. (National Oceanic and Atmospheric Administration Photo Library)

to flood and wind damage. Damage in this sector was almost total because such buildings are underdesigned for high wind velocities on the coast, and because they are often placed on unattached, uncemented concrete blocks with inadequate anchors and hold-downs (Miller 1990).

VALUE OF THE LOSSES

Nearly one-half the total dollar value of damage caused by Hurricane Hugo represented residential damage. South Carolina estimated the damage to residences at almost $3 billion (see table 6), of which approximately 45 percent was recovered through insurance claims. In fact, the total number of paid residential claims was two and a half times the number of total residential structures damaged, which may make it difficult to understand the relationship between damage estimates and insurance claims. There are a number of possible explanations for the discrepancy.

In some cases, individual owners may have received payments based on multiple claims on separate flood insurance, and/or windstorm and hail insurance, policies in addition to their regular home-owner policies. However, because there were only some fifty thousand of these special policies in force in the state, and less than 30,000 claims paid, at an av-

TABLE 8
LOSSES AND CLAIMS PAID
BY INSURANCE COMPANIES,
HURRICANE HUGO

	Homes	Mobile Homes	Total
Gross Losses ($ Millions)	$1,423	$172	$1,595
Paid Losses ($ Millions)	$1,349	$167	$1,516
Number of Claims	221,142	57,109	278,251
Average Claim	$6,100	$2,931	$5,448

SOURCE: South Carolina Insurance Commission, as reported in Fontaine Company 1991.

erage of twenty-seven thousand to thirty thousand dollars (Miller 1990), this does not account for much of the difference. Typically, in any disaster not all the minor damage is counted or recorded. Many individuals may make claims on their home-owner policies for minor damage, even though their losses were not represented in the official tally. For this reason, it is difficult to accurately represent the full extent of the storm damage. On one hand, it is unclear how many of the 111,000 damaged units tallied had insurance. On the other hand, it is not certain what portion of the 278,000 paid claims were for building damage directly attributable to the storm. See table 8.

If the twenty thousand mobile homes counted as damaged represent 90 percent of the mobile homes in the twenty-four-county area, then the fact that some fifty-seven thousand insurance payments were made to mobile-home owners indicates that either there was minor damage outside the federally declared disaster area, or there were multiple claims made by policyholders. Another possible explanation is the potential for fraudulent claims in a chaotic period after the storm, but the limited data are insufficient to justify any single explanation.

Whatever the actual total numbers of damaged units, it is clear from both the insurance and the Red Cross data that the great majority of the losses were minor in terms of structural damage. Further, many engineers reviewing the damage agreed that Hugo was a severe windstorm but one that produced damage far in excess of that which need have occurred. Peter Sparks's assessment is damning: "Most of the damage took place where wind conditions had a recurrence interval of between 20 and 50 years and was the result of owners, insurers, and government accepting forms of construction with wind resistance less than that recommended by the engineering profession more than 25 years ago" (1991, 24).

CONCENTRATION OF LOSSES

As in many disasters, losses were not evenly distributed over the counties declared federal disaster areas. After Hurricane Hugo, more than 70 percent of the building loss was concentrated in four counties, Charleston, Berkeley, Dorchester, and Sumter (Berkeley, Charleston, and Dorchester Council of Governments 1990a). Even within each of the four counties, building damage was concentrated in two or three towns or developed areas. Thus, in Charleston County, where 40 percent of all occupied housing units were damaged, the concentration of damage was in the Charleston metropolitan area; in the communities of North Charleston, Folly Beach, Mount Pleasant, Sullivans Island, and Isle of Palms; and along the northern coast in the area known as the Grand Strand.

In the two decades prior to the storm, the coast of South Carolina underwent an explosive development process driven by a tourist economy that produced 35 percent of the state's income (Miller 1990). The two housing types most heavily impacted were coastal vacation homes, built and developed in a largely laissez-faire regulatory context, and the substandard housing of the rural poor.

HOUSING LOSS RELATIVE TO LOCAL CONDITIONS

In the tri-county area of Berkeley, Charleston, and Dorchester Counties, the Council of Governments tracked local conditions as well as amassed storm recovery data. They found that the population was largely composed of young white families with modest incomes (median annual household income was twenty-nine thousand dollars). Housing was easily accessible because vacancy rates were high (7 to 8 percent, higher in rural areas), and both owners and renters paid a median amount of only 20 to 26 percent of their income for housing (U.S. Census 1990).

The housing stock was 64 percent single-family dwellings, 14 percent multifamily dwellings, and 22 percent mobile homes. What was damaged in the storm was fairly representative of the total housing in the counties. Median value of owner-occupied housing was $68,500; median rent was $357 per month. The census numbers alone suggest that housing costs in the tri-county area were lower than the national average. More important was the degree of change that coastal counties had experienced in recent decades. The population had tripled since 1960, with half the growth attributable to in-migration of young white families. The building boom of the 1980s was concentrated in coastal communities with higher incomes and higher property values, but at the same time mobile homes had become an increasingly popular form of housing between 1980 and 1990, and the number of mobile homes had doubled (Berkeley, Charleston, and Dorchester Council of Governments 1990a).

As such, the disparity between rich and poor became more pronounced, but each group found few impediments to development. Local governments welcomed the growth and put few restrictions on land use or building methods. It was not until the late 1980s and the instigation of the National Flood Insurance Program that some coastal communities adopted and enforced standard construction codes. At the same time, concern with increasing development near beaches and dunes, rising sea levels, and increased erosion led to the fear that tourism would be adversely affected, and the state passed the Beachfront Management Act in 1988. Of course, most of what was damaged during the hurricane was in place before these standards were adopted and enforced. Moreover, South Carolina is one of several states without standards for the installation of manufactured housing. Even in areas participating in the National Flood Insurance Program, there was widespread failure to enforce elevation and anchoring requirements (Miller 1990).

As a result of all factors combined, South Carolina took extensive losses in poorly built, relatively expensive beachfront vacation developments and in the rural homes of the marginal workers who served the tourist industry. Although some of the wind damage was unavoidable given the high velocities, much of the costly damage could have been avoided through the enforcement of simple building construction standards and prudent land use planning.

HOUSING RECOVERY

How did South Carolina's disaster victims recover? On the surface the recovery appears to have gone smoothly. State and local governments report that 90 percent of the damaged housing was repaired or replaced within one year (Fontaine Company 1991; Landis and Simpson 1992). Recovery statistics, like damage estimates, depend on who is counting and for what purpose. In general the pace of recovery depends on funding and management. Funding is a combination of the influx of capital from insurance, government programs, and private savings in conjunction with some degree of excess capacity in the building trades. Management

Figure 16. House Damaged by Flying Debris. Much of the damage to wood-frame structures is caused by such debris. Here, a foundation column pierced the roof. (National Oceanic and Atmospheric Administration Photo Library)

Figure 17. Typical Minor Roof Damage. Costly damage results from improperly secured roofs, because water soaks the interior finishes and contents. (Peter R. Sparks)

TABLE 9

PUBLIC EXPENDITURES ON HOUSING
ASSISTANCE AND REPAIR, HURRICANE HUGO

Agency or Program	Total ($ Millions)	Number Assisted
FEMA Individual and Family Grant	$70.2	37,566
FEMA Housing Repairs	$22.1	21,068
FEMA Housing Rental	$8.4	8,318
National Flood Insurance[a]	$365.0	11,113
SBA Home Loans	$94.0	Not available
HUD-CDBG	$1.5	Not available

SOURCE: Fontaine Company 1991.

[a] This is a total for the program, since claims for housing were not recorded separately from commercial claims.

of recovery is in part the availability and speed of service in state and federal recovery programs, and in part the efficiency of local government in regulating the rebuilding process.

Nearly half of the $6.4 billion in property damage resulting from the hurricane was covered by private insurance. Owners of single-family residences, including mobile homes, received $1.5 billion in insurance payments. There were over three hundred thousand claims, and the average payment was small, reflecting the high proportion of buildings with minor damage. See table 8 and figures 16 and 17.

In addition to the funds from private sources, more than $700 million flowed to South Carolina in the form of federal grants and loans. Of this, nearly $200 million went to housing: half by means of FEMA's Minimal Home Repair (MHR) program, Individual and Family Grant (IFG) program, and short-term rental assistance payments; and half by means of the Small Business Administration's low-interest loans for home repairs. See table 9.

The flow of insurance funds and federal assistance for housing repairs represents only a portion of the real cost of repairs. Many individuals dug into their own pockets to pay for repairs not covered by insurance or public assistance. Many others were ineligible for loans like those from the SBA because they could not support the additional debt. Some were simply too isolated to know about public assistance programs. Thus, the picture of housing recovery varies by locale and by income. In the Charleston metropolitan area and adjacent coastal communities, recovery of single-family homes moved ahead quickly; but there was a decrease in the supply of rental units, especially low-cost rental units, because many landlords chose not to repair damaged ones (Fontaine Company 1991).

Inland, the story was different again. Hurricane Hugo not only revealed the substandard construction of many buildings in South Carolina, it also revealed the substandard housing conditions of a substantial number of rural poor. Planning and providing for repair and replacement of housing for rural victims was left largely to private nonprofit agencies such as churches. County governments lacked redevelopment, planning, or housing agencies or capabilities. There was no local government effort to assist in rebuilding or even to subsidize rents for low-income persons needing to be rehoused after the hurricane (Monday 1992).

The NAACP, churches, and other organizations raised $1.5 million in cash and in-kind services to assist more than three hundred families who had slipped through the cracks. Habitat for Humanity and other organizations assembled volunteers, who helped rebuild hundreds of homes (Fontaine Company 1991). Often, the churches and ad hoc groups that formed attempted to rebuild damaged homes to a standard higher than that of their pre-Hugo state, especially when the homes did not have plumbing or electricity.

The housing recovery process occurred without the benefit of a plan. Neither the city of Charleston nor any of the surrounding counties developed a formal recovery plan, and little effort was made to alter the physical pattern or quality of development. In Charleston, city officials did not require permits or inspections for minor damage repair—in fact, the quality of the materials, design, and construction of residential buildings is questionable both inside and outside the city. Even after Hurricane Hugo, only one-third of the state's counties have adopted the Standard Building Code, as accepted by the state in 1987. Statewide efforts to mandate compliance have been resisted. In a region where only no government is considered good government, code enforcement and coastal development regulation are generally perceived as an intrusion on property rights (Miller 1990; Landis and Simpson 1992).

All told, recovery from Hurricane Hugo was a mixed bag. Middle-class owners in coastal communities generally collected some insurance and tapped into government grant and loan programs. They repaired their roofs and replaced their carpets, and many rebuilt their beachfront homes, swimming pools, and breakwaters before tougher coastal regulations were adopted or enforced. By contrast, apartment dwellers had difficulty finding alternative housing at the same rents, and the rural poor had little access to any form of public assistance and depended on help from private charities to repair and replace their damaged housing.

LOMA PRIETA EARTHQUAKE

On October 17, 1989, just one month after Hurricane Hugo devastated South Carolina, an earthquake measuring 7.1 rocked the San Francisco Bay Area. The epicenter was in the Santa Cruz Mountains, near a hill called Loma Prieta, about sixteen kilometers northeast of Santa Cruz and thirty kilometers south of San Jose. The earthquake occurred eighteen kilometers beneath the earth's surface, and it ruptured a forty-kilometer segment of the San Andreas fault. It was felt all the way from Los Angeles to the Oregon border and east to Nevada. The strong shaking lasted less than fifteen seconds and caused more than $7 billion in damage. See map 4.

The earthquake struck just after 5 P.M., but commute traffic was unusually light because many locals were glued to their televisions, awaiting the first pitch in the first game of the "Bay Bridge" World Series between Oakland and San Francisco. Instead of baseball, fans saw the cameras jolt and the TV blacken, and simultaneously they felt the earth move. In that brief period, a portion of the Bay Bridge and a one-and-a-half-kilometer section of elevated freeway collapsed in Oakland, more than ninety kilometers from the epicenter. See figure 18. Two other major highways in San Francisco were closed and a large number of buildings throughout the region were severely damaged. Although centered in a sparsely populated area, the quake was strong enough to distribute damage over many communities and governmental jurisdictions. After the event, ten counties were included in the presidential disaster declaration; however, damage was heaviest in two towns nearest the epicenter, Watsonville and Santa Cruz, where older commercial structures collapsed and individual wood-frame homes slid from their foundations. See figures 19 and 20. Similarly, San Francisco and Oakland each sustained the loss of older multifamily housing units and damage to commercial structures. See figure 21.

Why did the cities suffer such extensive damage, given that they lie about seventy kilometers from the epicenter? Although the location and size of the earthquake were no surprise to geoscientists, the fault displacement differed from the predominant horizontal movements of the San Andreas. In this earthquake, the rupture spread in both a northwest and southwest direction. The direction of the movement, combined with deep soil conditions, magnified the intensity of the shaking

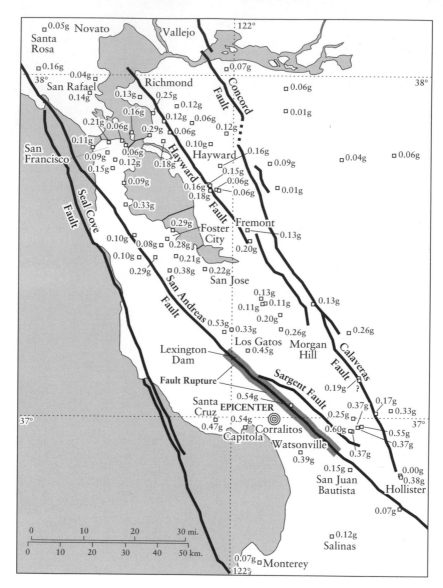

Map 4. Loma Prieta Earthquake Impact Area. The earthquake occurred on the San Andreas fault, about ninety kilometers from the San Francisco Bay. (EQE International, Inc.)

Figure 18. Aerial View of Cypress Freeway Collapse. A 1.6-kilometer segment of double-deck freeway collapsed in West Oakland. (Earthquake Engineering Research Institute's slide collection)

Figure 19. Pacific Garden Mall, Santa Cruz, California. More than twenty-five commercial buildings collapsed in downtown Santa Cruz. (Earthquake Engineering Research Institute's slide collection)

Figure 20. Damage to Single-Family Home, Myrtle Street. Single-family homes were knocked off their foundations, porches detached, and chimneys collapsed. (California Governor's Office of Emergency Services, Earthquake Program)

Figure 21. Damage to Unreinforced Masonry Hotel, Oakland, California. Ten downtown residential hotels, with a total of thirteen hundred rooms, were uninhabitable after the earthquake. Many residents were homeless because no alternative housing was available. (California Governor's Office of Emergency Services, Earthquake Program)

and resulted in severe as well as widely distributed damages. Thus, the earthquake was labeled a "site effects" earthquake because of the damage to structures built on fill or soft soils (EERI 1990; Housner 1990; Comerio 1994).

HOUSING DAMAGE RELATIVE TO OVERALL DAMAGE

Unlike hurricanes, earthquakes provide no early warning and no opportunity to evacuate the area. At 5:04 P.M. forty-two people who happened to be on the Cypress portion of Highway 880 lost their lives when the upper deck collapsed onto the lower deck. At 5:04 P.M., five individuals exiting their office in the Bluxome Building in San Francisco were killed by falling brick. Altogether, this large but not great earthquake killed sixty-two people, injured thirty-seven hundred, destroyed nearly four hundred businesses, and left more than twelve hundred people homeless (EERI 1990).

Damage from the earthquake was concentrated in three sectors: highways and bridges, residential structures, and public facilities. In reports to the Governor's Office and in numerous earthquake engineering damage evaluations, the overall physical damage has been estimated at $7.4 billion, although some researchers estimated that the actual loss was closer to $10 billion when uninsured property damage and secondary economic impacts were included in the tally (Steinbrugge and Roth 1994; Comerio 1994). As with Hurricane Hugo, the value of private property losses amounted to nearly half of the total, and loss of residential structures made up more than half of that amount. See table 10.

TABLE 10
ESTIMATES OF NET DAMAGES
FROM LOMA PRIETA EARTHQUAKE

Category	Damages ($ Millions)	Percentage
Private Property	$3,300	45%[a]
Public Facilities	$2,300	30%
Transit	$1,800	25%
Total	$7,400	100%

SOURCES: BAREPP 1990; Housner 1990.

[a] The value of damage to residential structures is estimated at about $2 billion. Insurance and public assistance provided about $1 billion in recovery assistance, and only 50% of the multifamily stock was repaired (Comerio, 1994).

HOUSING TYPES DAMAGED

Another means of assessing the residential damage as a component of the overall damage is to look at the buildings affected. Of the twenty-seven thousand structures damaged, the overwhelming majority were wood-frame structures. Only nine hundred were unreinforced masonry, a building type known to be susceptible to earthquake damage (Fratessa 1994). More than 75 percent of the buildings damaged were residential, and these included both wood-frame and masonry buildings. See table 11.

According to the best available information, in the Loma Prieta earthquake nearly 12,000 housing units were lost or severely damaged, and another 30,000 sustained some damage (Comerio 1994). See table 12. With the exception of those houses located near the earthquake's epicenter, the region's single-family housing stock escaped Loma Prieta relatively unscathed. A number of chimneys collapsed, some homes slipped off their foundations, and many houses experienced cosmetic plaster and stucco damage. Altogether, only forty-five hundred single-family homes were either destroyed or significantly damaged by Loma Prieta, and of the four cities that experienced substantial damage during the earthquake (San Francisco, Oakland, Santa Cruz, and Watsonville), only Watsonville experienced a significant loss of single-family housing.

The picture on the side of multifamily housing is different. More than 60 percent of the 12,000 housing units lost or severely damaged as a result of Loma Prieta were part of multifamily rental structures. Three-quarters of the units lost in San Francisco, all of the 1,300 units in Oakland, and one-third of the units in Santa Cruz were such rentals. Overwhelmingly, these units were occupied by low-income renters, which caused extraordinary problems in providing both emergency shelter and replacement housing. See table 12.

The Loma Prieta earthquake occurred minutes before the opening game of the World Series, which had already brought the national media to San Francisco. It is not surprising that television coverage of the event focused on the dramatic and photogenic damage to the Cypress freeway, the Bay Bridge, and the collapse of Marina district apartments. But the television picture in no way represented the whole story. There was extensive damage to older buildings throughout San Francisco. A total of 25,000 housing units sustained some damage, and of these 1,450 were red tagged or officially declared uninhabitable. Almost 5,000 were in need of substantial repair. Only 25 percent of those lost or substan-

TABLE 11

ESTIMATED NUMBER OF BUILDINGS DAMAGED,
LOMA PRIETA EARTHQUAKE

Single-Family Homes	20,000
Multifamily Structures[a]	~ 1,000
Public Buildings	~ 3,000
Commercial/Industrial	~ 3,000
Total	27,000

SOURCES: Fratessa 1994; Housner 1990; Wong 1993.

[a] There were approximately 24,000 units in the 1,000 buildings.

TABLE 12

NUMBER OF RESIDENCES DESTROYED
OR DAMAGED, LOMA PRIETA EARTHQUAKE

Destroyed or Had Major Damage	Single Family	Multifamily	Total
San Francisco	1,600	4,700	6,300
Oakland		1,300	1,300
Santa Cruz/Watsonville	2,000	1,000	3,000
Other	900		900
Subtotal	4,500 (40%)	7,000 (60%)	11,500

Minor Damage			
San Francisco	5,000	13,500	18,500
Oakland	2,000		2,000
Santa Cruz/Watsonville	7,000	3,000	10,000
Other	1,100		1,100
Subtotal	15,100	16,500	31,600
Total	19,600 (46%)	23,500 (54%)	45,100

SOURCES: Fratessa 1994; Housner 1990; Comerio 1994.

tially damaged were in the Marina district. Of the remaining 75 percent, half were in poorer downtown neighborhoods and half were distributed around the city.

In Oakland, the 1,300 units destroyed or significantly damaged comprised ten downtown single-room-occupancy (SRO) residential hotels and apartments. These units, like those in downtown San Francisco, had served as the last affordable housing resource for many minority and elderly residents in an urban community with high property val-

Figure 22. St. George Hotel, Fenced before Demolition. Four hundred residential hotel rooms in four buildings were destroyed in Santa Cruz. Most of the tenants were elderly. (Mary C. Comerio)

ues, high rents, and few options for those at the bottom of the economic ladder.

Nearest the epicenter was the city of Santa Cruz, a small seaside community and university town of forty-eight thousand. While on the whole the city suffered relatively little damage, the one exception was the loss of the historic Pacific Garden Mall, a six-block outdoor retail area dominated by local merchants in turn-of-the-century buildings offering a mix of local services along with coffee, books, and gifts for tourists and students. Thirty buildings had to be demolished and many others were significantly damaged. Included in these were four residential hotels with approximately 400 units housing an elderly and transient population. See figure 22. Outside of the downtown, many small housing units provided a source of affordable housing, while nearby mountain areas combined expensive custom homes and artfully built, but often technically substandard, houses. Something on the order of 10,000 housing units sustained some damage.

Watsonville is another small town, some thirty-two kilometers south of Santa Cruz, with a population of thirty thousand, half of which were

Figure 23. Mobile Homes, Watsonville, California. FEMA brought in mobile homes for use as temporary shelter in Watsonville when no alternative housing was available. (California Governor's Office of Emergency Services, Earthquake Program)

Hispanic farmworkers and cannery workers. The town had a small but thriving downtown, with stores and businesses catering to the Hispanic population and a concentration of older bungalows near the downtown commercial strip. Watsonville sustained the greatest single-family housing loss. Some 850 housing units (10 percent of the city's housing stock) were severely damaged or destroyed. These were small wood-frame houses and apartment buildings literally knocked off their foundations. Forty percent were owner occupied and more than 75 percent were affordable housing units. Largely occupied by the extended families of farmworkers and cannery workers, these houses typically had one permanent owner-tenant as well as informal subtenants who might be relatives or friends—some legal, some illegal; some permanent, some migrant workers. Because housing was in short supply before the earthquake, it was not uncommon to find twenty to forty persons living in one house, with some individuals and families in garages and chicken coops. In fact, during the damage inspections, officials found as many as 300 illegal dwellings. See figure 23.

HABITABILITY

In California, inspectors use a system of red, yellow, and green tags to evaluate the safety of structures after earthquakes. This system provides information to owners or renters as to an initial assessment of the structural integrity of the building, and it provides local and state officials with a preliminary understanding of the extent of the damage. Thus, red-tagged buildings have obvious structural hazards. Yellow tags on structures imply potential structural hazards, and green tags signify that the building was inspected and no structural hazards were found.

In fact, the tag color is not completely representative of the degree of damage. For example, a single-family home could be red tagged because the chimney is partially collapsed and represents a hazard, even if the rest of the house is undamaged. However, if the owner can have the hanging chimney removed and blocked off, the house will be considered safe for occupancy. By contrast, an apartment building could lose all the stucco finish on the exterior and much of the plaster inside, and be impossible to live in, but if no structural components of the wood framing failed, the building is not structurally damaged and it may be green tagged.

During the earthquake, the kind of damage and the habitability of housing units varied with the building types. Many of the older apartments and residential hotels in the San Francisco and Oakland downtowns were four-to-six-story unreinforced masonry buildings, with wood-frame floor and roof systems supported on thick brick walls. See figure 24. In many of these buildings, parapets and walls fell outward, x-cracks opened in the masonry (particularly between openings), and the masonry walls lost their residual capacity to carry loads. All buildings affected this way were declared uninhabitable and were difficult to repair. In other buildings, walls and plaster were substantially cracked, but no more than cleanup and moderate repair was needed before the buildings could be safely inhabited.

In San Francisco's Marina district, the multifamily stock was typically four-story wood-frame construction, with three stories composed of apartments over parking garages. Most of the failures came from structural weakness in the first floor, typically called a "soft" first story, which collapsed when the soft soils these were built on liquefied during the quake. These buildings too were significantly damaged, and they required major structural repairs before they could be occupied.

In single-family homes, the typical construction was wood frame, with many older, traditional styles involving a raised first floor supported by short piles or low walls called cripple walls. Typically, either the subfloor structure collapsed, or the house simply slid sideways off the foundation. In either case, the fall caused an otherwise sound structure to fracture many of its connections, both in the building itself and in its services.

Figure 24. Partial Damage, William Penn Hotel, San Francisco. This hotel, like many residential hotels in San Francisco, had extensive cracking and fallen plaster, requiring repairs and structural upgrading. (Mary C. Comerio)

These homes too were uninhabitable, although many families tried to stay in damaged houses where power and water services were uninterrupted, even if parts of the structure were unsafe. Only a very small number of mobile homes were affected by the earthquake (less than two hundred), and these had the same problems as single-family homes. Typically they were dislodged from their foundations and many components were cracked. In all cases, the severity of the damage varied from house to house, and the habitability depended on the speed in which the owner could make repairs and have services restored.

Overall, the 7,000 heavily damaged multifamily units, as well as some of those with minor damage, were uninhabitable for the long term, whereas the return to habitability for the damaged single-family stock took a few months to two years. Despite the fact that the actual number of damaged units was relatively small, amounting to less than 1 percent of the metropolitan area's housing stock, the impact in each of the affected communities was severe. The city of Oakland estimated that the earthquake added twenty-five hundred people to its homeless population. In San Francisco, the middle-class tenants who lost apartments in the Marina and outlying districts often found alternative rentals in other neighborhoods. Landlords offered breaks on the rent and waived security deposits. Department stores offered furniture at cost. There were no similar offers for the elderly, non-English-speaking, and transient populations from the Tenderloin and South of Market neighborhoods, and homeless shelters were already filled beyond capacity.

Similarly, in Santa Cruz and Watsonville, there was a limited supply of vacant housing, and people lived in emergency shelters for months. Although technically there were some vacancies in vacation rentals in the area's seaside communities, and the summer season was past, landlords were not eager to rent these units to farmworkers, and farmworkers were not comfortable with the distance between the vacation areas and their damaged homes and jobs. Thus, despite the numbers, the damage caused by Loma Prieta brought on a real crisis in the short- and long-term availability of affordable housing.

VALUE OF THE LOSSES

Although the estimated $2 billion value of losses to residential buildings represented about one-quarter of the total damage estimate, the figure in no way represents the replacement cost of a large segment of the affordable housing stock. At the same time, insurance settlements on single-family homes provide only a partial understanding of the value of the losses. According to a report by the U.S. Geological Survey, only 30 to 35 percent of the dwellings in the Loma Prieta study area had earthquake insurance (Steinbrugge and Roth 1994). Typical home-owner policies specifically do not cover damages from earth movement, although they do cover glass breakage and fire that results from an earthquake. At the time of the Loma Prieta earthquake, reimbursement for damage to structures and contents caused by an earthquake required a separate earthquake policy, which was relatively expensive and typically included a ten to fifteen thousand dollar deductible. Approximately $570 million was paid in forty-five thousand claims on single-family residences (65 percent of all insurance claims related to the earthquake), and yet the damage data only accounts for a total of twenty thousand single-family houses damaged. See table 13. Projecting that the twenty-six thousand earthquake policyholders are representative of only 35 percent of the damage, one might assume from the insurance data that some seventy-five thousand homes were damaged.

This discrepancy between damage estimates and insurance claims is similar to that in the Hurricane Hugo situation, where the number of claims was two and a half times the damage estimate. Here again, many

TABLE 13
LOSSES AND CLAIMS PAID BY INSURANCE COMPANIES, LOMA PRIETA EARTHQUAKE

	Home Owner	Fire Only	Earthquake	Total
Number Reported	35,670	725	55,112	91,507
Claims Paid	17,864	687	26,291	44,892
Paid Losses ($ Millions)	$162,839	$12,283	$397,727	$572,849
Average Claim	$9,000	$18,000	$15,000	Not applicable

SOURCE: California Department of Insurance, in Steinbrugge and Roth 1994.

of the same factors affect the data. Not all minor damage was recorded, and the low average amount paid makes it clear that many of the claims were small. At the same time, the rigor with which insurance companies investigated claims is uncertain. If a claimant was from the impacted area, and his or her claim was reasonable, it is unlikely that the agents challenged the relationship of the damage to the earthquake.

Much of the damage in unreinforced masonry and older wood-frame buildings was considered predictable by the engineering community: many engineers have written that there were "no surprises" in the performance of older, poorly designed structures (whether of wood or masonry). Building owners and public agencies, however, were surprised by the impact of that loss on communities. The governor ordered the preparation of a detailed plan to ensure the functionality of state facilities, and the Seismic Safety Commission documented the extreme frustration of public and private interests in obtaining financial assistance for housing recovery (Fratessa 1994; Mader 1994). In terms of damage to buildings, and particularly to housing, the economic and social consequences of the disaster were far greater than the physical impacts.

CONCENTRATION OF LOSSES

Ten counties were included in the federal disaster declaration, but the greatest housing damage was clearly concentrated in six or seven neighborhoods in four cities. In San Francisco, almost half the damaged housing was situated downtown. The worst damage struck the Sixth Street skid row area called South of Market, the same area where residential hotels on soft soils collapsed in 1906. And there was extensive damage to SRO hotels in the Tenderloin, an area north of Market Street, whose population is equally divided among Southeast Asian immigrants, the elderly, and transients, all of whom rent their rooms by the day or by the week. A similar population inhabited Oakland's damaged hotels, all located within a small, economically declining downtown with few services and public amenities. By contrast, most of the damage to middle-class housing in Oakland and San Francisco was scattered in small pockets around each city, with the exception of the heavy damage in the six-to-eight-square-block section of the Marina district.

In Santa Cruz, the lost four hundred units, located in four heavily damaged SRO hotels on the Pacific Garden Mall, comprised the most visible concentration of losses, although many smaller structures that had provided affordable housing were affected as well. Similarly, in the downtown core of Watsonville, where more than eight hundred small bungalows and apartments sustained heavy damage, housing loss was concentrated among a very low-income population in an agricultural community familiar with housing shortages.

HOUSING LOSS RELATIVE TO LOCAL CONDITIONS

The city of San Francisco has a population of 720,000 living in a forty-nine-square-mile area. Seventy-five percent of its residential units occur within multifamily buildings. Its housing is the most expensive in the nation, with a median house value of $295,000. It also has extraordinarily expensive rents, with the 1996 median for all units at $1,000 per month, and vacancies of less than 2 percent (Anders and Chao 1996). Yet despite the city's image as an elite, urbane, corporate address, median household income is only $33,400. San Francisco is a city with a very large ethnic population—211,000 Chinese and other Asians, 80,000 Hispanics, 80,000 African Americans. There is a significant economic gap between low-income minorities and middle- and upper-income whites.

With a population of 370,000 in ninety square kilometers, Oakland is a much larger city geographically, with lower housing densities, than San Francisco. While Oakland's downtown has lost business to new developments in suburbs beyond the hills—a natural boundary to the east, between urban and suburban areas—its position in the center of the Bay Area makes it an ideal housing choice for a variety of people. As in San Francisco, and as in much of the East Bay Area, there are enormous discrepancies between the incomes and home values of a largely white population in hillside homes and a predominantly minority population in flatland neighborhoods. Median rents in Oakland range from $500 to $600, compared to an $800 median in the whole of Alameda County, of which Oakland is a part. Home ownership is less costly than in neighboring counties, but Oakland's median home value is still $172,000 (U.S. Census 1990; Anders and Chao 1996).

By comparison, Santa Cruz and Watsonville are very small towns. Although the city of Santa Cruz and the surrounding areas house a primarily white middle-class population, the city has always been home to a large community of retirees living on fixed incomes, students, and individuals who chose the community for its relaxed lifestyle and who survive on limited incomes. Watsonville is an agricultural community, essentially segregated between the two halves of the population: established white families and Hispanic workers (both permanent and migrant).[1] Despite the obvious political and racial disparities, the economic status of the community is fairly common for California, with median incomes at $28,000, rents at $625 per month, and home values at $182,500 (U.S. Census 1990).

RECOVERY

Single-family housing recovery after Loma Prieta was fueled by a combination of federal disaster assistance, insurance settlements, and volunteerism. Data from insurance companies and federal disaster assistance agencies suggest that some fifty to sixty thousand home owners received some form of loan or insurance settlement, and perhaps two to three thousand others received some form of charitable assistance. See tables 13 and 14.

After insurance, the next-largest amount of reconstruction funding for single-family housing came from the Small Business Administration. The disaster assistance program provided $582 million in loans to home owners, businesses, and rental housing owners. Seventy percent of the loans were paid to home owners, which accounted for 53 percent of the funds. Small grants and loans were available from various FEMA programs, again largely targeted to home owners, except for portions of the Individual and Family Grant program, available for personal property losses. After the earthquake, the state of California realized that federal aid would not be sufficient, and it created the California Disaster Assistance Program (CALDAP), as part of the Department of Housing and Community Development, with loan funds targeted to both single-family and multifamily properties.[2]

TABLE 14

PUBLIC EXPENDITURES ON HOUSING
ASSISTANCE, REPAIR, AND RECONSTRUCTION,
LOMA PRIETA EARTHQUAKE

Agency or Program	Total ($ Millions)	Number Assisted
FEMA Housing Rental	$30.71	14,133
FEMA Mobile Homes	$4.00	150
FEMA Individual Family Grant	$46.06	29,855
FEMA Minimum Home Repair	$7.70	6,150
SBA Home Loans	$309.14	11,481
SBA Rental Property Loans	~ $126.50	Not available
CALDAP Home Loans	$43.31	810
CALDAP Rental Property Loans	$43.63	142
Red Cross Home Grants	$.90	68
Red Cross Multifamily Grants	$10.00	1,158
Red Cross Multifamily Predevelopment Loans	$2.25	832
FEMA Lawsuit Settlement for Affordable Housing Replacement	$23.00	1,500 units
Total	$609.25	

SOURCE: Comerio 1994.

While much of the minor damage to single-family homes was paid for by insurance and Small Business Administration loans, poor home owners, such as the Hispanic laborers in Watsonville, typically did not meet the SBA credit requirements for government low-interest loans. Those same owners almost certainly did not carry an expensive earthquake rider to their home-owner policies, if they had insurance at all. Since homeowners' insurance is a requirement of traditional mortgage lending, one tends to assume all homes have it. But in fact, in poor neighborhoods, where credit (lending and borrowing) is often done through relatives in a gray market, traditional underwriting criteria do not apply.

Similarly, many of the owner-built homes in the Santa Cruz Mountains, a building type exempted from some traditional regulations (Levin 1978), were not eligible for normal disaster recovery assistance. These too were outside the traditional lending and insurance framework. Despite these limitations, 75 percent of the damaged single-family houses were repaired or replaced within one year of the earthquake. How did it happen?

Watsonville received more than $1 million in donations from individuals, corporations, foundations, and its sister city in Japan. The Red Cross supplemented this fund with $2.5 million for affordable housing

Figure 25. Home Repair, Watsonville. Damaged homes in Watsonville were rebuilt with new foundations and cripple walls. (Mary C. Comerio)

and services for earthquake victims. City officials realized that most of the disaster victims would not qualify for SBA loans, and they made a decision very quickly after the earthquake to use this fund to help people rebuild. The city made grants of amounts between twenty and forty thousand dollars to anyone who needed funds for housing repair or reconstruction. See figure 25.

Numerous volunteer organizations and religious groups (e.g., the Mennonites, the Christian World Relief Committee, Habitat for Humanity, and other interfaith and nonprofit organizations) donated time and funds in the rebuilding effort. Many weekends were marked by volunteer construction workers involved in "barn-raising" new residences. The close-knit character of the Latino community and the willingness of neighbors to help in a variety of ways contributed to the spirit of self-reliance. The small-scale wood-frame construction made it easy for unskilled laborers to volunteer assistance in the rebuilding efforts, and the city's decision to waive permit fees and to be "easy on permits, and tough on inspections" allowed people to get on with the work without delay. Finally, since most victims had not lost their jobs to the disaster, there was an incentive to get back into their homes as soon as possible.

Figure 26. The Oakland
Hotel under Repair. Planned
structural improvements had
not begun when Loma Prieta
damaged this hotel. It took
more than seven years to
repair ten single-room-
occupancy hotels in Oakland.
(Mary C. Comerio)

Taken together, the resources available for home owners to repair or
rebuild single-family residences seem to have been adequate for a moderate disaster on the scale of Loma Prieta. As will be discussed in detail
in chapter 5, federal disaster assistance is primarily designed for home
owners. There is an implicit assumption that market forces (i.e., supply
and demand) will replenish rental housing stock as needed. The Loma
Prieta earthquake demonstrated the gaps in the conceptualization of disaster recovery programs and in the market's ability to replace affordable
housing. Thus, in each city, *who* lost housing was as important as how
much was lost.

Loma Prieta demonstrated that the loss of affordable housing was
greater than the capacity of any existing disaster or nondisaster housing
program. The state's CALDAP program became the funder of last resort, lending a total of $44 million to owners of rental properties and
$43 million to home owners over a five-year period after the earthquake.
See figure 26. Because CALDAP was a new program in a traditional housing agency, the mix of disaster assistance with housing assistance led to
complex and cumbersome regulations.

One situation following the demolition of a heavily damaged 160-unit hotel in San Francisco's South of Market area exemplifies the mismatch between funding regulations and recovery goals. After a long process involving foreclosure and purchase of the property by the Redevelopment Agency, the site was made available to a nonprofit housing developer. Before CALDAP granted funding for the project, it required one-for-one unit replacement. At the same time, this funding did not cover building code or quality upgrades. Thus, while units could be replaced they could not be improved. Moreover, the program provided limited support for development costs, and it imposed rent ceilings and tenant relocation costs. Since San Francisco zoning regulations for the site limited the height of new construction to eight stories in order to protect a nearby park from building shadows, the nonprofit organization could not fit more than 140 of the smallest units possible on the site. CALDAP's cumbersome requirements led to inordinate delays in the development process. Ultimately, the nonprofit developer resolved the funding Catch-22 by using CALDAP funds for only 40 percent of the project and making up the difference with a variety of funds from Community Development Block Grants, city loans, and foundation grants.

Despite these frustrations, CALDAP was the primary source of financing for the replacement of low-income housing in all areas after the earthquake. The program provided 810 home owners with a mean of $53,466 to repair or rebuild their homes, and 142 rental property owners with the funds to repair or replace housing. This funding assisted in the repair or replacement of about 2,800 units, for a mean of $15,000 per unit. Unfortunately, the CALDAP program provided assistance for fewer than half the affordable units damaged, and the contribution was less than half the real cost of replacement or repair. With the cost of new housing units in urban areas of California ranging from $80,000 to $140,000 per unit in 1990 (Bay Area Economics and ARCH Research 1993), owners were required to support the cost of residential rebuilding outside the traditional disaster recovery programs.

The frustration experienced by local governments and affordable housing advocates over the lack of resources for low-income victims took expression in the form of a frontal attack on FEMA and the American Red Cross by San Francisco Mayor Art Agnos. The media blitz that followed and a lawsuit against FEMA by the Legal Aid Society of Alameda County led to two unusual one-time solutions to the affordable housing repair crisis.

The lawsuit claimed that FEMA discriminated against low-income victims because the agency enforced the "proof of tenancy" and a thirty-day residency requirement for temporary housing assistance, which automatically disqualified SRO dwellers. While the strictly legal recourse to the grievance would have been to ask FEMA to provide the funds to the people concerned, Legal Aid recognized that the temporary assistance funds would not solve the problem since no comparable units were on the market. Therefore, Legal Aid decided to ask for money to replace units lost in the earthquake. The final settlement of $23 million was determined by multiplying the number of SRO units lost by an average unit value of $10,500. The funds were divided among Alameda, San Francisco, and Santa Cruz in proportion to their losses, and, overall, 1,200 to 1,500 units were actually rebuilt (Comerio 1994; Dietz 1995).

In a separate action, the American Red Cross responded to the political pressure to keep in the Bay Area all relief funds raised for Loma Prieta victims and to use some of the $84 million raised for housing recovery purposes (American Red Cross 1991). The ARC set aside $13 to $15 million for housing recovery projects, including $900,000 for grants to low-income home owners, $10 million for multifamily projects, and $2.25 million for what is known as "gap" financing, or predevelopment loans to nonprofits to start the development process.[3]

In the end, many of the damaged buildings were purchased by nonprofit housing developers skilled in patching together funding from multiple sources. In most cases, the disaster recovery funding covered 20 to 50 percent of the rebuilding costs, and the remaining costs were paid by traditional low-income housing programs such as Community Development Block Grants. Unfortunately, these funds are typically available only to the nonprofit community, and they provided no assistance to landlords of privately owned buildings.

Further, there were no special appropriations from the U.S. Office of Housing and Urban Development for disaster recovery. HUD provided very little assistance, despite a February 1990 memorandum from the regional administrator of Region IX (an area of western states) to HUD Secretary Jack Kemp describing the crisis and recommending additional allocations of Section 8 Rental Housing Vouchers and rental rehabilitation program funds to affected cities. The agency's only action was the allocation of 500 rental-assistance vouchers and 664 moderate-rehabilitation vouchers to the area. This did not represent an extra allocation but only an attempt to speed up existing allocations, which, because of bureaucratic delays, did not materialize until the summer of 1990.

The Loma Prieta earthquake deepened the already existing crisis in affordable housing in the Bay Area. It was apparent that the normal single-family-oriented housing recovery system of SBA loans augmented with Individual Family Grants and Minimal Home Repair Grants from FEMA, and other grants and loans from state and local governments, combined with insurance, would not be sufficient to enable housing recovery. Because the earthquake hit hardest in low-income housing in the San Francisco, Oakland, Santa Cruz, and Watsonville downtowns, the market was not able to provide alternative or replacement housing at affordable rents without some public assistance. Despite the efforts of the state and non-profit agencies, less than half of the low-income housing units destroyed by the earthquake were replaced or rebuilt (Comerio 1994).

HURRICANE ANDREW

Hurricane Andrew slammed into south Florida in the predawn hours of Monday, August 24, 1992, and damaged 1,760 square kilometers (1,100 sq. mi.) as it traveled across the peninsula and into the Gulf of Mexico, hitting southern Louisiana before dissipating. Andrew was classified as a category 4 storm, with sustained winds of 145 miles (232 km) per hour and gusts up to 175 miles (280 km) per hour. Andrew's storm surge set a record high for Florida: 16.9 feet (5 meters) in Biscayne Bay at S.W. 160th Street. See map 5.

The storm battered the coast but caused its most severe damage inland when the eye of the storm made landfall just east of Homestead Air Force Base, about 19 kilometers south of Miami. The area hardest hit bordered on the Everglades and Biscayne Bay National Park. There are two incorporated cities in the vicinity, Homestead (population 26,800) and Florida City (population 5,800), and acres of subdivisions that sprawled during the 1980s into the unincorporated areas south of North Kendall Drive, along U.S. Highway 1.

The impact on residents and businesses was staggering. Hurricane Andrew inflicted heavy damage in an area more than 64 kilometers in diameter. Street and highway signs were blown away. Loss of power, water, communications, and sewage facilities contributed significantly to the overall impact. Florida Power and Light reported that more than 20,000 kilometers of local power distribution lines and 960 kilometers of high-power feeder lines were down, affecting 1.4 million customers.

Virtually all economic activity in the devastated area of south Dade County ceased after the storm. Eight thousand of the county's sixty thou-

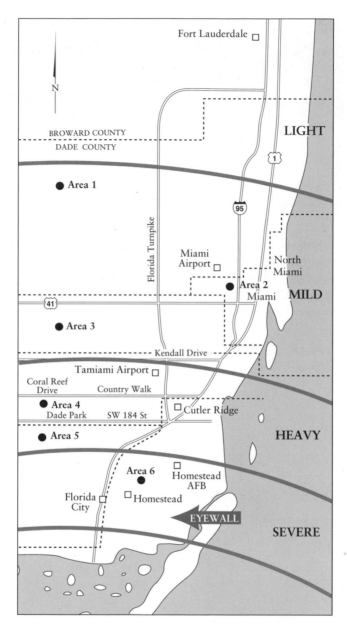

Map 5. Hurricane Andrew Impact Area. The hurricane battered south Dade County, Florida, but missed downtown Miami. The most severe damage was in the area of Homestead Air Force Base. (EQE International, Inc.)

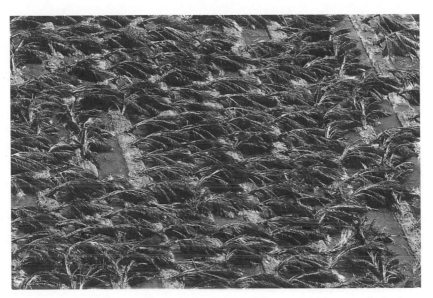

Figure 27. Bowled-Over Young Palm Trees in Homestead Nursery. Agricultural damage was extensive throughout south Florida—80 percent of the farms and ten thousand acres within nurseries were damaged—impacting jobs as well as property values. (© *The Miami Herald*/Chuck Fadely)

sand businesses were damaged. Most significant, Homestead Air Force Base was virtually leveled. The base itself had accounted for fourteen thousand military and civilian jobs and annually contributed more than $4 million to the local economy. Damage to agriculture was estimated at over $1 billion. Acres and acres of lime trees, mangos, and other tropical fruits were uprooted, causing short- and long-term loss of income for growers and workers alike. See figure 27. Finally, tourism, an industry that brought in $500 million per year, was impacted—not only by damage to hotels and restaurants but by the perception that south Florida was a place to avoid for some years. See figure 28.

In Louisiana, thirteen offshore oil and gas production platforms were destroyed, along with houses and other buildings, but fortunately the storm avoided the cities of New Orleans and Miami, and in this way both states were spared even greater devastation (EQE International 1992; Florida Governor's Disaster Planning and Response Committee 1993; Mesa 1993).

Hurricane Andrew was the third most powerful storm to hit the United States in its recorded history, exceeded only by Camille in 1969 and the Labor Day storm that struck the Florida Keys in 1935. Andrew tops the

Figure 28. Aerial View of Country Walk Area of South Dade County. Here, nearly all homes suffered some damage and many were completely destroyed. (© *The Miami Herald*/Joe Rimkus Jr.)

charts as the costliest hurricane of this century, with estimates of the losses ranging between $22 and $25 billion (see chapter 1, table 4). Clearly, all of the "most costly" storms are a product of recent development on the coastal areas. Fortunately, modern forecasting, with its ability to predict and monitor the path of hurricanes, has minimized the death toll of recent hurricanes.

HOUSING DAMAGE RELATIVE TO OVERALL DAMAGE

The physical damages caused by Hurricane Andrew in Florida have been estimated at nearly $23 billion, with the largest single area of loss (46 percent) concentrated in residential structures. The residential impact is more dramatic when the value of damage to structures and contents is tallied, amounting to almost 70 percent of the total losses. This is consistent with the fact that the area hardest hit was made up of the residential suburbs south of downtown Miami. Commercial structures and contents; vehicle losses (including autos, boats, and airplanes); agriculture; and federal, state, and local government losses all follow, with about $1 billion in losses in each category. See table 15.

TABLE 15
ESTIMATES OF DAMAGE IN FLORIDA
FROM HURRICANE ANDREW

Category	Damage ($ Millions)	Percentage
Residential Structures	$10,481	46.0%
Residential Contents	$5,385	23.0%
Commercial Structures	$1,142	4.5%
Commercial Contents	$1,080	4.5%
Vehicles	$1,109	4.5%
Agriculture	$910	4.5%
State and Local Government	$2,273	10.0%
Federal Government	$1,151	4.5%
Nonprofit	$15	~
Total	$22,649	100%

SOURCE: West and Lenze 1994.

While residential losses clearly dominated the financial losses, the fact that nearly three-quarters of the losses were covered by insurance lessened the blow. The closure of Homestead Air Force Base, the loss of twenty-one thousand jobs (on the base and in the surrounding community), and the permanent dispersion of some twenty-five to thirty-five thousand households had long-term impacts on south Dade County. Despite the "silver lining" of every disaster—the jobs, income, and revenue generated in the region by reconstruction funded by insurance and federal aid—these benefits are short term and do not offset the longer-term losses in farm, military, service, and government incomes (West and Lenze 1994).

In the agricultural sector, for example, tropical fruit trees such as limes, mangos, and avocados "fell like tumbleweeds" and were not replaced. Similarly, all farm equipment, packinghouses, and nurseries in south Dade County were about 95 percent damaged (Mesa 1993). Together, this brought about a long-term change in employment patterns for agriculture workers and for the services that supported these modest-income families. The demand for construction and repair services helped the local economy for two to three years but did not replace the agriculture and military jobs displaced (West and Lenze 1994), which in turn affected the residential recovery.

HOUSING TYPES DAMAGED

South Dade County had 80 percent of the total residential losses in Hurricane Andrew. The Federal Emergency Management Agency estimated

TABLE 16

NUMBER OF RESIDENCES
DESTROYED OR DAMAGED,
HURRICANE ANDREW

	Destroyed	Major Damage	Minor Damage	Total	Percentage
Single Family	8,373	37,245	40,632	86,250	63%
Apartments/Condos	10,719	13,995	13,889	38,603	29%
Mobile Homes	8,974	1,100	519	10,593	8%
Total	28,066	52,340	55,040	135,446	100%
S. Dade County Total	48,900	—[a]	58,900	107,800	80%

SOURCE: Project CHART 1994.

[a] Major damage is included in the total destroyed.

that a total of 135,000 residential units were affected by the storm, of which 80,000 (59 percent) were destroyed or substantially damaged. These units were largely modest single-family homes. While some expensive homes in high-income communities were affected, the majority of the damage was in the southernmost part of Dade County, where 70 percent of the homes were valued below $75,000.

In south Dade County, some 47,000 units were destroyed or seriously damaged, and 60,000 sustained some minor damage. The number of apartments and condominiums was proportionally greater in the south Dade County area (41 percent of the total destroyed or seriously damaged, compared to 30 percent overall) because of the concentrations of multifamily housing for air force base personnel and agriculture workers in the areas hardest hit. See table 16.

HABITABILITY

The damage to residential buildings in Hurricane Andrew was very much like that in Hurricane Hugo. See figures 29 and 30. There was widespread water damage, and this was by far the most costly factor in both hurricanes. The prevalence of water damage is a function of failure in roof coverings and openings (i.e., doors and windows). The large quantities of flying debris broke a great number of unprotected windows. In turn, damage to the openings contributed to the level of structural failure through internal pressurization. Damage to roofs was commonly associated with

Figure 29. Children Playing on Makeshift Swings amid Debris. Children in Homestead, Florida, were determined not to let Andrew get them down. (© *The Miami Herald*/Angel E. Valentin)

Figure 30. Aerial View of Damage to Manufactured Homes. A mobile home park near Harris Field in Homestead was devastated by the storm. (© *The Miami Herald*/David Walters)

Figure 31. Waterfront Condominiums with Roof and Window Damage. Multifamily structures comprised more than 40 percent of the housing losses in Hurricane Andrew—some were beachfront condominiums, but the majority were apartments for moderate-income service personnel. (National Oceanic and Atmospheric Administration Photo Library)

inadequate attachment of roof sheathing, especially in gable-roof homes, which experienced much greater damage than the more aerodynamic hip-roof homes. See figures 31 and 32.

Overall, the high level of residential damage was caused by a combination of factors. While the South Florida Building Code contained numerous requirements for hurricane-resistant construction, the hurricane winds exceeded the design wind speed specified in the code. Hurricane straps, the most obvious preventive measure, were generally installed in an effective manner; however, inspectors found that less obvious details, such as fastener spacing on roof sheathing, which ultimately determines the structural capacity of the roof system, were not in compliance with the codes. Further, the combination of gable roofs, poor quality materials, and unprotected openings led to the high degree of roof and water damage (NAHB 1993).

As a result, a high proportion—some 80,000 units, or 59 percent of the total units damaged in the hurricane—was largely uninhabitable. Ex-

Figure 32. Wind-Damaged Home with "I SURVIVED ANDREW" on Roof. A home owner broadcast a message from the remains of his house. (Raul De Molina, Sygma)

act data for damage and habitability were hard to generate. Sometimes local officials found people living in a portion of what looked like a destroyed house. In other cases, the roof might be intact, but closer inspection would show the house to be a vacant shell. Single-family dwellings, apartments, and mobile homes all sustained heavy damage in the areas of Cutler Ridge, Homestead, and Florida City, but to the north even homes with lesser damage were without utilities and basic services for months after the storm.

VALUE OF THE LOSSES

West and Lenze estimate that damage to residential structures and their contents made up nearly $16 billion of the $22 billion in losses in Florida (1994). Approximately $4.9 billion of this amount was for uninsured losses. These figures are confirmed in reports from Metropolitan Dade County Project CHART, the Coordinated Hurricane Andrew Recovery Team (Project CHART 1994) and the Florida Department of Insurance (1993). Florida home owners received almost $11 billion in insurance

TABLE 17

LOSSES AND CLAIMS PAID BY INSURANCE COMPANIES,
HURRICANE ANDREW

	Home Owners	Fire Policies	Mobile Homes	Total
Claims Paid	280,000	24,267	11,779	316,246
Paid Losses($ Millions)	$9,973	$932	$180	$10,875
Average Claim	$34,800	$38,100	$15,200	$34,400

SOURCES: Florida Department of Insurance 1993; Insurance Institute for Property Loss
Reduction 1995.

TABLE 18

PUBLIC EXPENDITURE ON HOUSING
ASSISTANCE, REPAIR, AND RECONSTRUCTION
AS RESULT OF HURRICANE ANDREW

Agency or Program[a]	Total ($ Millions)	Number Assisted
FEMA Temporary Rental Housing[b]	$141.2	~ 68,000
FEMA Individual Family Grant	$198.0	~ 63,500
FEMA Minimum Home Repair	Not available	Not available
SBA Home Loans	$398.8	17,902
SBA Rental Housing Loans	~ $100.0	Not available
National Flood Insurance	$18.0	Not available
HUD Section 8 Vouchers	$183.0	4,000
HUD CDBG/Home	$196.0	Not available
Total Federal Housing Assistance	$1,235.0	

SOURCE: Project CHART 1994.

[a] Additional resources included federal funds to repair damage to 1,600 of 2,500 HUD-owned units,
a State of Florida Housing Reconstruction Fund that provided $172.8 million in home repair loans,
and $23 million raised by We Will Rebuild (a developer-business coalition) for local community re-
building efforts.
[b] Includes mobile homes and rental housing vouchers.

payments, and $1.2 billion (56 percent) of the $2.2 billion of the federal
dollars spent in Florida was used for housing assistance. See tables 17
and 18.

CONCENTRATION OF LOSSES

Although four counties in Florida, totaling over 15,500 square kilometers, and two Louisiana counties were declared federal disaster areas, the
great majority (80 percent) of the losses were concentrated in the southernmost portion of Dade County, south of North Kendall Drive. The Met-

ropolitan Dade County Planning Department Research Division produced an Impact Area Profile one month after the storm (in September 1992), which describes the area hardest hit by Hurricane Andrew. See map 5.

The developed area of south Dade County runs about 29 kilometers from north to south, and 24 kilometers from east to west, and it straddles U.S. Highway 1. The area includes both urban and rural communities and a diversity of rich and poor, with structures ranging from high-rise offices at Dadeland in the north to farmworker trailer parks southwest of Homestead. To the west of the developed area lies Dade's prime agricultural land.

The area's 355,000 residents represent about 18 percent of the county's population and generally reflect its ethnic and cultural diversity. But south Dade differs from the rest of the county in that there are more family households, more children, and fewer elderly persons. Racial and ethnic segregation is evident in the housing patterns. The black population is clustered in older black communities along U.S. 1, in Richmond Heights, Perrine, Goulds, Homestead, and Florida City. The more recently arrived Hispanics live in less segregated areas, but concentrations are apparent in South Miami Heights, Leisure City, and the more recently developed suburb, the Hammocks, on the western edge of Kendall Drive.

At the time of the hurricane, there were about 136,000 dwellings in the area (18 percent of the dwellings in the county), of which 75,000 were single-family detached homes, 6,000 were mobile homes, and the remainder were townhouses, duplexes, and other attached units. *Two-thirds* of all the units were owner occupied and the remainder were rentals. Vacancy rates ran about 8 percent. A disproportionate share of the rentals was located in the hardest hit area at the southern edge of the county, including Homestead, where the owner/renter mix was 58/42 percent, closer to the county average.

At the same time, incomes and the values of homes in the southernmost portion of the county were lower than average. More than half of the households in the areas with severe damage (see map 5) earned less than twenty-five thousand dollars annually. Seventy percent of the homes in these areas were valued below seventy-five thousand dollars (80 percent of the county median home value of eighty-five thousand dollars). The families hardest hit in south Dade County were also larger than those in the rest of the county. Over half of them were minorities, and 42 percent were renters. Thus the poorest populations in the poorest quality housing lost their homes and their jobs in Hurricane Andrew (Metropolitan Dade County Planning Department 1992; 1993; 1994).

Figure 33. Reconstruction in Homestead. Streets and homes were rebuilt on existing subdivision lots. (Catherine J. Firpo)

HOUSING RECOVERY

Given that the storm caused disproportionate losses to lower-cost housing, the recovery is complex and hard to evaluate. The housing market in Dade County was temporarily severely tightened. Apartment vacancy rates plummeted to record lows of virtually zero in south Dade. Approximately 100,000 residents left Dade County. Among those who stayed, much doubling up took place. At the same time, a wide variety of housing assistance was made available from many sources, both public and private.

Insurance paid for the majority of the single-family housing losses, and Project CHART (1994) estimates that overall, 75 percent of the housing lost was restored to 90 percent of its prestorm value within two years. See figures 33 and 34.

FEMA provided over 3,600 mobile homes and travel trailers to disaster victims, and in conjunction with the U.S. Department of Agriculture the county developed a mobile home park for migrant farmworkers within ninety days of the storm. See figure 35. HUD made available eight thousand Section 8 rental vouchers for disaster victims, about half of which were extended until September 1996, four years after the storm. HUD also managed the repairs of sixteen hundred of the twenty-five hundred HUD-assisted affordable housing units in the county.

Figure 34. Typical Home with New Roof, South of Miami. Insurance companies paid for roof replacement in communities south of Miami. (Catherine J. Firpo)

Figure 35. Temporary Farmworker Housing South of Homestead. Temporary and new farmworker housing was financed by the Department of Agriculture. (Catherine J. Firpo)

At this point it is clear that the combination of insurance settlements and almost $400 million in SBA home loans has eased the financial burden of rebuilding for middle-class and moderate-income home owners. The picture of what has actually happened to low-income home owners and renters in the southernmost part of south Dade County is less clear. County officials have commented that while low-priced homes are under construction, these are being built by developers and sold to newcomers to the area. The closure of Homestead Air Force Base and the upheaval in the agriculture industry, combined with the absolute lack of housing choice, forced some thirty-five thousand people to permanently relocate out of the area, and about one-quarter of those left the state.

In an Economic Development Plan prepared by Arthur Andersen and Company for the Metro Dade County Office of Community Development (1994), the authors included a microanalysis of the Redlands-Gould area, the Homestead area, and the Southwest Kendall-Perrine-Cutler Ridge area. In these areas, twelve developments have been started since the hurricane, offering low-priced homes with an average price of seventy to eighty thousand dollars. Buyers are using Federal Housing Administration, Veterans Administration, Sur Tax, or Hurricane Assisted finance programs, the latter two state programs allowing modest-income buyers to enter into the market. The buyers are largely blue-collar, first-time buyers moving from central Dade County, particularly the city of Hialeah, or they are already living in south Dade.

Despite the many "as is" sales of uninsured homes, and the loss of multifamily rental housing, the total number of housing units in south Dade appeared to be back to prestorm levels two to three years after the hurricane. The recovery was primarily a middle-class phenomenon, fueled by insurance, federal aid, and in-migration to new, relatively affordable developments. The changes in the jobs market and the limited number of rental units available has driven the poorest population out of south Dade County.

NORTHRIDGE EARTHQUAKE

On Martin Luther King's birthday, January 17, 1994, at 4:31 A.M., a magnitude 6.8 earthquake, nineteen kilometers below the earth's surface, rocked the San Fernando Valley and the Los Angeles Basin for fifteen seconds. The buried thrust fault, one and a half kilometers from the campus of California State University at Northridge, or about thirty-two

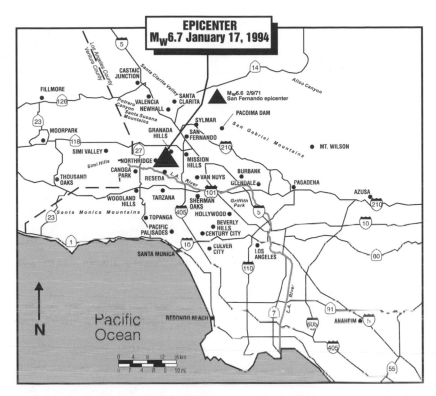

Map 6. Northridge Earthquake Impact Area. The earthquake was centered
in the San Fernando Valley, a largely residential area thirty-two kilometers
northwest of downtown Los Angeles. (EQE International, Inc.)

kilometers west-northwest of downtown Los Angeles, caused extensive
damage from Anaheim in Orange County to Valencia in Ventura County,
and from Santa Monica to Glendale in Los Angeles County. See map 6.
Media attention was focused on the collapsed Northridge Meadows
apartment complex and fires and flooding from collapsed water and gas
mains, as well as some large commercial structures that failed.

Although the earthquake was the same size and approximately the same
location as the 1971 San Fernando (Sylmar) earthquake, it was much more
damaging because of the density of development, which had increased in
the ensuing twenty-three years. Peak ground acceleration reached .9g (the
horizontal component) in four locations between Santa Monica, which
lies 24 kilometers to the south, and Sylmar, located 13 kilometers to the
north. Because the earthquake was caused by a relatively unknown fault,

the vertical motion was also significant in this earthquake, and it contributed substantially to the heavy damage to buildings (Moehle 1994;
EERI 1994; EQE International 1994; Todd 1994; and Housner 1994).

The losses were predominantly in the San Fernando Valley, a moder-
ately dense suburb where most of the residential structures were built after World War II. The greatest proportion of damage from the earthquake
occurred to two-to-four-story wood-frame residential buildings, strip
malls, and mini malls built between 1940 and 1976. While there was
certainly damage to hospitals, offices, schools, and numerous other building types of varied construction, almost all the building-related deaths,
as well as the significant structural and nonstructural losses, property
losses, and business losses, occurred in wood-frame residential and commercial structures. As noted by the Earthquake Engineering Research Institute, "These building types represent the low end of our design and
construction spectrum, both architecturally and structurally, and a huge
volume of construction" (EERI 1994, 32).

HOUSING DAMAGE RELATIVE TO OVERALL DAMAGE

The Northridge earthquake was the most destructive earthquake in the
United States since the great San Francisco earthquake in 1906, and the
first to be centered directly under an urban area since the 1933 Long
Beach earthquake. Fortunately it struck while most of the city slept, and
so the death toll was mercifully low. Only fifty-seven fatalities were attributed to the earthquake, of which sixteen occurred as a result of the
collapse of the Northridge Meadows apartment building. See figure 36.

Overall, this was an earthquake that severely damaged buildings.
Wood-frame housing sustained the greatest portion of the earthquake damage: damage to such homes comprised about 50 percent of the overall estimated $25 billion in losses; wood-frame homes represented 90 percent
of the total number of buildings affected. There were some ninety-three
thousand residential structures with nearly 450,000 units inspected in Los
Angeles, Ventura, and Orange Counties, but 95 percent of the damage was
located in Los Angeles, with more than 80 percent in the San Fernando
Valley. There were about ten thousand other damaged structures. Of these,
six thousand were commercial and industrial and four thousand were mu-
nicipal buildings, schools, and university and medical buildings (Comerio
1995; Comerio, Landis, and Firpo 1996).

The earthquake caused the collapse of 7 freeway bridges, and more

Figure 36. Collapse of Northridge Meadows Apartment Building. Sixteen people died in the collapse. (© J. Scott Smith)

Figure 37. House Pulled Apart by Landslide. Landslides caused a few dramatic losses of single-family homes, but the majority of houses damaged suffered only minor cracking and broken glass. (© J. Scott Smith)

Figure 38. Damaged Historic Unreinforced Masonry Building, Santa Monica. Unreinforced masonry buildings in Santa Monica were heavily damaged. The city had not begun implementation of a retrofit program at the time of the earthquake. (© J. Scott Smith)

Figure 39. Typical Carport Collapse, San Fernando Valley. Nearly one-third of the insured losses were of appurtenant structures such as carports and garden walls. (Mary C. Comerio)

Figure 40. Partial Collapse, Multifamily Structure with a Soft First Story. Modern wood-frame apartments with tuck under parking were particularly vulnerable to a soft first-story collapse. (© J. Scott Smith)

than 250 others were damaged. Although traffic was disrupted briefly, the state Department of Transportation was able to move quickly and repair all the freeway damage within three to four months. There was much less freeway damage than had been experienced in Loma Prieta, and the agency had the repair technology in place as a result of research conducted after Loma Prieta. See table 19.

TABLE 19
ESTIMATES OF DAMAGE FROM
NORTHRIDGE EARTHQUAKE

Category	Damage ($ Millions)	Percentage
Residential Buildings	$12,651	49%
Commercial Buildings	$4,854	19%
Public Buildings, Local Government Buildings, and Other Local Government Expenditures	$6,502	25%
Freeways and Bridges	$655	3%
Miscellaneous	$1,042	4%
Total	$25,700	100%

SOURCES: California Department of Insurance, U.S. Office of Management and Budget, and California Governor's Office of Emergency Services, in Comerio, Landis, and Firpo 1996.

There were some dramatic building failures in medical buildings, shopping malls, and parking structures built of nonductile concrete and concrete framing, such as the Kaiser Medical Building, the Northridge Fashion Mall, and the parking garage at California State University at Northridge. These were near the epicenter and built with materials and construction details known to be hazardous in earthquakes. By contrast, the biggest surprise of the disaster was the discovery of failures in the welded connections of about one hundred steel-frame buildings. Although the number of buildings affected was small, the potential impact of such hazards in a building type thought to be safe in earthquakes is a serious issue for architects, engineers, and researchers. Still, nonengineered wood-frame low-rise construction accounts for the greatest portion of any suburban building stock and is the type that clearly sustained the greatest damage in the Northridge earthquake.

HOUSING TYPES DAMAGED

Seven times as many apartments as homes were damaged in the Northridge earthquake in Los Angeles County.[4] See figure 37. There were seven thousand single-family homes and twenty-seven thousand multifamily buildings (with 49,000 units) given red and yellow tags. Again, the great majority of tagged dwellings were located in the city of Los Angeles (see table 20), although Santa Monica, with more than 2,600 tagged units, certainly had its proportionate share of the residential damage. See figure 38. By comparison, less than five hundred single-family homes in Ventura and Orange Counties combined were red and yellow tagged.

TABLE 20

NUMBER OF RESIDENCES DESTROYED
OR DAMAGED IN LOS ANGELES,
NORTHRIDGE EARTHQUAKE

	Red Tagged	Yellow Tagged	Green Tagged	Total	Percentage
Single Family	1,000	6,000	57,000	64,000	14%
Multifamily	15,000	34,000	327,000	376,000	84%
Mobile Homes	5,000	—[a]	4,000	9,000	2%
Total	21,000	40,000	384,000	449,000	100%

SOURCE: Comerio 1995; Seismic Safety Commission 1995.

[a] Major damage is included in the total destroyed.

HABITABILITY

The majority of the residential stock in the San Fernando Valley was built in the 1960s and 1970s. This valley, where most of the damage occurred, is relatively densely populated with wood-frame houses and apartment buildings in the one-to-four-story range. Most of the houses are one- and two-story, slab on grade, with semidetached garages or carports, swimming pools, and concrete-block garden walls. See figure 39. Some of the older houses have a slightly elevated first floor supported above the foundation by a cripple wall. The apartments and condominiums are typically designed so that the first floor is partially devoted to "tuck-under" parking, with two to three stories of residential units above. The first-floor garages are typically built of masonry or concrete walls and pipe columns supporting a concrete slab. The units above the slab are then built of wood.

Because wood buildings are both flexible and well connected, with many interior walls that act structurally, life-threatening collapses seldom occur. However, the soft first stories of the apartments with tuck-under parking are vulnerable, as was demonstrated in the Marina district apartment building failures in the Loma Prieta earthquake. This was by far the most common failure in the Northridge earthquake. See figure 40. The difference is that the Marina district apartments were 1920s-vintage buildings on bad soils, and the Northridge buildings were modern buildings on average soils. See figure 41. The second most common and dramatic failure was the loss of stucco sheathing on the exterior and drywall on the interior. See figure 42. Clearly these materials could not withstand the shear loads, and most were built at a time when a plywood underlayer was not required.

Although one might assume that newer buildings built after 1976 did better because of the improved seismic requirements in the 1976 Uniform Building Code, this was not the case for much of the wood-frame construction. While an increase in design requirements for certain building materials did increase the use of plywood, the allowable shear loads for plywood, stucco, and drywall have remained quite constant since the 1950s. There were changes in the allowable loads for drywall in the 1988 Uniform Building Code, but the Los Angeles code did not adopt these until 1991, and these were only applied to engineered buildings. Much conventionally framed dwelling construction came under a prescriptive part of the code for nonengineered buildings that had not been reviewed or changed for many years (EERI 1996).

Figure 41. Damaged Garden Apartments. Modern building codes did not prevent significant damage to wood-frame apartments, a result of poor design and construction practices and code deficiencies. (© J. Scott Smith)

Figure 42. Stucco Failure in Collapsed Multifamily Building. After soft first stories, the second major cause of damage was insufficient shear strength in stucco walls. (© J. Scott Smith)

As a result, wood-frame residential buildings were damaged in proportion to their distribution in the building stock by age. In other words, 53 percent of the vacated single-family homes were of the vintage 1940 to 1975, when 66 percent of all single-family homes were built in the San Fernando Valley. Similarly, 50 percent of the vacated multifamily stock was from the same era, when 58 percent of the apartment stock was constructed. The more contemporary residential buildings failed in direct correlation to their proportion in the building stock (Comerio 1995). Recent research suggests that when all other factors are accounted for, older structures—those built prior to 1950—actually outperformed newer construction (Comerio, Landis, and Firpo 1996). While the primary determinants of damage are ground shaking, soil conditions, and construction quality, another factor that may explain the damage to modern houses may be the change in house styles in the 1960s, including the introduction of split levels, two-car garages, and open-plan living rooms.

While the damage pattern suggests that all residential construction is vulnerable, irrespective of age, vulnerable is a relative term. It is clear from the limited number of collapses that basic life-safety criteria are being met in the modern codes for wood-frame construction, but the volume of damage, the cost of repairs, and the disruption to the lives of thousands cannot be overlooked in developing future code standards.

Although more than 450,000 units were inspected for damage, only a small portion of those were uninhabitable. The city of Los Angeles made a specific count of vacated units. In addition, the city used inspectors' rough preliminary estimates of the value of the damage to gauge the number of units that had more than five thousand dollars in damage. The city called these units "at risk" because city housing officials were concerned that units with high damage-repair costs could be lost from the housing stock if tenants were unwilling to stay, and if owners could not obtain financing for the repairs. The city estimated that 20,000 units were vacant and uninhabitable. Because these were predominantly in apartment buildings, there were in fact 30,000 units in the complexes with the vacated units. These additional 10,000 were obviously "at risk," as were seventeen thousand single-family homes and an additional thirteen thousand apartments with damages estimated at more than five thousand dollars per unit. All together, there were some 60,000 units uninhabitable or very heavily damaged, about 14 percent of the total damage tally.[5]

VALUE OF THE LOSSES

Significant earthquake damage to buildings is not always structural. Furniture and appliances are overturned, plaster and drywall cracked, windows and dishes broken, light fixtures knocked to the ground, porches and carports detached. Thus, in terms of real economic damage to residential structures, the number of heavily damaged units (whether termed "at risk" or red or yellow tagged) represents only the tip of the iceberg. Inspectors in Los Angeles County were asked to estimate the economic value of damages as part of their inspection reports. While these estimates were preliminary and limited to the inspector's judgment based on a cursory review of the damage, they provided an insight into the actual damage and an understanding of the magnitude of damage in housing units. The mean and median damage estimates for Los Angeles County are shown in table 21, and they represent a reasonable, if low, estimate of the value of the damage in inspected units.

Two years after the earthquake, losses and claims reported by insurance companies were wildly out of sync with the inspection estimates of $1.5 billion in damages. Insurance companies have reported nearly four hundred thousand earthquake-related claims (of which two-thirds are residential), with paid claims totaling more than $12 billion. The discrepancy is similar to those in Hurricanes Hugo and Andrew, in that the number of claims was two to three times the number of single-family homes inspected. This is partially a function of the inspection process, done as a safety assessment rather than a realistic damage assessment. In the Northridge event, the problem was compounded by the manner in which claims were estimated and settled by the insurance industry (Comerio, Landis, and Firpo 1996; Eguchi et al. 1996). See table 22.

Like the city government of Los Angeles, the insurance industry looked

TABLE 21

MEAN AND MEDIAN DAMAGE ESTIMATES
PER UNIT BY TAG COLOR,
NORTHRIDGE EARTHQUAKE

	Red Tagged	Yellow Tagged	Green Tagged
Single Family, Mean	$75,000	$31,900	$9,300
Single Family, Median	$135,700	$12,000	$3,000
Multifamily, Mean	$43,300	$9,600	$2,100
Multifamily, Median	$20,000	$3,333	$250

SOURCE: Comerio 1995.

TABLE 22
CLAIMS PAID BY INSURANCE COMPANIES,
NORTHRIDGE EARTHQUAKE
(AS OF MAY 1995)[a]

Policy Type	Claims Paid	Value ($ Millions)	Average Loss
Earthquake-Only Policy	6,687	$412,275	$61,653
Earthquake Rider on Home-Owner Policy	110,805	$4,550,152	$41,065
Earthquake Rider on Fire Policy	9,169	$246,988	$26,937
Earthquake Rider on Mobile Home Policy	5,494	$102,309	$18,622
Earthquake Rider on Condominium Policy	20,717	$272,432	$13,150
Earthquake Rider on Rental Policy	9,652	$80,636	$8,354
All Residential Policies	162,524	$5,664,793	$34,855

SOURCE: California Department of Insurance, in Comerio, Landis and Firpo 1996.

[a] As of September 1996, the California Department of Insurance reports that the final total number of claims is approximately 20% higher than described in this data set. Thus, the total number of residential claims is approximately 195,000 claims; the value paid amounts to $7,808,000.

at the information available after the Northridge event and estimated its losses to be about $2.5 billion (Eguchi et al. 1996). As claims continued to be made, six to eighteen months after the event, the industry was forced to revise its loss estimate upward, until two years later the final tab for insured losses was in the $12.5 billion range, of which some $7.8 billion was for residential losses (Comerio, Landis, and Firpo 1996).

A number of factors played a role—including bad judgment in estimating losses and an unexpected willingness to settle claims quickly. A few years earlier, when three thousand homes were incinerated in the Oakland Hills fire in 1991, and a similar number was lost in the Malibu fire of 1993, many insurance companies took a long time to settle claims. The public perception, fueled by media reports, was that insurance companies were stingy and uncooperative. The bad press was also the product of a multiyear battle with John Garamendi, a liberal insurance commissioner who forced a number of consumer-friendly requirements on insurance companies, including rebates on auto insurance premiums.

It appears that after the Northridge earthquake, companies were in a less combative mood, particularly since they did not perceive the losses to be extraordinary. Other reasons for the hike in the number of individual claims settled included:

1.   The loss estimation process: companies estimated losses on the basis of prevailing wages and code-approved construction practices, and because of a "line of sight" rule developed by the insurance commissioner, the cost of refinishing everything within the line of sight of the damage was included in the settlement.

2.   The payouts for appurtenant structures, contents, and temporary living expenses: damage to detached garages, carports, and garden walls was all covered as part of the policy, as were all interior finishes. Together these payouts represented 48 percent of all claims.

3.   Copycat claims: not all the late claims were a result of "hidden" damage but were a function of neighbors reviewing the windfalls of others and "recognizing" their own minor damage as "loss."

Thousands claimed the need for a few nights in a hotel, even if they stayed with their in-laws. On the property itself, a collapsed unreinforced concrete block garden wall would cost ten thousand dollars if replaced to code by a contractor. This became the offset for the deductible for most claimants. Other flimsy detached structures (especially carports) also contributed to the claim value. Both the insurers and the SBA put out the word that any glass breakage on carpet would require the carpet to be replaced, so nearly all were. Nearly everyone in the valley got a new television set, and many had their homes redecorated as a result of small cracks in the plaster. Needless to say, extensive finish work also drove up the cost of claims.

There were certainly many homes with serious damage, but the combination of stringent estimating rules, agents who were generous in the description of the damage, and victims who saw an opportunity to collect on what they perceived as an overpriced insurance product combined to drive the costs out of sight. Is the $7.8 billion in paid claims really representative of the damage value? Some researchers think not. In an unpublished study for the insurance industry, Haresh Shah found the actual damage to be about 70 percent of the paid claims, for many of the reasons discussed above.

CONCENTRATION OF LOSSES

Although the residential damage caused by the Northridge earthquake was spread over a three-county area, the vast majority of the damage was concentrated in fifteen neighborhoods in the central and western portions of the San Fernando Valley area of Los Angeles. These neighborhoods came to be known as "Ghost Towns" because in relatively small areas of six to eight square blocks more than 60 percent of the total housing stock was lost. In six of the Ghost Towns, nearly all of the housing was lost (Comerio 1995).

There were only thirty-eight census tracts in Los Angeles County with one hundred or more vacated units, accounting for 12 percent of the housing stock in these tracts. Again, the majority of these were in the valley. The overall housing loss in the San Fernando Valley, which contains almost half the housing in the city of Los Angeles, was only 3.2 percent, and the overall loss in the county was less than 1 percent.

As such, the earthquake did not create a housing crisis in the city or county of Los Angeles, but it did create the potential for a crisis in the Ghost Towns and the areas of concentrated loss. Understandably, people did not want to move far from their jobs, their children's schools, their churches, their friends, their dry cleaners, and local grocery stores. Generally, disaster victims have so many new things to manage that the desire for consistency with predisaster social patterns is very high (Wickham 1997) In earthquakes, unlike hurricanes, there is less likelihood for the entire infrastructure to be demolished at the same time, so it is easier for victims to choose to remain close to home.

HOUSING LOSS RELATIVE TO LOCAL CONDITIONS

Given the neighborhood concentration of damage, and the desire, even among renters, to stay close to home, the potential for a housing shortage in localized areas was very high. In this instance, Angelenos were lucky. The recession that had gripped Southern California since the late 1980s had produced a soft rental housing market. The multifamily housing vacancy rate in the San Fernando Valley before the earthquake was 9.3 percent. Citywide, the multifamily vacancy rate was 8.9 percent.

In the areas where the greatest concentrations of damage occurred, there was a surplus of vacant apartments. While the earthquake vacated nineteen thousand units, there were fifty-four thousand vacant units in the valley before disaster struck. As a result, there were places nearby for earthquake victims to live. This explains why the number requiring emergency shelter was low, relative to the amount of housing damage. Further, the unprecedented infusion of temporary housing assistance from FEMA, HUD, and the city of Los Angeles, combined with the availability of apartments, accounts for the relative speed with which victims found alternative housing.

While the process of distributing temporary housing assistance was muddled by the large number of families seeking assistance, by the need for eligibility checks, and by overwhelmed staffs at the Disaster Application Centers, the majority of individuals and families displaced by the earthquake found housing within three to four weeks. Compare that to the 1989 Loma Prieta experience, in which three emergency shelters in Oakland were converted to homeless shelters because no alternative housing for SRO hotel victims was available, in which the Red Cross operated some shelters in Santa Cruz County for a record sixty-six days, and in which two months passed before FEMA agreed to supply trailers in the town of Watsonville (Comerio 1994; 1995).

Despite the good fortune of available alternative housing near the areas of greatest damage, it is important to underscore the dire conditions within the Ghost Town neighborhoods. In these areas, whole blocks were damaged and vacant. The spoiled food and garbage inside the buildings attracted rodents and posed a public health hazard. The empty buildings attracted looters, vandals, squatters, drug dealers, prostitution rings, and gangs, whose trespassing caused additional damage. The threat of fire increased. Burglaries increased. The remaining neighbors were overwhelmed. How long could they live adjacent to derelict and dangerous structures? How could they continue their lives when neighborhood-serving businesses began to close for lack of customers?

Within two to three months after the earthquake, it was clear that serious blight conditions were imminent, if not inevitable. The city requested and received funding from FEMA for a security plan for the Ghost Towns. All vacant buildings were fenced and boarded, swimming pools were drained, debris was removed, and a round-the-clock security force patrolled the areas. At the same time, the Housing Department compiled a listing of all the damaged buildings within the Ghost Towns and worked directly with individual property owners on their plans to repair, rebuild, or sell their damaged buildings.

What kind of housing does the San Fernando Valley have? Aside from having almost half of the city's entire housing stock, it is characterized by the second highest home-ownership rate (48.2 percent) in any area of the city, and a very high rate of new rental construction that accounts for almost one-quarter of the city's rental stock. Rent-stabilized units (that is, units built before 1978 whose rents are regulated by the City of Los Angeles Rent Stabilization Ordinance) comprise 52 percent of the stock, while subsidized rental units account for only 6 percent. Single-family rental units account for another 17 percent of the rental stock, a share that is well above the citywide average of 12 percent (Hamilton, Rabinovitz, and Alschuler 1994, 18).

As such, the housing in the San Fernando Valley is generally middle class, and the rental stock is quite modern, although there are obvious variations in unit valuation across the valley. Among the fifteen Ghost Towns, residents of three had preearthquake median household incomes of more than fifty thousand dollars, residents of eight had median incomes of thirty to forty thousand dollars, and residents of only four had median incomes below twenty-five thousand dollars. The middle- and upper-income Ghost Towns are largely white and balanced between renters and owners. By contrast, the four impoverished Ghost Towns have a majority of nonwhite residents. Housing there is nearly 100 percent rent stabilized, with median rents between $500 and $650 per month, well below the 1993 citywide asked-for median of $682 per month (Comerio 1995; Hamilton, Rabinovitz, and Alschuler 1994).

HOUSING RECOVERY

Five years earlier, the Loma Prieta experience had focused attention on the lack of recovery programs for multifamily housing, and in 1994 the most severe Northridge losses appeared to be concentrated in apartments in the San Fernando Valley. The federal government was acutely aware of the post–Loma Prieta, post–Hurricane Andrew critiques of FEMA's response to the earlier disasters. At the same time, the Clinton administration was anxious to provide some economic assistance to the ailing economy in Southern California. So, disaster response happened quickly.

Temporary housing assistance was mailed directly to households in the highly damaged areas. HUD was on the scene from day one and provided unprecedented assistance, making twenty thousand Section 8 housing vouchers available for emergency shelter.[6] The recession had created high vacancies in multifamily apartments, so temporary housing was not a significant issue. However, despite the aggressive federal response to requests for short-term assistance, there was still no federal program for repair of multifamily housing, recessionary economics prevented many owners from qualifying for SBA loans, CALDAP (the state loan program developed after Loma Prieta) was bankrupt, and the voters of California turned down a temporary tax increase and a bond issue to fund recovery loans. See table 23.

In the months following the Northridge earthquake, the combination of preearthquake economic conditions—high rental vacancies, declining

TABLE 23
PUBLIC EXPENDITURE ON HOUSING
ASSISTANCE, REPAIR, RECONSTRUCTION
AS RESULT OF NORTHRIDGE EARTHQUAKE

Agency or Program	Total ($ Millions)	Number Assisted
FEMA Temporary Rental Housing	$380,758	119,583
FEMA Individual Family Grant	$214,307	214,227
FEMA Minimum Home Repair	$841,250	287,778
SBA Home and Renter Loans	$2,480,973	98,847
HUD Section 8 Vouchers	$200,000	12,643
HUD CDBG/Home	$605,000	Loans: 1,563
		Units: 13,000
Total Federal Housing Assistance	$4,722,315	

SOURCES: FEMA Status Report, U.S. Office of Management and Budget, the Urban Institute, Los Angeles Housing Department, in Comerio, Landis and Firpo 1996.

property values, declining rental income, high mortgage debt, and severe reduction of owner equity—made it clear that rental housing repairs would not take place without significant public intervention. It was also clear that the city of Los Angeles would serve not only as the lender of last resort but, in most cases, as the lender of first resort.

The city coordinated a successful effort to garner $321 million in Supplemental Disaster Relief Funds from HUD to assist property owners whose request for SBA and FEMA's Individual and Family Grant program had been declined. Table 24, published by the Los Angeles Housing Department in its report, *Rebuilding Communities* (1995), shows the allocation of federal funds and how they were being used for residential earthquake recovery.

The city of Los Angeles also worked directly with HUD officials on advance allocations of housing block grant funds so that other lending efforts could be undertaken (Rabinovitz and Comerio 1996). In addition to funding single and multifamily property repairs, the city targeted funds for acquisition and rehabilitation of damaged properties, loans to individual condominium owners and condominium associations, special assistance to coach and mobile home park owners who were unable to secure FEMA assistance, and loans to lenders to increase the supply of private loans to buyers of foreclosed or distressed properties. The result was a set of highly targeted programs based on data used to identify the concentrations of damaged units, in conjunction with the understanding of unmet lending needs. See figures 43 and 44.

TABLE 24
FUNDS ALLOCATED TO EARTHQUAKE HOUSING REPAIR THROUGH LOS ANGELES HOUSING DEPARTMENT

Funding Source	Total Allocated	Available for Loans	Administration Costs	Program Use
HOME Supplemental	$58,995,000	$53,353,500	$5,641,600	Citywide single and multifamily
HOME Presidential	$22,467,000	$22,467,000	$0	Multifamily Ghost Town only
CDBG Supplemental A	$40,209,400	$40,209,400	$0	Citywide single and multifamily
CDBG Supplemental B	$200,000,000	$195,000,000	$5,000,000	Citywide multifamily
Totals	$321,671,400	$311,029,800	$10,641,600	

SOURCE: Los Angeles Housing Department 1995.

Figure 43. Repairs to Multifamily Building with Soft First Story. Owners of apartments in the Willis-Natick Ghost Town were among the first to begin repairs with HUD-financed loans made by the Los Angeles Housing Department. (Mary C. Comerio)

Figure 44. Foundation Repair to Single-Family House. Insurance paid for the repair and refinishing of two hundred thousand homes, like this one in the West Adams area. (Mary C. Comerio)

HUD funds, combined with some SBA loans and private lender for-
giveness of a portion of the original mortgage debt, provided recovery
funding for two-thirds of the targeted twenty thousand units (mostly
Ghost Town and south-central Los Angeles properties) within two years
after the earthquake; less than five hundred units have been demolished.
While detailed statistics are not available, city housing officials investigated one neighborhood where they had low response to their loan programs, and they found that only two or three out of two hundred damaged buildings had not been repaired. The rest had been completed with
private funds.

Thus, it appears that within two years after the event, with a combination of private funding, lender participation, and an aggressive public lending program on the part of the city of Los Angeles, all but about
ten thousand of the sixty thousand seriously damaged units had been repaired. Given the level of insurance settlements and Small Business Ad
ministration loans, it is clear that the minor damage in single-family homes
has all been repaired. What remains uncertain is the level to which many
of the privately funded multifamily units have been repaired. Owners may
have done the work necessary to make the units habitable, but nonessential repairs may have been ignored, and as a result the quality of units,
especially affordable units, may have declined (Comerio 1996; Urban Institute and Hamilton, Rabinovitz, and Alschuler 1996).

COMPARISON TO OTHER
RECENT AMERICAN DISASTERS

Hurricanes Hugo and Andrew and the Loma Prieta and Northridge
earthquakes stand out as major disasters, if not in terms of lives lost
then certainly in terms of cost to repair or replace buildings and infrastructure. What makes these different from the $15 billion great mid-
western flood of 1993; or Hurricane Iniki on the island of Kauai in
1992, with its smaller but highly concentrated losses; or the California wildfires in Oakland in 1991 or Malibu in 1993? Primarily, it is
the combination of the quantity and concentration of housing damage
relative to the local market. When a disaster impacts the displaced victims' capacity to find alternative housing, and/or their capacity to finance repairs, it is truly a major disaster. Other costly disasters or in-
cidents of highly concentrated damage may not trigger a sheltering or
a financing crisis.

HURRICANE INIKI

Just weeks after Hurricane Andrew hit southern Florida, Hurricane Iniki struck Kauai in the Hawaiian Islands, on September 12, 1992. The hurricane's direct hit on the island killed four people and caused approximately 90 percent of the island's wood-frame buildings to sustain some damage. However, most of the damage was light to moderate, leaving windows broken and roofs damaged. The buildings most heavily damaged were homes along the waterfront, typically those that were older, poorly designed and/or poorly built, and weakened by dry rot. By comparison, many newer, well-designed and well-engineered houses and condominium projects suffered little damage (EQE International 1992).

The total estimated loss on Kauai was approximately $1.5 billion (FEMA 1993b; 1993c), and the Red Cross tallied thirteen thousand damaged homes, of which approximately fourteen hundred (11 percent) were destroyed (NAHB 1993). Despite the concentration of damage in an island community, there was not a tremendous need for alternative housing, in part because much of the damage was light, and in part because most of the units were vacation housing and not occupied year round. Financing repairs was not difficult. Many owners carried insurance, and for others FEMA recognized the hardship presented by the island's isolation and limited housing alternatives, and increased the maximum grant.

THE GREAT MIDWESTERN FLOOD OF 1993

By most traditional measures, the flooding in the spring and summer of 1993 along major rivers and their tributaries in the upper Mississippi River basin was a major event. Losses ranged from $12 to $16 billion. Although the great majority of the damage was concentrated in agricultural and transportation sectors, some fifty thousand housing units were damaged, and an equal number experienced flooded basements as a result of storm sewer backups. The duration of the flooding forced people in the floodplain areas out of their homes for an extended period. Was it a housing disaster?

There was not a serious problem with alternative housing for disaster victims. The flooding was spread over nine states in largely rural communities. While there were concentrations of damage in Chicago, St. Louis, and Kansas City, the majority of displaced residents were distributed over a vast geographic area. See figure 45. In addition, most were able to return to their homes after the floodwaters receded, and many

Figure 45. Missouri River Flooding in Communities West of St. Louis, 1993. This aerial view, looking southwest along the Missouri River on July 29, 1993, was taken a few days before the peak of the flood. In the foreground the twelve-hundred-acre Earth Island development is protected by levees, while much of the Chesterfield Valley is underwater. (Surdex Corporation)

were able to make minor repairs with financial assistance from national flood insurance, SBA loans, and FEMA grants (Interagency Floodplain Management Review Committee 1994).

The most innovative approach to financing repair of housing damage came in the form of a government buyout of damaged homes in designated floodplains. The program used funds from a combination of FEMA hazards mitigation and demolition programs, and HUD Community Development Block Grant programs, to buy out residential properties and help families relocate to higher ground. Altogether, some ten thousand floodplain properties formerly in small towns were purchased by the federal government and new housing built in new communities (Missouri Emergency Management Agency 1995; Brown 1996). While this is a valuable model for future floodplain management, it would be nearly impossible to translate into similar action in hurricane- and earthquake-prone regions, where the frequency and location of disasters is hard to predict.

THE OAKLAND AND MALIBU FIRESTORMS

The fall fire season in California is relatively predictable. The long dry summers turn trees and grasses to tinder, and a strike of lightning or a careless match can start a raging fire. Residential developments on hills and in canyons at the urban edge, the interface between cities and wildlands, are particularly vulnerable. This was clearly the case on October 20, 1991, when a wind-whipped brushfire spread over the hills of Berkeley and Oakland. See figure 46. In ten hours, eighteen hundred acres were blackened and some twenty-eight hundred dwelling units (of which twenty-five hundred were single-family homes) were destroyed (Woodbridge 1994; Comerio, Landis, and Firpo 1996). A similar event occurred in Southern California two years later, when more than ten thousand acres of wildland burned and three thousand homes in the Malibu area were destroyed.

Although in both cases the concentration of damage in a single neighborhood was both dramatic and shocking, the fire did not cause a crisis in housing. In both, the losses occurred in affluent communities where victims were able to accommodate themselves temporarily with friends or in hotels, and over the longer term in rentals in nearby communities. The homes were insured and residents were able to make choices between rebuilding or selling out and moving. The recovery did not always go smoothly, and numerous rebuilding problems surfaced in the private and the public sector. Many long-term residents were shocked to discover the limitations inherent in their home-owner policies and were frustrated by local government's attempts to impose new regulations on rebuilding efforts. Still, despite the frustration for individuals, the overall housing impact of the disaster was minor.

In determining the impact of a disaster, neither the intensity of the earthquake, hurricane, or other natural disaster, measured in scientific terms;

Figure 46. Single House Remaining after 1991 Oakland Hills Fire. Few houses survived the intense heat and flames that devastated three thousand homes in the Oakland and Berkeley Hills. (California Governor's Office of Emergency Services, Earthquake Program)

nor the number of buildings damaged; nor the estimated cost to rebuild is a good measure of the significance of the disaster. Simply put, the traditional "death and dollars" measure of disaster impact is insufficient. The density of development and the concentration of damage, as well as the physical and market conditions of the building stock at the time of the disaster, are more important.

A more accurate measure of the severity of a disaster has to include the scale of area impacted, the number of buildings affected, and the value of losses, together with local economic, social, and market conditions. These can be measured in terms of:

1. Amount of housing damage as a percent of the overall damage

2. Types of housing damage (single-family, condominium, or rental units, primary residences or vacation units)

3. Portion of the damaged stock that is uninhabitable

4. Value of the housing loss and the degree to which it is insured

5. Concentration of damage within a housing market

6. Social and economic condition of the area impacted

Together, these factors provide a better assessment of the severity of the disaster in housing terms and indicate the need for and availability of temporary alternative housing for displaced families, as well as the funds likely to be available for repairs and reconstruction.

The significance of local conditions is particularly clear in the aftermath of the Loma Prieta and the Northridge earthquakes, two disasters in urban settings where large numbers of multifamily housing units were affected. In each case, the availability of suitably sized, suitably priced undamaged units affected the government's capacity to provide temporary housing. After Loma Prieta, more generous rental assistance from FEMA would not have helped victims, because there were no comparable units available for displaced low-income victims. After Northridge, a surfeit of housing assistance was available, as was a surfeit of vacant available units. Thus, in each disaster, market forces dominated the success of the temporary-housing process.

That market forces and local social and economic conditions dominate recovery efforts is also evident in the rebuilding experience after each of the four recent urban disasters. Repair or replacement of affordable housing requires deep subsidies with or without disaster losses, whereas the speed of repairs for damaged single-family homes and rental housing is determined by the availability of funds combined with local market forces.

The use of a broader set of criteria in measuring disaster loss is not specific to the American experience. In the next chapter, the experience of housing losses after earthquakes in Mexico City and Kobe, Japan, will be described in the context of various traditional approaches to disaster relief and recovery. Despite differences in the victims' economic status and the local development conditions, the Mexican and Japanese housing losses were very much alike. While both governments pursued similar temporary-housing strategies, their approaches to rebuilding represent opposite ends of the spectrum. In chapter 4 these international cases, together with the American ones, will be used to assess the successes and failures of government assistance and recovery programs and to suggest alternative strategies to address disaster-created housing problems.

CHAPTER 3

Evaluating American Disaster Recovery in the Global Context

Earthquakes, hurricanes, volcanic eruptions, cyclones, typhoons, floods, and drought have destroyed communities and forced resettlement and rebuilding in nations around the world. Some geographic areas are of course more disaster-prone than others. The regular recurrence of storms and floods in countries such as Egypt or Bangladesh, for example, has forced the rural populations to live lightly on the fertile plains, investing more in their agriculture than their homes (Oliver-Smith 1990; 1991; Zaman 1991).

Many of the world's hazardous areas, once sparsely populated, have developed because of the growth of cities and industrial centers, which have attracted large populations to live and work in harm's way. Since the turn of the twentieth century, seventeen urban areas have been seriously damaged by earthquakes and hurricanes. More than half of these events have occurred in the last twenty-five years (see table 25). This chapter briefly reviews the housing loss and recovery issues from disasters in the past twenty-five years that have shaped much of the international and domestic thinking on disaster relief and recovery. Next, the chapter focuses on the recent experiences in Mexico City and Kobe, Japan. In these cases, the housing losses are comparable to those in recent American experience, but each city followed a very different approach to the recovery process. In each event, a substantial amount of multifamily rental housing was lost in the city centers, and most households did not have insurance. In Mexico, the government intervened to replace one

TABLE 25

PRINCIPAL URBAN DISASTERS

	Number of Deaths
1900 Galveston, Texas, Hurricane	6,000
1906 San Francisco, Earthquake and Fire	3,000
1906 Valparaiso, Chile, Earthquake	1,500
1923 Tokyo, Japan, Earthquake and Fire	143,000
1963 Skopje, Yugoslavia, Earthquake	1,100
1964 Anchorage, Alaska, Earthquake	131
1967 Caracas, Venezuela, Earthquake	236
1972 Managua, Nicaragua, Earthquake	12,000
1976 Tangshan, China, Earthquake	655,000
1985 Mexico City, Earthquake	7,000
1986 San Salvador Earthquake	1,800
1988 Leninakan, Armenia, Earthquake	30,000
1989 Hurricane Hugo	49
1989 Loma Prieta Earthquake	65
1992 Hurricane Andrew	52
1994 Northridge Earthquake	57
1995 Kobe Earthquake	6,000

SOURCE: G. L. Berlin 1980; Pomonis in Earthquake Reconstruction Programme 1990; UNCRD 1995.

hundred thousand units within two years, while in Kobe the reliance on market economics could mean that much of what was lost will never be replaced.

The chapter concludes with an assessment of the patterns in disaster recovery assistance common to both American and international experience, ranging from doing very little to doing too much. Because disaster relief and recovery assistance are typically driven by simplistic assessments of loss (the "death and dollars" index) combined with the politics of aid, disaster relief and recovery efforts are often ill-suited to the needs of the victims or the affected community. While this view is commonly held by researchers who evaluate the quality of disaster assistance for developing countries, the same critique is rarely applied in the United States or other developed nations.

APPROACHES TO RECOVERY IN URBAN DISASTERS

Despite the enormous rebuilding costs after the four recent urban-centered disasters in the United States, none truly devastated a city and its housing stock, as happened in San Francisco at the turn of the century,

Tokyo in 1923, and Tangshan, China, in 1976. The 1906 earthquake destroyed half of San Francisco's housing and eliminated two-thirds of the jobs in the city. Three hundred thousand people were evacuated and one-quarter of those never returned. To house those who remained, the army brought in eight to ten thousand tents. One year after the event, private builders had produced sixty-two hundred two- and three-room cottages, which housed twenty thousand people (Haas, Kates, and Bowden 1977, 71). The remainder of the rebuilding was privately financed.

The heroic and fast-paced efforts to rebuild San Francisco have been perceived as a triumph of private enterprise and public will. The myth of a city rising from the ashes was largely promoted by the railroads and newspapers for economic and political reasons (Hansen and Condon 1989). In fact, in the years following 1906, San Franciscans faced many of the same problems inherent in modern recovery circumstances: insurance companies failed to pay claims, labor and materials suppliers charged exorbitant prices, changes in building codes were perceived by owners as reactionary and irrational, and delays in public decisions on widening streets and reorganizing infrastructure frustrated expedient building replacement plans (USGS 1907, 59–60).

Although the experiences of rebuilding San Francisco following the devastation in 1906 and Tokyo following the Great Kanto Earthquake and fire in 1923 are important historical references, it is difficult to draw meaningful comparisons between rebuilding approaches in the early twentieth century and those of today. The recovery experience after urban disasters since the 1970s provides more useful comparisons because the building and infrastructure conditions are more closely related to those of contemporary cities. There are, since the 1970s, four basic recovery models: (1) the complete redevelopment of a devastated area by a national government; (2) the infusion of outside aid targeted to low-income housing, provided by either governments or charities; (3) a limited-intervention approach, which assumes that private insurance will cover some losses, property prices will adjust to the new circumstance, and government will provide some supplemental assistance for the poor; and (4) a complete reliance on market forces to adjust and adapt after a disaster.

Over the past thirty years, the redevelopment model has only been used in the most dire of circumstances, as when an earthquake completely destroyed the city of Tangshan in China in 1976, and another virtually destroyed the cities of Spitak and Leninakan in Soviet Armenia in 1988. The targeted infusion of outside capital has been most commonly used when a devastating disaster has occurred in a major city or impacted a large region in a developing country. The limited intervention model has been the basis of U.S. disaster policy, while the laissez-faire market approach has been the de facto policy in Japan since the Kobe earthquake.

THE REDEVELOPMENT MODEL

In the case of Tangshan, an industrial city of a million people was reduced to rubble by a magnitude 7.8 earthquake. The city was located at a major junction in the national railway system, and it was an important link in the national telecommunications network. Although it formed as an industrial center, it was also part of an important agricultural district in Hebei Province. More than half the industrial production was concentrated in heavy industries, including coal mines, electrical energy generation plants, and steel, cement, and locomotive production. Given the city's importance, the Chinese government began plans for a new city on the old site, but one planned on a grid system with lower density and separate zones for industrial, warehouse, cultural, and administrative functions.

Residential areas were planned as 118 neighborhood districts of 5,000 to 10,000 inhabitants, each with self-contained schools, services, theaters, and shops. In the immediate aftermath of the earthquake, emergency housing was built from the masonry rubble of damaged buildings, but some 300,000 people were evacuated to temporary shelters in parks in Beijing and Tianjin. Construction of the new city of Tangshan, which began in 1979 with the help of fifty-three construction companies brought in from all over the country, was completed in 1985; an average of twenty to thirty thousand households per year were resettled into new quarters (Chen et al. 1988; Arnold 1990; Lagorio 1990).

In the case of the 1988 Armenian earthquake, Spitak (population 25,000) was leveled and Leninakan (population 250,000 and the region's second largest city) was 80 percent destroyed. See figure 47. Although these cities were small towns by Russian standards, they were the major cities of a region in which one hundred villages were destroyed and five hundred were damaged by the earthquake. In Leninakan, eleven thousand blocks of mid-rise, concrete-frame residential flats were destroyed. Much engineering analysis has focused on the poor performance of these buildings. There is general agreement that the damage resulted from

Figure 47. Housing Damage in the Armenian Earthquake, 1988. Damage to concrete-frame buildings with masonry infill walls was extensive. (California Governor's Office of Emergency Services, Earthquake Program)

Figure 48. Reconstruction of Housing in Armenia. Although government funds were pledged for reconstruction of housing in Leninakan, Spitak, and surrounding communities, the dissolution of the Soviet Union left most construction projects unfinished. (Antonios Pomonis, University of Cambridge)

inappropriate designs combined with poor construction-quality control
(Arnold 1990).[1]

To this remote region, United Nations aid organizations and nongovernmental organizations (NGOs) sent relief supplies and various
forms of temporary housing to assist survivors, but in the bitter winter the only practical solution was to move survivors to more hospitable
climates. More than 170,000 Armenians were evacuated—more than
half to other republics of the Union of Soviet Socialist Republics. On
December 24, 1988, the Russian Council of Ministers made a decision
to rebuild the cities and to commit the resources necessary to complete
the program within two years (Novosti 1989; Lagorio 1990; Rost 1990).

This ambitious plan included providing 4 million square meters of private housing (approximately eighty thousand units), 78 million square
meters of school buildings, and forty-eight hundred hospital beds, and
associated clinics (Rost 1990). Unfortunately, the tragic internal conflicts
that plagued Armenia and Azerbaijan, combined with the breakup of the
Soviet Republic, left the reconstruction program stalled midstream.
Buildings under construction in 1991 remain unfinished and unoccupied
in 1996. See figure 48.

The model in which a national government takes responsibility for
the creation (or re-creation) of a city is rare in both disaster and nondisaster situations. The newly developed capital cities such as Brasilia and
Chandigar and the newly created British towns in the 1960s and 1970s
are examples of efforts that required long-term financial and political
commitments. As in the creation of new towns, strengths and weaknesses
of the complete redevelopment approach in Tangshan and Armenia are
evident. In Tangshan, a centralized government managing a centralized
economy needed the mineral and industrial resources of the region. The
commitment to rebuild the city was economically driven, and it was ac-
complished in a political system where the redirection of resources was
not contested. In the Armenian situation, the social commitment to rebuilding was admirable but infeasible in light of the larger political and
economic forces in the region and nation. Unfortunately, the focus on a
grand plan for rebuilding left the locals with half-finished buildings when
centralized funding and management collapsed.

THE CAPITAL INFUSION MODEL

In Skopje (1963), Managua (1972), Guatemala City (1976), and San Salvador (1986), earthquakes destroyed substantial portions of the residential

building stock but left important infrastructure as well as financial and employment sectors reasonably intact. Although individual losses as well as social and economic conditions in each city clearly differed, what these cities had in common was an infusion of outside capital, in the form of international aid, combined with outside expertise, to develop the plans for rebuilding housing for low-income populations.

Skopje, which suffered the loss of 90 percent of its housing, was transformed into a twenty-four-kilometer linear city. Housing was built in planned estates, on agricultural land away from the city center and away from the rubble and debris. In time, industry filled in between the housing estates, and the center was redeveloped according to a modern decentralized plan designed by architect Kenzo Tange (Ladinski 1995). In Managua, 43 percent of the housing stock was destroyed and another 25 percent was damaged. Three-quarters of the housing loss was concentrated in the core of the city, where two-thirds of the population had low and lower-middle incomes, and one-third had middle and upper incomes. Fearing epidemics, authorities relocated the population to towns outside the city and encircled the damaged zone with barbed wire. Building permits and lending were frozen to stop individual rebuilding projects, as outside aid institutions built thousands of modern housing units in the redeveloped zone (Haas, Kates, and Bowden 1977).

In each of these cases, as well as in numerous rural disasters, social scientists and housing advocates criticized the misfit between institutionally planned and built postdisaster housing and local needs (Anderson and Woodrow 1989; Aysan and Davis 1992; Coburn and Spence 1992; Cuny 1983; Oliver-Smith 1990). Researchers and aid organizations suggested the need for a link between disaster aid and economic development, and they recognized the need for a more careful evaluation of *what* was needed and *how* it was delivered. Thus, after the 1986 El Salvador earthquake, where forty thousand low-income barrio dwellers lost their housing, aid organizations rejected large-scale redevelopment plans in favor of a locally managed self-help rebuilding program. NGOs organized access to supplies of building materials and used locally based training programs to help disaster victims rebuild their own housing (Durkin and Hopkins 1987; Solo 1991). The change in approach came as the World Bank and U.S. Agency for International Development promoted the notion that the state should act as an "enabler" rather than a provider in response to urban sheltering problems in developing countries (Cohen 1983; Aysan and Davis 1992; Hodges and McCray-Goldsmith 1994).

In fact, the self-help approach to rebuilding after disasters has been difficult to implement because the need for immediate shelter is often over-whelming. The model has evolved to include mixing some new con-struction by outside contractors with local self-help. This has become the dominant standard for the provision of international aid, particu-larly in developing countries. After recent earthquakes in Manjil, Iran, and in Luzon, Philippines, both of which struck in 1990, as well as af-ter the Maharashtra earthquake in India in 1993, international aid or-ganizations typically brought in Western-style building systems to sup-ply about half of the housing needed in the hardest hit areas and worked with NGOs to supply construction materials and training in other areas (Earthquake Reconstruction Programme 1990; U.N. Habitat 1990; Sidhu 1993). While specific problems are bound to arise in the applica-tion of the model to varying political and social circumstances, the con-cept of a less intense intervention has become generally accepted. Dis-aster aid in the 1990s still involves an infusion of outside cash, but the outside experts tend to value low-key and local rebuilding solutions over Western industrial methods.

THE LIMITED INTERVENTION MODEL

The changes and improvements in international disaster aid to cities and rural regions in underdeveloped countries have no equivalent in disaster assistance in the developed world. In part, this is because there have been few major losses in developed countries, and in part because developed countries tend to manage relief for large and small disasters through in-ternal policies and programs. For example, the earthquakes that devas-tated small towns in the Friuli region of northern Italy in 1976, and parts of Naples and the surrounding region in southern Italy in 1980, caused significant localized housing losses. It was expected that the Italian gov-ernment would make provisions for disaster relief and rebuilding assis-tance for its own citizens, just as the American government did in the af-termath of floods, tornadoes, hurricanes, and earthquakes in cities and towns throughout the nation.

Typically, developed nations rely on private insurance to compensate individuals and businesses for private losses. Government programs are generally designed to assist in the repair and replacement of public infra-structure and to provide some minimal degree of disaster relief to assist individuals with personal losses. This was the case after the 1964 An-chorage, Alaska, earthquake and Hurricane Camille in 1969, the two most dramatic contemporary disasters in American communities before the two earthquakes and two hurricanes described in the previous chapter.

Although the intent of supplementing insurance with government assistance appears to be reasonable, recent experience has shown the degree to which the system is unbalanced in urban settings. This system tends to favor creditworthy home owners over poor or financially strapped home owners, and it completely overlooks all rental housing. In addition, the government's supplemental programs assume that private insurance is both available and affordable to rental property owners as well as home owners. In the absence of such insurance, the government is left with the dilemma of how to supplement the supplements with nondisaster programs.

THE MARKET MODEL

The simplest of all postdisaster recovery strategies, the market model assumes that the real estate market will sort out the winners and losers in the aftermath of a calamity. In this model, there is the inherent assumption that while the federal government in developed countries (or outside aid organizations in underdeveloped countries) will provide assistance to restore local infrastructure, individuals and property owners must cope with their losses based on their own personal and financial circumstances.

Given the absence of disaster insurance in Japan, the market model is evident in Kobe's struggle to recover from the earthquake. The national government quickly funded repairs of the transportation system and public utilities, but cash infusions for the redevelopment and replacement of the housing stock have not been funded.

URBAN DISASTERS OUTSIDE THE UNITED STATES

Outside the United States, only two major urban disasters have occurred in recent years, both of them earthquakes. The recovery program after the earthquake in Mexico City in 1985 produced one hundred thousand repaired and/or rebuilt housing units in two years. The program has been a peculiar amalgam of cash infusion models, combining outside aid to a developing country with an internally managed, government-directed program. By contrast, recovery after the 1995 Kobe earthquake followed the market model and the repair of housing has languished. These two cases are particularly interesting because the scale of the housing losses is comparable to that in American disaster experience, and because the differing approaches to housing recovery represent possible futures for U.S. disaster recovery policy.

MEXICO CITY EARTHQUAKE

At 7:19 on the morning of September 19, 1985, an 8.1 magnitude earthquake shook Mexico City for a period of approximately two minutes. This was followed by a second large earthquake the next afternoon, which added to the human and material losses. The earthquake occurred on the subduction zone between the North American and Pacific Plates. The epicenter was located off the coast of Michoacán, about four hundred kilometers from Mexico City. See map 7. While the earthquake was felt across a wide region, from Oaxaca to Veracruz to the south and east, and to Guerrero to the north, damage in the Michoacán coastal area was light.

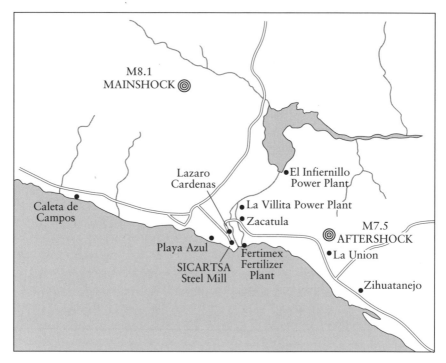

Map 7. Mexico City Earthquake Impact Area. The destruction was caused by an earthquake whose epicenter was off the coast of Michoacán, four hundred kilometers away. (EQE International, Inc.)

Figure 49. Typical Pancake Collapse of Concrete Building, Mexico City.
The columns of mid-rise concrete buildings collapsed, and floors pancaked
one upon the other. Soft soils amplified the ground shaking, causing massive
failures in a variety of building types. (California Governor's Office of
Emergency Services, Earthquake Program)

The majority of damage was concentrated in the historic center, in a
limited area of about six square kilometers within Mexico City. While
many colonial monuments survived, much of the modern construction
as well as the slums in these areas were severely damaged, the result of a
combination of factors. The long duration of the earthquake, combined
with lake bed soil conditions, produced unusually long shock waves. These
two-second cycles of quaking created a harmonic resonance with certain
building types, magnifying their sway and leading to structural failure.
See figure 49. Five- to fifteen-story concrete buildings were particularly
susceptible, but buildings of all sizes were damaged in the intense shaking (Armillas-Gil 1986; EERI 1988; 1988a; 1989; Echeverria 1990).

HOUSING DAMAGE RELATIVE TO OVERALL DAMAGE

Although Mexico City has a long history of damaging earthquakes, the
scale of the damage that occurred on September 19 was completely unexpected. According to official records, more than 600 buildings suffered
complete or partial collapse, more than 2,000 had serious structural dam-

TABLE 26

ESTIMATE OF DAMAGES IN MEXICO CITY

	Damage ($ Millions)	Percentage
Government (property and displaced workers)	$8,500	68
Infrastructure	$2,000	16
Buildings (64% housing)	$1,000	8
Indirect Losses	$1,000	8
Total	$12,500	100

SOURCE: Bilateral Technical Cooperation Project 1989.

age, and a total of 5,728 was reported to have some level of damage. As a result of this damage, some thirty thousand people were left homeless. The exact number killed in the earthquake will never be known: government estimates place the total number of fatalities at seven thousand,[2] but in the days after the earthquake twenty thousand people were reported missing. Although some of the missing were reunited with family members, a more precise number of the permanently missing has never been established. Even one year after the earthquake, newspaper accounts citing estimates by charitable organizations and other NGOs continued to contradict official estimates, placing the death toll closer to twenty thousand and the number of homeless as high as two hundred thousand (*Mexico City News*, 19–23 September 1986).

The extreme ground deformations caused by the amplified shaking of soft soils under Mexico City had a severe impact on infrastructure and services. Roads were impassable for days. The Metro closed 13 of its 101 stations. Water supplies and communications networks were badly damaged, affecting service to more than a quarter of the city's population. Overall, the total economic loss was estimated at $4 billion (U.S.), of which around 25 percent was in structural damage to buildings, 50 percent in damage to infrastructure, equipment, and building contents, and 25 percent in indirect expenses. In addition, the government estimates that public losses amounted to $8.5 billion (U.S.) as a result of damage to public buildings and lost jobs for 150,000 government workers (Garcia-Perez 1986). See table 26. Because Mexican government reports do not disaggregate these estimates of direct and indirect losses, it is difficult to estimate the housing portion of direct losses as a percentage of total losses.

The physical losses to buildings affected all sectors. Two major hospitals collapsed and 704 schools were damaged. Eight percent of the city's hotel rooms were lost, theaters and cinemas were damaged, and facto-

TABLE 27
ESTIMATES OF RESIDENTIAL BUILDINGS DAMAGED, MEXICO CITY

	Multifamily Buildings	Estimated Housing Units
Official Government Count[a]	3,745	76,000
Japanese Reconnaissance Team[b]	5,000	100,000
Newspaper Accounts[c]	Not available	180,000

[a] Damage survey cosponsored by the Mexico City Federal District and United Nations agencies, 1986.
[b] Investigative report by the Tokyo Metropolitan Government, in Aritake et al. 1986.
[c] Collection of earthquake-related articles on the one-year anniversary of the event, in *Mexico City News*, 19 September through 30 October 1996.

TABLE 28
TYPES OF BUILDINGS DAMAGED, MEXICO CITY

	Destroyed	Severe Damage	Medium or Minor Damage	Total
Residential	577	1,638	1,530	3,745
Schools	43	206	454	703
Stores	161	171	134	466
Public Offices	38	82	55	175
Private Offices	28	69	73	170
Hospitals	5	22	14	41
Recreational	9	9	17	35
Manufacturing	7	6	6	19
Other	86	93	195	374
Total	954	2,296	2,478	5,728

SOURCE: Armillas Gil 1986.

ries suffered nearly $900 million in damages. The government itself was hard hit, with 1.7 square kilometers (more than 1 square mile) of office space seriously damaged. Still, among all the buildings damaged, residential structures comprised the major loss. Two-thirds of the damaged buildings surveyed by government inspectors were residential (see tables 27 and 28). Given the discrepancies in various reports of the damage, and the tendency to undercount instances of minor damage, it is likely that at least twice the number of residential structures reported had some degree of damage.

Figure 50. *Viviendas* before Earthquake. Much of the housing in the historic center of Mexico City consisted of tiny units around a central courtyard, with shared facilities for cooking and bathing. (Christopher Arnold)

HOUSING TYPES DAMAGED

Two very different kinds of housing were damaged in the earthquake. The first was large, multistory apartment buildings such as the Nuevo Leon building and the Multifamiliar Juarez, each of which collapsed and killed thousands of inhabitants. Nuevo Leon was a thirteen-story building, part of Nonoalco Tlatelolco, the largest housing development in Latin America. Built in the early 1960s within a historic district, the complex included 102 apartment buildings, with 120,000 inhabitants in 12,000 units. It was part of a government low-cost housing program designed to alleviate severe overcrowding and unsanitary conditions of the central city. The units were managed and rented by the National Popular Housing Fund (FONHAPO) and the Institute of Social Security for State Workers (Kultenbrouwer 1986; Geis and Arnold 1987; Gonzalez-Karg 1988; Bilateral Technical Cooperation Project 1989). Similarly, the Mul-

Figure 51. Wooden Bracing for Damaged Buildings. Most *viviendas*
would have been considered uninhabitable before the earthquake, even
though most had been occupied by the same families for twenty to
thirty years. (Christopher Arnold)

tifamiliar Juarez was another government housing project in the Colonia Roma. When originally built, there were 19 buildings in the complex
with 1,200 apartments. So much was destroyed by the earthquake that
the majority of the buildings were demolished and only 288 units were
repaired (Fuentes 1986).

The second type of building damaged was the much smaller apartment buildings known as *viviendas,* or tenements. Often these were very
old, very run-down mixed-use buildings with commercial and industrial
uses within the building. In some cases the *viviendas* comprised a set of
individually rented rooms surrounding a common courtyard with shared
cooking and bathroom facilities. See figures 50 and 51. In all cases, families had occupied the same units for twenty to thirty years, paying very
low rents, an average of forty-five hundred pesos monthly, the equivalent of 9 percent of the monthly minimum wage. The buildings were
small, averaging 20 units per building, and in very poor condition, of-

ten lacking plumbing maintenance and other basic services (63 percent lacked toilets; 29 percent had shared kitchens). A planning study of the Cuauhtemoc and Venustiano Carranza *colonias* (neighborhoods) after the earthquake found that on average 8 to 10 people were living in units of twenty-three square meters, and 79 percent of the units in the areas damaged were smaller than forty square meters (Anaya-Santoyo and Rafael-Hernandez 1986).

HABITABILITY

The damage to some of the high-rise structures (in particular the Nuevo Leon and Multifamiliar Juarez) was so severe that demolition was the only solution. In the Tlatelolco complex, only 32 of the buildings had structural damage and were vacated for repairs, while 60 buildings with minor damage to elevators, windows, plumbing, and finishes remained inhabited during repairs (Gonzalez-Karg 1988). In the case of the *viviendas*, most would have been considered uninhabitable before the earthquake. In fact, the housing shortage in Mexico City was dire. In the year before the earthquake, planners estimated that Mexico City faced a housing shortage equivalent to 30 percent of the existing housing stock.

After the event, surviving occupants of the most severely damaged units were clearly homeless and in need of alternative shelter. The government built four hundred provisional camps to accommodate the homeless in public streets, parks, and other public lands. Here, twenty-two thousand families lived in rectangular, corrugated sheet metal dwellings the size of a one-car garage. Kitchen and bathroom facilities were shared by groups of twenty families. See figures 52 and 53. Another twenty thousand families received temporary rental assistance (Direccion General de Renovacion Habitacional Popular 1987a; Gaddis 1986). Perhaps many more damaged units should have been vacated, but the prospect of homelessness was worse than the prospect of living with precarious damage, and some families simply returned to living in their damaged buildings. In Colonia Morelos, for example, one of Mexico City's poorest barrios, buildings were heavily damaged and 4,000 dwellings were deemed uninhabitable. But in this neighborhood, the death toll was mercifully low, and the area received less government attention than others. Tenants feared that landlords would evict them if they abandoned their buildings, so many stayed, and community groups eventually organized a self-help repair program (*Mexico City News* 1986a, b).

Figure 52. Temporary Housing in Metal Sheds. Such housing was placed on all available sites and in public rights-of-way near damaged properties. (Christopher Arnold)

Figure 53. Daily Life in Temporary Housing. Families carried on with daily life for two years while repairs were under way. (Christopher Arnold)

VALUE OF THE LOSSES

A study prepared shortly after the earthquake by the Economic Commission for Latin America (CEPAL) noted that the great majority of damage was sustained by apartments and government offices. Business and industry were relatively unscathed by the disaster. Insurance covered about 60 percent of whatever damages were sustained by private businesses. Similarly, telecommunication losses were also covered by insurance. By contrast, only 4 percent of the government losses and none of the residential losses were covered by insurance (Friedman 1986; Smolka and Berz 1989). In Mexico City, the minimal rents paid by families in dilapidated buildings meant that residential properties were virtually worthless, damaged or undamaged. As a result, it was clear that private owners had no reason to rebuild or even repair their buildings.

CONCENTRATION OF THE LOSSES

With the exception of the two high-rise projects, the majority of the residential damage was concentrated in seventy-eight *colonias,* an area approximately thirty-six square kilometers (14 sq mi), within three of the sixteen districts that comprise the Federal District of Mexico City. The heavily impacted area included 14 percent of the housing stock, with 250,000 inhabitants (Garcia-Perez 1986; Direccion General de Renovacion Habitacional Popular 1987a). Still, this is a tiny portion of the Fed-

TABLE 29

DISTRIBUTION OF DAMAGED DWELLINGS
AND RECONSTRUCTION BY DISTRICT,
MEXICO CITY

District	Percentage Damaged Dwellings	Percentage Repaired Dwellings by RHP
Cuauhtemoc	56%	60%
V. Carranza	18%	34%
G. Madero	>1%	6%
B. Juarez[a]	17%	—
Other[a]	9%	—
Total	100%	100%

SOURCE: Direccion General de Renovacion Habitacional Popular 1987a.

[a] The B. Juarez district lost one very large public housing project, the Multifamiliar Juarez. Damage noted for other districts includes damage to Nuevo Leon and Tlatelolco. These were repaired in separate programs.

eral District and of Mexico City. The metropolitan area has a population of 24 million, and Federal District houses 9 million of those. The districts of Cuauhtemoc, V. Carranza, and G. Madero together house one-third of the population of the Federal District. Thus, as a portion of the several million buildings subject to shaking, the percentage of buildings severely damaged was low. Even in the areas of severest shaking, less than 5 percent of the buildings were seriously damaged and less than 2 percent of the population was displaced (Bilateral Technical Cooperation Project 1989). See table 29.

HOUSING RELATIVE TO LOCAL CONDITIONS

The highly concentrated housing loss in Mexico City (officially estimated at seventy-six thousand units in four thousand buildings; unofficially estimated as two to three times greater) is particularly dramatic when viewed from the perspective of housing conditions within the center of the Federal District. Architects and city planners had long recognized the conditions of blight in dense and dilapidated neighborhoods, but in-migration to the capital city, low wages for workers, and high construction costs had prevented the development of adequate housing supplies in either the public or the private sector.

However, from the perspective of the inhabitants of Cuauhtemoc and other central districts, inexpensive rents; strong family and community ties within the neighborhood; and access to transportation, jobs, and shopping made the conditions tolerable and the neighborhoods desirable (Miraftab 1995). From one perspective, the areas affected by the earthquake were slums, but from another these were popular communities in desirable locations for established working-class and middle-class Mexican families.

The unique political conditions of the Federal District are as important as the social conditions of the areas damaged. Mexico has had a highly centralized federal government, a powerful president, and a dominant political party representing not only the elite but the interests of farmers, laborers, and many other middle-class groups. Within this form of governance, Mexico City has unique and special status. The mayor is appointed by the president, and often the demarcation between federal and local administrative functions and services is blurred (Dynes, Quarentelli, and Wenger 1990). As home to 20 percent of the country's population and producer of 44 percent of the gross national product (GNP), Mexico City is clearly more than a capital city: it is Mexico.

RECOVERY

Given the political and social conditions in place at the time of the earthquake, it is not surprising that some scholars and politicians feared that the disaster might be exploited by the military to enhance its power. This was one of a larger set of political concerns about the consequences of the earthquake for political stability. Dynes, Quarentelli, and Wenger (1990) hypothesized that the social disruptiveness of the disaster could create a new political constituency, the victims, poised to make demands as had laborers, peasants, the urban poor, and others in the past. At the same time, long-standing social divisions could also fuel hostilities. This situation inside Mexico City could not be separated from Mexico's precarious position in the international context. At the time of the earthquake, Mexico had a $97 billion foreign debt, and the price of oil, the staple of the economy, was falling like a stone.

Thus, Dynes and his colleagues believed that "highly visible . . . politically motivated assistance to a small number of disaster victims was seen as important. . . ." For Mexican officials, "the consequences of having large numbers of victims needing longer term assistance could provide a politically explosive situation for which there were no easy solutions" (1990, 16). It is in this context that the organized response to replace the damaged housing was conducted.

Institutions responsible for reconstruction of the earthquake damage were rapidly created. The National Reconstruction Commission, headed by the president, was formed on 4 October, with subcommittees set to focus on priorities such as decentralization of health and education, social services, public safety, financial affairs, and international aid. Out of these, four different government housing programs were established, each with a broad-based decision-making capacity and the participation of academic, social, professional, and technical groups as well as community leaders.

The most extensive of the four programs was the Renovacion Habitacion Popular (RHP), developed to rebuild or repair 48,800 housing units in the hardest hit neighborhoods. To organize the rebuilding program, the federal government ordered a decree to expropriate 3,569 plots and created the RHP as a legally autonomous temporary agency with a two-year life span (Garcia-Perez 1986). This was a momentous decision, one that acknowledged the rights of families to remain in their neighborhoods, made possible in part because residents organized and decisively rejected alternative housing proposals, including one to move the entire refugee population to a new town site ten kilometers away.

Figure 54. New Low-Rise Housing under Construction. Nearly forty-eight thousand new units were built in two years. (Christopher Arnold)

Displaced residents from the designated renewal areas were given a Certificate of Rights entitling them to short-term rental assistance or access to temporary housing built in public rights-of-way within their neighborhoods, and entitling them to low-interest loans for the purchase of rebuilt units, thus converting them from tenants to owners.[3] More than 280 architectural and engineering firms were engaged to conduct damage assessments and develop plans for the expropriated sites. Reconstruction plans were jointly developed by technicians and the community, with the understanding that a basic prototypical housing unit and building were the foundation for every plan for every site. See figure 54.

The basic apartment was a forty-square-meter unit with two bedrooms, living-dining room, and kitchen and bath with hot and cold running water, in a three-story building with a single entrance gate. The gates became the focus of design competitions, and architects adjusted the massing and colors of the individual buildings to create urban and social spaces. See figures 55, 56, and 57. The prototypical schemes allowed for the processing of eight hundred building permits per month, and construction methods were monitored by a single team of project engineers and inspectors who were part of the RHP organization (Direccion General de Renovacion Habitacional Popular 1986; 1987; Echeverria 1990).

Figure 55. Repaired Masonry Housing Structure. Nearly thirty-eight thousand damaged buildings were repaired at the same time. (Christopher Arnold)

Figure 56. Completed New Infill Housing. Prototypical floor plans were adjusted to meet the dimensions of specific infill sites. (Christopher Arnold)

Figure 57. Interior Courtyard of New Housing. On larger sites, new housing was grouped around courtyards, with distinctive social spaces and entry gates. (Christopher Arnold)

The funding for the overall program came in part from Mexican government housing programs (40 percent), and the remainder from World Bank loans (60 percent). The government's capacity to manage the postearthquake programs was helped by concessions from the International Monetary Fund (IMF). At the time of the earthquake, Mexico was supposed to pay back about $900 million in principal on its foreign debt. Instead, Mexico received a ninety-day postponement, and then the IMF agreed to lend the country another $1.6 billion while indefinitely postponing principal repayments (Friedman 1986).

In addition to RHP, three additional reconstruction programs were developed in the same period. See table 30. The first came about as a result of the considerable pressure Tlatelolco residents put on local authorities to repair the damaged public housing units. Here too a technical advisory committee was formed to incorporate the input of residents into the repair plans. In the course of the program, 6,300 units received minor repairs, 4,200 were structurally strengthened, and 730 units in eight buildings were demolished and rebuilt. Nine high-rise buildings were reduced to three stories and shops and service quarters

TABLE 30
SUMMARY OF RECONSTRUCTION PROGRAMS,
MEXICO CITY

Program	Minor Repair	Upgraded	New or Rebuilt	Total Housing Units
RHP	490	6,220[a]	42,090[b]	48,800
Tlatelolco[c]	6,346	4,214	730	10,560
Phase I[d]	16,077			16,077
Phase II[e]		4,439	5,153	12,000
NGOs				7,456
Total Units[f]				94,893

SOURCE: Direccion General de Renovacion Habitacional Popular 1987a.

  [a] Of these, 2,500 were restorations of historic buildings.
  [b] Of these, 2,300 were prefabricated units.
  [c] Nine of the high-rise buildings were reduced to three stories. In addition to the residential repairs, 189 shops and 1,893 service quarters were built.
  [d] Phase I was a credit program for individual repairs.
  [e] Phase II was also a credit program, for rehabilitation or reconstruction; 504 shops also received funds.
  [f] Most new and repaired buildings averaged 12 to 13 units per building.

were added to the community (Bilateral Technical Cooperation Project 1989).

An additional rehabilitation program for damaged buildings, known as Phase I, was created, based on a credit system for those who inhabited the damaged dwellings after the time of the earthquake. Out of twenty-two thousand families who asked for credit, sixteen thousand benefited from the program, and others were helped either through the RHP or nongovernmental organization housing programs. By July 1986, however, government agencies recognized that a significant number of families from the damaged *viviendas* were left unserved by RHP and Phase I. Financing for a new program was developed through the National Popular Housing Program (FONHAPO). In this program, known as Phase II, fifty-one hundred families received credit for new housing and forty-four hundred received financing for rehabilitation. Construction in these programs was carried out by government and private agencies (Garcia-Perez 1986; Bilateral Technical Cooperation Project 1989). In total, the government of Mexico City built or repaired nearly 88,000 housing units in the course of two years. NGOs contributed another 7,000 units (see table 30), and countless citizens repaired the cracks in their own housing units with the help of family and friends. By any standard, the housing recovery in Mexico City is a remarkable achievement. Unfortunately, it is also one that would be difficult to replicate in either the developing or the developed world.

The special relationship between the national government and the city cleared the path for a high-level decision to assign senior ministers to the managerial task. At the same time, the victims, a cohesive working- and middle-class community with long-standing ties to the central city, were vocal advocates for their own housing concerns. Financially, Mexico's status as a developing country, and therefore its eligibility for World Bank funds, combined with its special relationship to the United States, provided the financing for the ambitious program. Thus, the political need was matched with the administrative potential to tackle the problem, and the financing followed the traditional model for developing countries: the infusion of capital from outside sources.

In most countries, the divisions between national, state, and local governments complicate the distribution of disaster aid. In developed countries, no one would expect that the United States or Japan, for example, would qualify for a World Bank loan. Indeed, when an equally devastating earthquake struck Kobe in 1995, the recovery picture was markedly different.

THE GREAT HANSHIN EARTHQUAKE

At 5:46 A.M. on January 17, 1995, one year to the day after the Northridge earthquake, a 7.2 magnitude earthquake struck the Hanshin and Awaji regions of Japan. The epicenter was located in Osaka Bay, between the northern tip of Awajishima Island and the mainland, approximately twenty kilometers southwest of central Kobe. See map 8. Although the duration of the earthquake was only eight to twelve seconds, the shallow focal depth (between ten and twenty kilometers) contributed to the high level of ground shaking, causing urban earthquake damage on a scale never before experienced by a large modern city (Asano 1995; Comartin, Greene, and Tubbesing 1995; RMS and FAA 1995).

The area most affected by the earthquake included Kobe City, located on the southern portion of Hyogo Prefecture, the northern portion of Awaji Island, and several sites on the eastern part of Osaka Prefecture.[4] The area resembles the San Francisco Bay, with commercial development concentrated on the flat lands adjacent to the bay, and residential development extending into the surrounding hills and mountains.

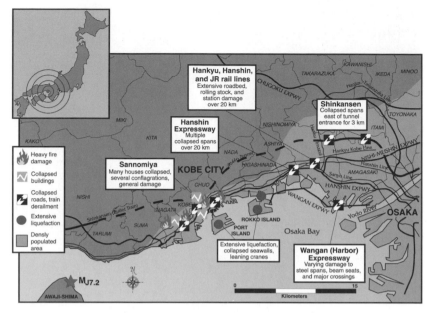

Map 8. Kobe Earthquake Impact Area. With the epicenter directly under the city, the Kobe earthquake was one of the most destructive in Japanese history, second only to the 1923 Great Kanto Earthquake and fire. (EQE International, Inc.)

HOUSING DAMAGE RELATIVE TO OVERALL DAMAGE

Kobe is a major port and shipbuilding city, with vital links to the nation's transportation system. Damage to the port was extensive, rail tracks were twisted, and a 650-meter section of elevated freeway collapsed, paralyzing the region's transportation network. Ground liquefaction and fires shut down urban utilities. Electricity, water, telephone, and other lifelines were cut off for an extensive period. Immediately following the earthquake, large-scale fires broke out simultaneously in numerous locations, particularly in the Nagata, Suma, and Hyogo wards. Building damage was extensive, particularly in older wooden homes built with heavy tile roofs and light traditional framing. These collapsed and killed sleeping inhabitants. In all, fifty-five hundred people died, and more than forty-one thousand were injured.

Destruction of offices and commercial buildings was most intense along the fault, and many concrete buildings toppled from damage to first-floor columns or suffered collapse of an intermediate floor (usually the third to the fifth, where column size was reduced). See figure 58.

Figure 58. Narrow Street with Buildings Fallen, Kobe. Many concrete buildings collapsed from damage to first-floor columns. (Laurence Kornfield, City of San Francisco)

Figure 59. Damaged Tile Roofs. Heavy tiled roofs, designed as storm protection, collapsed killing thousands of sleeping residents. (Catherine Bauman)

Figure 60. Nagata Ward after Fire. Narrow streets are all that remain of the densely built area. (Catherine Bauman)

Figure 61. Damage to Multifamily Four-Story Structure. More modern apartments were damaged alongside older wooden structures, which constitute the majority of Kobe's housing stock. (Catherine Bauman)

Overall, four hundred thousand housing units in 192,000 residential buildings, along with 500 public buildings and 3,100 other buildings, were severely damaged in the earthquake (Asano 1995; Funahashi 1995; UNCRD 1995).

Housing damage represented more than 95 percent of the building damage (see figures 59, 60, and 61) and well over 50 percent of the total value of the damage to the Hanshin region (see table 31). The fires alone destroyed 7,500 residential buildings (with ninety-three hundred households). The degree of physical damage to wooden houses was the worst in Japanese history, with the exception of the Great Kanto Earthquake and fire in Tokyo in 1923. Two hundred thousand buildings collapsed or partially collapsed at that time, and another 200,000 sustained some degree of damage (see table 32).

TABLE 31

ESTIMATE OF NET DAMAGE
IN KOBE, JAPAN

	Damage (Trillion Yen)	Damage ($ Millions)	Percentage
Buildings (including residential)	5.8	$52,200	59%
Transportation (highway, rail, harbor)	1.9	$17,000	19%
Education, Health, Public Facilities	.6	$5,400	6%
Utilities/Public Works	.85	$7,600	8.5%
Commerce, Industry, Agriculture	.75	$6,800	7.5%
Total	9.9	$89,000	100%

SOURCE: Hyogo Prefecture estimates, in UNCRD 1995, 195.

TABLE 32

RESIDENCES DESTROYED OR DAMAGED,
KOBE, JAPAN

	Buildings	Households
Burned Out	7,456	9,322
Collapsed	92,877	179,202
Severely Damaged	99,829	227,135
Total Destroyed	200,162	415,659
Partially Damaged	~ 200,000	Not available

SOURCE: Unpublished Hyogoken Province Damage Statistics, July 15, 1996, as assembled by Professor Kunio Funahashi, Osaka University. Note: these are comparable to the May 21, 1995, damage statistics published in UNCRD 1995, 41.

HOUSING TYPES DAMAGED

There are two types of traditional wood dwellings in Japan, the Shink-abe and Ohkabe, and these constituted 60 percent of the housing in Kobe City (UNCRD 1995).[5] Both consist of a post-and-beam structural system with exterior and interior mud walls. Both use heavy tile roofs as a protection against wind and storms. The most evident difference in the two is in the framing of the roof truss and its connection to the walls. Still, neither had the structural integrity to resist the earthquake's lateral forces. The lack of diagonal bracing, the heavy roofs, and deterioration from age contributed to the loss.

These older wooden structures were concentrated in center city wards, those least desirable to middle-class families. Instead, the inhabitants were typically elderly or students, and often there were concentrations of working-class immigrant laborers (who made up 10 percent of the Cho and Nagata wards), squatters,[6] and *buraku,* historically the untouchable caste, still poor and not fully integrated into Japanese society (Japanese NGO Forum 1996).

The fatality statistics in the heavily damaged wards are an indicator of the social characteristics of the inhabitants: 53 percent were more than sixty years old. The older people not only inhabited the older housing, but often they slept on the ground floor, and they were crushed when the upper floors collapsed. In addition, the death rate among people in their early twenties was high compared to that of young people below this age. This can be explained by the fact that there were colleges in two of the wards, and students were living in inexpensive rooming houses. By contrast the death rate of people in their late thirties, as well as that of young children, was low, perhaps because young families had left the area for newer housing (UNCRD 1995, 45).

HABITABILITY

Clearly, all of the four hundred thousand housing units that collapsed were rendered uninhabitable. There was very little information collected on the two hundred thousand buildings with partial damage, but it is safe to assume that these were comparable to other buildings with minor earthquake damage. That is, only a small percentage (typically less than 10 percent) were left completely uninhabitable, while others could be occupied once some of the broken plaster and glass was cleared and partial repairs were undertaken.

Figure 62. Temporary Housing in Office Building Parking Lot. The government built forty-eight thousand temporary housing units in parking lots and on undeveloped land on the outskirts of Kobe. (Catherine Bauman)

In the aftermath of the earthquake, displaced victims lived in all manner of temporary shelter (in schools and parks and public buildings) for months while the Japanese government built forty-eight thousand temporary housing units to house one hundred thousand people. See figure 62. Eight months after the earthquake, temporary shelters were officially closed, but twelve shelters, renamed "waiting centers," still housed about two thousand displaced victims (Eadie 1996). New temporary housing was clustered in parks and school yards in the damaged neighborhoods, but the great majority of the camps were built in outlying areas of Kobe, two hours away by bus or train. The sites were carved out of vacant land in residential areas or sometimes set in the parking lots of office structures. All were far from medical and shopping facilities, and all resembled refugee detention centers.

The units were extremely small, prefabricated boxlike structures, twenty to twenty-six square meters, equipped with toilet and bathing facilities. Because the local governments gave priority to those who were elderly or disabled or who were single parents, the elderly and disabled accounted for 70 percent of the population in many of the camps, a circumstance that separated this particularly needy population from families and services. Moreover, given the number of units destroyed, even

Figure 63. Playground Equipment Used as Temporary Housing. Every piece of usable open space was commandeered for housing, including this shelter constructed by a homeless resident. (Charles Eadie)

forty-eight thousand temporary units were insufficient to meet Kobe's housing needs. Victims fashioned makeshift housing using playground equipment as a framework for shelters or tacking tarps and tents onto damaged buildings. See figure 63. Many others simply relocated to other cities (Tomioka 1997; Eadie 1996; Japanese NGO Forum 1996).

VALUE OF THE LOSSES

While the estimated $150 billion in property damage was unprecedented, the final impact of the event on the Japanese insurance industry will be less than the impact on the U.S. insurance industry following recent disasters such as Hurricane Andrew and the Northridge earthquake. With total insurance payments for the damages in Japan estimated at only $6 billion, there appears to be a major disparity between property values and insurance coverage. See table 33. In part, this is because the Japanese government, along with a handful of insurance companies in business in Japan, recognized the difficulty of insuring against earthquakes in a country in which all the buildings are vulnerable. Thus, residential owners can buy only a limited earthquake rider to the basic fire policy, and the indemnity covers about 30 to 50 per-

TABLE 33
RESIDENTIAL CLAIMS PAID
BY INSURANCE, KOBE, JAPAN

Value of Property Loss	~ $150 billion
Estimated Claims Paid	~ $6 billion
Number of Claims	Only 7% of home owners purchased earthquake insurance
Average Claim	Limited to 30 to 50% of replacement value; claims capped at $100,000 (U.S.); Prorated: total loss pays 100% of insurance available, half loss pays 50% of insurance available, partial loss pays 15–25% of insurance available

SOURCE: EQE International 1995a, 83–84.

cent of the structure's replacement value, capped at one hundred thousand dollars U.S.[7]

In addition to the fact of limited coverage available, claims were categorized into one of three groups: total loss, half loss, and less than half. Thus, if the damage was categorized as half loss, the amount paid was prorated at 50 percent of the sum of the total insured. Therefore, the payment would amount to only 15 to 25 percent of the value of the structure. Contents were not covered unless they were totally destroyed, and only minor allowances were made for incidental expenses. Nationally, only 7 percent of Japanese home owners have bought this insurance, and in Kobe the coverage was less than 3 percent (EQE International 1995a).

Thus, while the impact on the insurance industry has been minimal, the impact on Japanese property owners has been severe, although not dire. Because the bulk of the value in Japanese residential properties is in the land rather than the structure, an owner maintains substantial equity (and theoretically, borrowing power) after an earthquake. This is reinforced by the fact that the Japanese are less heavily mortgaged than their American counterparts. Still, the *capacity* to borrow is not the same as the *will* to rebuild.

Owners must want to return to their former neighborhoods and must believe that market forces make rebuilding possible and profitable. Middle-class, middle-age families with children (i.e., those for whom jobs or social ties make a location desirable) are more likely to pursue rebuilding of a damaged home, particularly if the real estate economy is good. Unfortunately, central Kobe was losing this population to the suburbs be-

fore the earthquake. At the same time, a weak economy had dampened
real estate investments. In general, other population groups—elderly
owners or families without job security—are the least likely to seek financing and struggle with rebuilding after a disaster. These are more likely
to accept their losses, sell their land to speculators, and move on. Similarly, renters will not be willing to wait for replacement housing; they
will find alternative housing in the market, with rental rates and available vacancies determining their choice of units and locations.

CONCENTRATION OF THE LOSSES

Damage from the earthquake was concentrated in a narrow strip of soft
soils about two kilometers wide and 30 kilometers long. Researchers have
estimated that 40 percent of the wooden buildings and 35 percent of the
nonwooden buildings in the high-impact area were damaged (UNCRD
1995, 193–94). The worst housing damage was concentrated in the Nagata, Nada, Chuo, and Suma wards of Kobe City and in Nishinomiya
City. In the seven wards situated along the waterfront, 40 to 60 percent
of the housing was completely destroyed. These seven wards—from west
to east: Tarumi, Suma, Nagata, Hyogo, Chuo, Nada, and Higashinada—
make up only 30 percent of the land area of Kobe City but hold 70 percent of the city's population and 74 percent of the housing units (Japan
National Census 1995, 305–13). All told, the housing damage impacted
at least half the population of Kobe City and 20 percent of the population in Hyogo-ken Province.[8]

HOUSING RELATIVE TO LOCAL CONDITIONS

The Hanshin region is a sprawling urban center whose economic output
represents 10 percent of Japan's GNP. As part of this area, Kobe has re-
tained its importance as a port and transportation hub. However, as in
other older cities, housing growth has generally occurred in suburban
regions. An industrial and shipping center, Kobe City houses a mix of
working-class immigrants and middle-class families in densely populated
neighborhoods, where new condominiums are built next to older traditional structures.

   Given the economic growth and job creation in the region, rental vacancies in Kobe were very low, even before the earthquake. And, given
the historic structure of central Kobe neighborhoods, with their narrow
streets and fully built-out small lots, it is not surprising that inner-city

wards have population densities of six thousand to twelve thousand persons per square kilometer—less dense than in Mexico City, but nine to ten times that of the average American city. Thus, the housing stock was old and very crowded, and demand was high; but land and building costs were also high, so new housing was largely unaffordable to average workers.

RECOVERY

Because Kobe's earthquake was the most recent of all the disasters described in this book, its recovery is the least complete. Information cited here is based on conditions eighteen months after the event. Given the scale of the damage, it is impossible to expect that great strides have been made to date in housing reconstruction, but past experience suggests that trends observed one to two years after the event set the pace for the recovery.

Within a month after the event, the Japanese government organized reconstruction committees, passed necessary legislation, and issued construction bonds to raise the funds necessary to finance the reconstruction of roads, harbors, and water supply and sewage systems, and deficit bonds for temporary housing and rubble disposal (Asano 1995; UNCRD 1995). One year later, trains were running on all three railroads, bridges to the islands had been repaired, the massively damaged Hanshin expressway and the harbor highway were repaired, and 40 percent of the berths in Kobe Harbor were usable. With temporary berths and twenty-four-hour operations, the port was handling 70 to 80 percent of its preearthquake capacity. Twenty million tons of rubble had been removed from the city. Large industries (such as shipyards, as well as steel, machinery, and rubber manufacturers) were back in full operation, although smaller manufacturers were having a harder time. Shoe and apparel makers, sake breweries, and roof slate manufacturers located in the hardest hit areas were reported to have resumed only 50 percent of their preearthquake production. Needless to say, tourism has not resumed (Hyogo Cultural Center 1996).

Despite the impressive scale of construction in the public and business sectors, repairing Kobe City continues to be a daunting challenge. One year after the event, local streets remained closed and traffic still crawled around demolition and construction sites. Amid the construction and repairs, some buildings stood untouched, with glass shards hanging from unboarded windows, their repairs complicated by multiple ownerships, death of the owners, or lack of funding. Visitors describe the city as resembling a large-scale urban renewal project, with gaps in the urban fabric where major buildings once stood, and whole neighborhoods cleared and vacant (Eadie 1996). See figure 64.

Although some individuals have begun the process of repairing or rebuilding their housing (see figure 65), the process of recovery is complicated by two significant factors: a government plan to redevelop about half of the heavily damaged neighborhoods, which will widen streets and regularize lots, regrouping building and landowners into larger condominium schemes; and the simple lack of both public and private funds for repairs.

In the heavily burned neighborhoods, where housing and small shops and workspaces were densely packed onto tiny lots of twenty square meters, some owners have built temporary housing, and a few are replicating the crazy-quilt pattern with three- and four-story structures built of steel, mini versions of downtown buildings. See figure 66. In about half of these areas, the government has forbidden permanent reconstruction in order to redefine the lot pattern, widen roads, establish open spaces, and cluster housing in condominiums. Needless to say, the process of negotiating the land adjustments between owners and the government, and among potential owners that the government hopes to introduce into the new condominium arrangements, are complex and time consuming. In these areas, it will be years before the redevelopment plan is complete.

In other areas, where the earthquake has left some buildings intact while demolishing others, the vacant lots are constant reminders of individual and community losses. Here, as in those portions of the heavily damaged areas where the government has taken a laissez-faire attitude toward the rebuilding, the financial and social circumstances of the owners determine their capacity to make repairs. Few had insurance, and there are no agencies like FEMA or SBA in place to provide loans and grants to victims. Some tax reductions or exemptions were initiated as emergency measures, and small disaster loans have been made available to repair the "public portions" of condominiums (e.g., halls and elevators). But, essentially, the Japanese government does not provide any loans for private property.

Residential real estate market trends favoring growth in the suburbs rather than in the city have made financing residential buildings difficult, even though interest rates have remained very low. Those who were able or willing to deplete their life savings to rebuild their homes found they had to wait months to find a private contractor (Eadie 1996).[10] As a

Figure 64. Cleared Area with Temporary Buildings. Amid downtown high rises, several blocks had been cleared of debris. (Catherine Bauman)

Figure 65. Patched-Over Damage along Narrow Street. In residential areas with partial damage, the "standards of repair" have been determined by individual owners. Blue plastic tarps are a common sight. (Charles Eadie)

Figure 66. New Housing under Construction. Some owners have begun to reconstruct their homes. While wood frame is still the conventional building material, a number of home builders have chosen to mimic downtown high-rise steel-frame construction. (Catherine Bauman)

result, gangs and speculators have been buying up heavily damaged sites (Kristof 1995). At the same time, there remained thousands of occupied buildings with damage ranging from cracks to missing walls. Ubiquitous blue tarps covered holes in walls and roofs as residents grappled with the problems of funding repairs.

Equally complex has been the fate of those inhabiting temporary shelters. The government developed a plan to build 125,000 housing units in three years. Half were planned as publicly owned, affordable rental housing; half were expected to be private developments. Unfortunately, this plan had no solid financial commitment from the central government. With the total cost of reconstruction estimated at 15 trillion yen ($135 billion), initial government commitments have been focused on public infrastructure. See table 34. Worries over devaluation of the yen and Japan's weakened economic position in the world market—products of recession, not the earthquake—may limit public commitment to private sector losses. In addition, the general experience in past disasters

TABLE 34
PUBLIC EXPENDITURE
ON RECOVERY AND REPAIR,
KOBE, JAPAN, ONE YEAR LATER

	Completion	Expenditure
Debris	90% removed	2.4 trillion yen allocated
Transportation	100% repaired	Included above
Port	40% usable	Included above
Major Industry	100% recovered	Included above
Small Business	50% recovered	Not available
Tourism	Unrecovered	Not available
Temporary Housing	48,300 units built (occupied by 100,000)	Not available
Permanent Housing	125,000 units planned (half public, half rental)	Part of 5–8 trillion yen government package, not passed or allocated as of 1996

SOURCES: Hyogo Cultural Center 1996; UNCRD 1995.

has shown that government commitments to recovery wane as time passes, and demands from other sectors and other regions take precedence.

Thus, it appears that Kobe's elderly and poor citizens may reside in makeshift temporary housing until they die, or until they can find alternative housing on their own. Home owners may live in damaged structures for years as they rely on personal and private finances to repair or rebuild homes. Those with free title to their lots may sell or rebuild, but those in redevelopment areas must wait until the government plans are complete in order to make realistic decisions. According to a report for the Kansai Electric Power Company prepared by an international advisory team at the New York–based Institute of Public Administration (1995, 26), planning for redevelopment areas could take five to ten years, in part the result of Japanese custom, but in larger part because national government programs are unsuited to disaster response, and powerful bureaucracies will act in Kobe's interest only if the situation matches their broader interests.

The repair of housing in Kobe will likely be more a product of market forces than a product of government programs. This condition is made poignantly clear in two quotes from Takumi Ogawa, deputy mayor of Kobe, in charge of rebuilding the city. At an international forum on the recovery efforts, held eight months after the event, he said, "Every day is like fighting a battle. We have had a weak life since the earthquake" (Eadie

1996, 1). Six months later, it was reported that Mr. Ogawa had committed suicide. He was quoted as saying before his death, "I have stumbled against the mass of Japan's bureaucratic system—how little power the city was given by the nation" (*San Francisco Chronicle*, 16 March 1996, p. A12).

PATTERNS IN RECOVERY ASSISTANCE

The aftermath of a natural disaster poses enormous challenges to the citizenry affected, local businesses, and local governments. While some want to rush to replace what they had before, others see opportunities for change and improvement. The majority of postdisaster assistance from governments and charitable organizations is typically directed toward emergency relief, the restoration of infrastructure, and perhaps temporary shelter. The recovery phase is the least investigated and the least understood component of postdisaster aid. There has been little research on the efficacy of programs designed to assist victims in rebuilding their homes and businesses.

In the past two decades, some studies have attempted to define recovery and evaluate the impact of various approaches at the community level. Some research has examined individual and household coping behavior (Bolin 1985; Bolton, Liebow, and Olson 1993; Phillips 1993), while some has focused on the process of reconstruction and the factors that constrain or facilitate the process (e.g., Haas, Kates, and Bowden 1977; Rubin, Saperstein, and Barbee 1985; Anderson and Woodrow 1989; Berke, Kartez, and Wenger 1993). Although some attention has been given to the economic justification for federal assistance (Dacy and Kunreuther 1969; Friesema et al. 1979; Kunreuther 1973), and some to issues of program implementation (May and Williams 1986), the majority of the research on recovery has accepted existing institutional models for planning, managing, and financing reconstruction after disasters.

Only the source of capital has varied, depending on the country or the circumstances. In developing countries, the primary source of funds is international aid from governments and relief charities. In the developed countries, financing for recovery comes from federal treasuries, taxes, and bonds in the public sector, and from insurance and private borrowing in the private sector.

The work of recovery is presumed to be in the planning and public works mechanisms for approval and oversight of a large volume of construction projects. For decades, government and aid organizations have based their disaster recovery efforts on Western development models. In the 1980s, international aid organizations became more sensitive to the links between disaster aid and development aid, and they now undertake careful assessments of both damage and need before offering aid (Anderson and Woodrow 1989; Kreimer 1991). In recent disasters, institutions have begun to look for models and processes that expedite recovery, promote sustainability, increase mitigation of hazards, and promote equity, all without increasing the victim population's economic and social vulnerability. In developing countries, responsible disaster aid has come to be identified with responsive development planning.

This approach to disaster aid promotes directing financial resources into the hands of the victims and allowing them to make their own decisions. At the same time, the approach strives to encourage local institutions to develop enlightened, fair, unobstructive planning and building regulations before, as well as after, a disaster. The difficulty with this concept is that it assumes an uninterrupted supply of both cash and wisdom.

Given that future disasters in both the developing and developed nations are likely to have enormous impacts on urban housing, disaster recovery models need to be rethought. Neither governments nor aid agencies nor insurance companies can provide unlimited funds to replace individual and community losses, but together these entities can develop recovery plans that address the complex relationships between the distribution of damage and local housing markets and conditions.

Ultimately, models for recovery assistance need to grow from the social and physical patterns of disaster damage. For governments facing situations like those in Mexico City, Kobe, San Francisco, and Oakland after earthquakes damaged a critical segment of the affordable housing stock, the targeted rebuilding program implemented by the Mexican government provides an important example of a recovery policy designed to stabilize a critical housing situation. While it could be argued that the RHP program favored some neighborhoods and some households over others, it is important to acknowledge that the quickly devised and implemented program averted a serious housing crisis in the old center of the city.

In a similar way, the Los Angeles city government recognized the need for targeted funds for repairs to multifamily housing after the Northridge earthquake and appealed to HUD for special appropriations. The difference here was that HUD could help only within a limited set of existing programmatic boundaries, while at the same time other disaster assistance programs were providing funds to home owners, who were also collecting from their insurance policies.

Although it is true that each disaster exacerbates predisaster problems, the location and extent of damage determine which problems will be exacerbated. Public, private, and charitable recovery assistance programs need the flexibility to respond to the *singularity* of a particular loss experience with a variety of programs for a variety of needs.

CHAPTER 4

Catastrophe Index

*When Is a Natural Disaster
a Housing Crisis?*

Disasters in the last decade have captured national and international attention. For the first time in almost a century, American housing losses
have reached the same scale as those typically experienced in developing countries. The difference is that in developing countries the death toll
is enormous and the cost to rebuild is marginal, whereas in the developed world the number of deaths caused by housing loss is typically
smaller, but the economic cost of repairs is staggering.

While casualties even in recent American disasters remain low, the unprecedented number of housing units lost has created increased pressure
for expanded public assistance and, at the same time, increased pressure
from private insurers to limit disaster coverage in high-risk areas like
Florida and California. Who will pay to repair the damage and replace
the losses in future disasters? How can government draw the line between
public and private responsibility for losses? These policy questions cannot be resolved without a better understanding of the kinds of losses that
can be expected in future natural disasters.

Recent disasters demonstrate that in urban settings, housing loss is
the single greatest component of all losses, and timely housing recovery
is a component of economic recovery; but experience also demonstrates
that not every disaster is a *housing* disaster. A housing disaster is not simply a function of the number of units lost. A housing disaster results when
there is no reasonable alternative housing available for victims, and/or

there is no capacity to finance within a reasonable time frame the repair or reconstruction of units lost.

This chapter will compare within the context of local conditions the losses in Hurricanes Hugo and Andrew and the Loma Prieta and Northridge earthquakes, and argue that the standard "death and dollars" measures of loss are insufficient for assessing the true magnitude of housing losses in urban disasters. Recent experience will be used to demonstrate a more realistic method of loss assessment that includes consideration of the intensity of loss in terms of habitability in various types of housing, and the concentration of losses, as well as the social and economic conditions.

To demonstrate how a better understanding of housing loss could lead to improved recovery policy and planning, this chapter will consider what is likely to happen if a disaster of truly great intensity strikes. What are the similarities between the earthquakes in Mexico City and Kobe and the predictions for a large magnitude earthquake on the Hayward fault in the San Francisco Bay Area? From these comparisons, five critical factors will be proposed for use in evaluating housing loss and developing recovery programs.

COMPARING CONDITIONS
AND REEVALUATING LOSSES

Loss of lives and destruction of buildings and other property are the inevitable outcomes of earthquakes, hurricanes, floods, volcanic eruptions, and other natural phenomena that occur in places where people have settled. In terms of lives lost or families left homeless, the recent American disasters described in this book were moderate compared to their international counterparts.

Financially, however, the magnitude of these U.S. disasters was shocking. Successively, each has been rated the most expensive natural disaster in history. In the five-year period between 1989 and 1994, Hurricanes Hugo and Andrew, the Loma Prieta and Northridge earthquakes, and the massive flood on the Mississippi River and its tributaries caused more than $75 billion in damage combined, half of it to residential structures. By comparison, the Kobe earthquake, while similar in magnitude to that of the Northridge earthquake, caused many more deaths, destroyed substantially more buildings, and represented a financial loss of more than $150 billion.

It is not surprising that, in a world where the population has grown exponentially and become urbanized, earthquake and hurricane hazards grow more important every year. In 1950, only 54 percent of the population in the developed world lived in urban areas. In developing countries, the figure was only 17 percent. By the year 2000, 75 percent of the population in developed countries and 47 percent in developing countries will live in urban areas (UNDIESA 1987).

In the United States, the population density of hurricane-prone areas such as the South Carolina coast and earthquake-prone areas such as the California coast has increased more than 75 percent in the last thirty years (ISO 1994). Even though the seismicity of a region or the weather patterns remain constant, the uncontrolled and rapid increase in urban development is not counterbalanced by an increase in preparedness. In California, in terms of population and economic development, the disaster potential is now at least ten times what it was at the time of the 1906 San Francisco earthquake (Bertero 1994).

Given the concentrations of the world's population, it is undoubtedly true that any natural disaster in any urban area will cause unprecedented damage and suffering. In the aftermath of such an event, one would expect that other seismically vulnerable or hurricane-vulnerable urban areas would take heed. The potential for losses in infrastructure (in transportation, energy distribution, sanitation, and telecommunications) and in buildings, particularly housing, is staggering. And yet, there seems to be little aggressive policy to mitigate hazards or limit development in hazardous areas. In part, this is a result of a certain myopic sense that it will not happen here (or it will not happen to me) by cities as well as people. And in part, it is a result of the fact that cities have no viable means of measuring and understanding what has happened in other cities and therefore find it difficult to anticipate what their own problems may prove to be.

Housing comprises 60 to 75 percent of any urban land use. It seems obvious that substantial losses in housing would have an impact on the housing/jobs balance, on the tax base, and on services. But because economists traditionally measure loss at the regional level, mechanisms to adequately characterize the magnitude of the housing impact prove to be difficult to devise (Cochrane 1996; West 1996).

In a comparison of the four American disasters by their overall losses, housing loss consistently represents half of the total dollar value of disaster losses. Only in the case of Loma Prieta, where transportation and infrastructure losses dominate, do housing losses drop to 25 percent of the total value of losses. See table 35. Ironically, despite the fact that Loma

TABLE 35

COMPARISON OF LOSSES IN FOUR AMERICAN DISASTERS

	Hugo September 1989	Loma Prieta October 1989	Andrew August 1992	Northridge January 1994
Total Damage Value (Billions)	$6.4	$7.5	$22.6	$25.7
Percentage Housing Loss	46%	26%	46%	52%
Housing Units Destroyed or Severely Damaged	36,000	11,500	80,000	60,000
Total Housing Damage	112,000	43,000	135,000	500,000[a]

SOURCE: See chapter 2 of this book.

[a] The total number of residential units inspected after the earthquake was 445,000. Of these, 64,000 were single-family homes. Two years later, 265,000 households collected on private insurance claims, 98,000 received Small Business Administration loans, and 288,000 obtained small grants from the Federal Emergency Management Agency for minimal home repairs. Assuming some overlaps between government assistance and private insurance, an estimated 500,000 units were damaged (Comerio, Landis, and Firpo 1996).

Prieta had the smallest number of units damaged and the lowest dollar value attributed to housing loss, it was the only disaster that caused a serious housing crisis in the areas affected. After the Loma Prieta earthquake, the majority of victims displaced by severe damage to their housing could not find alternative housing, nor could they or their local communities replace much of what had been lost.

To understand how this can be, it is useful to look beyond the numbers of units damaged and loss values to local circumstances at the time of the disaster: to the "geography" and the "demography" of the losses in order to determine when a natural disaster is, in fact, a housing disaster. The catastrophe index for housing should not be based solely on numbers of units damaged or replacement costs but also on the answers to two questions: How and where will victims who have lost their homes be rehoused in the short term? How and where will the owners of damaged units find the funds to repair or rebuild their damaged homes? The answers to these questions can help to determine whether the natural disaster has caused a housing crisis or, put another way, when a natural disaster is a housing disaster. These questions ought to be the basis on which governments and charitable relief agencies determine the nature of the relief and recovery aid that is appropriate and necessary. Most disaster assistance is based on the numbers alone, and not on a careful understanding of the urban circumstances that may help or hinder recovery. If the intensity of loss and/or the local housing conditions preclude alternative housing for victims or financing for recovery, then the disaster is truly a housing disaster.

THE GEOGRAPHY AND DEMOGRAPHY OF HOUSING LOSS

If the concentration of losses (e.g., the percentage of housing damaged) in a particular neighborhood or town is high and the intensity of loss (the ratio of units lost to the total number of units in the area) is significant, the loss can overwhelm the availability of alternative housing in the area, and then there is clearly a short-term housing crisis. This is most evident in rural areas of developing countries when an earthquake levels entire villages made up of houses built of masonry, stone, and adobe. This was the case in the 1993 earthquake in the state of Maharashtra, India, where 32 villages completely collapsed (Kagami et al. 1994; Sidhu 1993), and in the 1990 earthquake in Iran where nearly one hundred thousand units in 273 villages were completely destroyed (Earthquake Reconstruction Programme 1990). Similarly, in 1988 in Soviet Armenia,

100 villages were destroyed along with 80 percent of the housing in the cities of Spitak and Leninakan (Arnold 1990; Rost 1990).

Although less visibly dramatic, the same sheltering problems affect the victims of urban disasters when there is no equivalent alternative housing. In the case of urban settings, the issue is not simply whether there is any alternative housing available, but whether there is housing similar in type and cost to that which was lost, within a reasonable distance of what was lost. In Mexico City, one might expect that the loss of some seventy-six thousand housing units could be absorbed in a city where the city's central core alone houses a population of 10 million people. In fact, this was not the case. Given the severe housing shortage in the Federal District, there were no alternative rentals available. Victims of the earthquake were long-term residents who understood the value of a central location. After the disaster, they organized and refused to be relocated to the outskirts of Mexico City, where they would have been without access to their jobs, families, and social networks.

In rural settings, the need to develop immediate solutions to the problem of alternative housing is more obvious than in urban disasters, where existing housing alternatives seem probable. In urban disasters, the number of units lost is less significant than the concentration of loss and the intensity of that loss, not only within a limited geographic area but within a particular segment of the housing market. If the market is soft and there are vacancies in units of similar size and cost, the issue of alternative housing is moot, as was the case in Los Angeles. By contrast, in a situation where an entire segment of a market is lost, as was the case when single-room-occupancy housing units were lost in the downtowns of Oakland, San Francisco, and Santa Cruz after the Loma Prieta earthquake, even a small number of damaged housing units can cause long-term homelessness.

Beyond the ability to temporarily rehouse disaster victims, the capacity to garner the financial and psychological resources to rebuild is the second component in evaluating housing loss. The financial and physical capacity to rebuild is related not so much to the concentration and the intensity of loss as to the local social and economic conditions. Five characteristics of the housing stock and its inhabitants are crucial to understanding the capacity of the private sector to absorb the displaced tenants and the cost of repair and reconstruction.

1. *The Composition of the Housing Stock*   Perhaps the single most critical issue in determining the recoverability of damaged housing is whether the housing lost or damaged is in single- or multifamily structures. Single-

family housing is most typically owner occupied, and most typically in-sured to some degree. For the owner, the house is his or her home and likely the single greatest investment that he or she will ever make. Unless the owner has just purchased or just refinanced the home in the months before the disaster, he or she is likely to have a substantial equity invest-ment in the property. As such, the personal and financial incentives to re-pair damage, or even to replace a total loss, are very high.

By contrast, multifamily rental housing offers shelter for rent to ten-ants and a cash flow to its owners. When this kind of housing is dam-aged in a disaster, the tenants simply want to replace their personal losses and find equivalent shelter at an equivalent price, preferably nearby. Own-ers have little incentive to repair or rebuild their buildings unless the cost of repairs can be passed on in increased rent. Multifamily-owned hous-ing, in the form of condominiums or townhouses, is extraordinarily dif-ficult to repair or rebuild. Despite the individual owners' financial in vestment, the complexity of sharing the costs and responsibilities among numerous owners and lenders usually proves to be overwhelming. Thus, in an urban disaster, the degree to which there is a housing recovery cri-sis will depend on the proportion of units damaged in single- and mul-tifamily stock.

2. *The Age and Physical Condition of the Housing Stock*   The age of buildings is commonly used by engineers and risk analysts as an indica-tor of vulnerability. Because older residential structures were built with less modern building codes, they are presumed to be more susceptible to damage, especially if not maintained. Before 1950, houses in California were not required to be bolted to their foundations and Florida codes did not include design factors for wind resistance. In recent research on housing losses, age was not the dominant factor influencing loss (Com-erio 1995; Comerio, Landis, and Firpo 1996; Sparks 1991; Saffir 1991). Criteria for wind and seismic resistance in contemporary building codes for nonengineered structures (e.g., most small wood-frame construction) typically lag behind requirements for other building types (EERI 1996). Limited structural requirements, combined with contemporary design styles (open-plan living areas, large garage openings, big picture windows) and shoddy workmanship led to significant damage in modern homes and apartments in all the recent American disasters.

The overall condition of the damaged stock also helps determine the degree of severity of the housing crisis. Whether single- or multifamily, if the damaged housing is relatively modern (i.e., post–World War II) and

well maintained, it is likely to carry a traditional mortgage, be fully occupied, and be financially viable, and therefore be both desirable and re-
pairable. If, however, the housing lost is old and decayed or even modern but run down, it is likely to rent at below market rates, it may or
may not carry traditional financing, and it is not likely to carry insurance. Thus, the poorer the housing quality, the more difficult it will be
to repair or replace, because the owners may have limited financial capacity and the market for such properties is limited.

3. *The Housing Market and Vacancy Rates*   No matter what the condition of housing in a particular area, the market for housing will drive
values and vacancy rates. In a community where there is high demand
and limited housing choice, property values and rents will rise. In a soft
market, property values fall, rents drop, and vacancies increase—even
in good buildings. Thus, the degree to which the housing loss in any urban disaster is a crisis depends, in some ways, on the local housing market at the time of the disaster. If, for example, a disaster occurs in an area
with high vacancies, it may happen that residents displaced by the disaster will not have difficulty finding alternative shelter; but the owners
of damaged apartments may have little financial incentive to rebuild in
a soft housing market. By contrast, in an area of high demand and market rate rents, it may be easier for owners to finance repair costs.

Many factors contribute to the overall conditions of the housing market and an individual owner's ability to rebuild. If jobs are lost because
key industries are damaged beyond repair, the housing market is likely
to soften and the short-term need will diminish as people relocate. If the
local economy is weak even before disaster strikes, the market will provide little rebuilding incentive. In other words, disasters do not completely
change predisaster economic conditions; instead they simply magnify
trends or conditions in place before disaster struck.

4. *Rebuilding Cost/Debt Ratio*   Ultimately, whatever the general market conditions, rebuilding decisions are made on a building-by-building
basis by individual owners. The amount of damage is translated into the
repair or rebuilding cost, which must be reviewed relative to the existing debt on a house or multifamily structure. If the damage is substantial, and the owner's debt/equity ratio is high because the property was
recently purchased or recently refinanced, or because market value has
dropped since the time of purchase, it will be very difficult for an owner
to absorb additional debt, and remain "in the black." A home owner

may find that the cost of repairs pushes his or her total debt well beyond the resale value of the home, while an apartment owner's repair cost, combined with the initial mortgage, may be substantially higher than the rental income a building can generate. While these are financial conditions specific to individual buildings, the aggregate impact on overall reconstruction can be gauged based on the estimates of damage to the housing stock, in combination with local market and housing conditions.

5. *Social and Economic Status of Victims*   Who was affected by the disaster is often as important to recovery potential as the value of the building damage. A home-owner or renter population with significant social and economic ties to the locale will be more aggressive advocates of repair. Middle- and upper-middle-class families whose jobs are nearby and whose children are settled in a school will have a vested interest in repairing homes or reestablishing themselves in apartments nearby, and they will have resources to commit. Low- and moderate-income home owners or renters, who already spend a disproportionate share of their income on housing, may not be able to secure loans for repair or find the extra funds for rental and security deposits required to relocate, without some assistance. Elderly and young renters may find it easier to move on than to wait for repairs. Similarly, in neighborhoods populated by recent immigrants, or by other, more transient populations, residents may not have the resources or the commitment to pursue the recovery of their buildings or their neighborhood.

Together, these five characteristics of the housing stock and its inhabitants describe a great deal about the geography of the damage and the demography of the victims. In combination they provide a powerful set of indicators necessary to assess the degree of crisis that an urban disaster has wrought in the housing sector. If these characteristics of the damaged stock can be assembled quickly from census and housing-market data after a disaster, local governments can assess the likelihood that short-term sheltering needs will reach crisis proportions. At the same time, an assessment of the extent of damage overlaid with market and social conditions will indicate the extent to which private recovery financing, in terms of insurance and loans, may be available, thus indicating the degree to which outside assistance may be necessary to avoid a recovery crisis.

In fact, the extent to which recovery can be predicted by the amount, type, and location of the housing damage (the geography of the damage) and the social and economic characteristics of the building owners and tenants (the demography of the damage) is tempered by one unique and unpredictable factor: the local political will to recover and to succeed. Numerous studies (Rubin, Saperstein, and Barbee 1985; Anderson and Woodrow 1989; Kreimer and Munasinghe 1991; Landis and Simpson 1992) have demonstrated that knowledge, leadership, and the ability to act on the part of local government contribute to disaster recovery. While political will can sometimes overcome the most dire sheltering and financing problems, in the end political will alone is not enough. The will to recover must be combined with a real understanding of the loss situation and a realistic financial recovery plan if political will is to have an impact on the outcome.

In light of these points, were the four cases described in chapter 2 really the housing disasters their "numbers" make them out to be? By the numbers, Hurricane Andrew and the Northridge earthquake were by far the largest disasters in U.S. history, damaging a significant number of relatively modern houses, multifamily apartments, and condominiums in the suburbs of major American cities. By the numbers, Hurricane Hugo and the Loma Prieta earthquake caused less than one-third the amount of housing damage caused by Andrew and Northridge. Did they cause a housing crisis in their communities? If we look at the ability to rehouse victims, and the ability to finance recovery, we find a much more complex picture of housing impacts than the disaster-loss numbers portray. See table 36.

COMPARISON OF THE CASE STUDIES

HURRICANE HUGO

In 1989, the majority of the housing damaged in South Carolina was single-family homes and vacation condominiums. Half the total damage was concentrated in four coastal counties, where 25 percent of the existing housing stock was affected. Was short-term alternative housing a problem? No. Despite the apparent concentration of damage, vacancy rates were high and much of the most severely damaged, and therefore uninhabitable, housing was in coastal vacation units. Was recovery financing a problem? Only partially. Nearly half of the residential damage was covered by insurance. Federal assistance in the form of temporary housing rental assistance grants and Small Business Administration repair loans were available to home owners. Although recovery was reported to be nearly complete within a year of the disaster, about one-

TABLE 36

COMPARISON OF HOUSING LOSS
AND RECOVERY IN FOUR AMERICAN DISASTERS

	Hugo September 1989	Loma Prieta October 1989	Andrew August 1992	Northridge January 1994
Housing Units Destroyed /Major Damage	36,000	11,500	80,000	60,000
Single Family	71%	40%	63%	11%
Multifamily	11%	60%	29%	88%
Mobile Homes	18%	0%	8%	>1%
Uninhabitable	32%	25%	59%	13%
Value Residential Losses (Billions)	$3	$2	$15.5	$12.7
Residential Insurance Paid (Billions)	$1.5	$0.57	$10.8	$7.8
# Insurance Claims Paid	278,000	45,000	316,000	265,000
Value of Public Assistance for Housing (Billions)	$0.5	$0.6	$1.2	$4.7
Vacancy Rate	8%	<1%	10%	9%
Concentration	25% Berkeley, Charleston, Dorchester, Sumter Counties	>1% Oakland/ San Francisco; 10% Watsonville/ Santa Cruz	6% South Dade County	3% San Fernando Valley (1.5% of Los Angeles)
Recovery	90% in 1 year	Single family: 90% in 1 year; multifamily: 50% in 7 years	75% in 2 years, limited rebuilding of multifamily	80% in 2 years; 20% without financing

SOURCE: See chapter 2 of this book.

quarter of those affected had little access to any rebuilding assistance. Rural poor, particularly those in mobile homes and marginal apartments, depended on private charities for repairs and reconstruction assistance.

LOMA PRIETA EARTHQUAKE

The housing damage from the Loma Prieta earthquake was concentrated in the downtown areas of two major cities—Oakland and San Francisco—and the two small towns Santa Cruz and Watsonville. In proportion to the area's housing stock, the losses appeared to be minimal: less than 1 percent of the total housing in San Francisco and Oakland, 10 percent in Watsonville and Santa Cruz. However, 60 percent of the heavily damaged units were in older single-room-occupancy hotels and apartments serving an elderly, transient, and low-income population. Was there a short-term alternative housing problem? Yes. In each city, vacancy rates were extremely low and there was no alternative housing at the bottom of the market rents. Even in Watsonville, where the damage occurred primarily to single-family homes, the owners and renters were low-income farmworkers unable to afford the vacant vacation rentals in nearby coastal towns and fearful of hostility and outright discrimination.

Was recovery financing a problem? Yes. In normal times, the ability to finance the construction of affordable multifamily housing is limited, and after the disaster only one state program was created to provide special recovery financing. Substantial numbers of the urban low-income renters became homeless, further taxing an already overtaxed social service system. Five years after the event, only 50 percent of the affordable housing lost had been replaced. Farmworkers, without insurance and without a steady income, typically did not qualify for federal government SBA loan programs designed to assist middle-class home owners. Like the rural poor in South Carolina, they had to rely on volunteers and private charities for rebuilding assistance.

HURRICANE ANDREW

South Dade County is a typical suburb, yet apartments and mobile homes comprised one-third of the housing lost. Six percent of the housing stock and 18 percent of the population in the county were affected. Was there a short-term alternative housing problem? Yes. Because the storm damage virtually flattened a large area, even a 10 percent prestorm vacancy rate in the county could not accommodate all the displaced victims. Home owners and renters needed to find alternative housing, and they had to travel some distance to find it. For two years after the hurricane, the market tightened, vacancy rates dropped to less than 1 percent in the county, and rents increased. Further, the loss of Homestead Air Force Base, a major employment center, meant that many victims lost their jobs as well as their homes. Immediately after the event, one hundred thousand people left the area; seven thousand households (approximately twenty-five thousand people) permanently relocated.

Was recovery financing a problem? Only partially. Although the majority of the homes destroyed or damaged were small and occupied by moderate-income families, they were fairly new and the market was strong. Most homes had insurance, and $10.8 billion was paid out in insured losses. Two years after the event, 75 percent of the damaged single-family housing had been repaired or replaced. Three years after the event, 90 percent had been rebuilt. It is less clear what happened to apartment reconstruction. With the loss of the air force base, many apartments were unnecessary, and five years after the event their sites surrounding the base remained vacant. Where multifamily units have been built in Homestead and Florida City, they appear to be aimed at the influx of new workers who have taken the agriculture and construction jobs created by the disaster.

NORTHRIDGE EARTHQUAKE

The Northridge earthquake in 1994 affected the largest number of housing units in any recent American disaster. A majority of the substantially damaged units was concentrated in fifteen neighborhoods. In these areas, dubbed Ghost Towns, while 60 to 90 percent of the housing was lost, the damaged units represented only 3 percent of the housing in the San Fernando Valley. The problem of alternative housing was smaller than disaster managers expected. The slowdown in the Southern California economy had created a vacancy rate of 9 percent in the valley, and there were fifty-four thousand vacant units before the earthquake. Within a month, renters at varying income levels found alternative housing near their damaged neighborhoods at rents comparable to what they had been paying before the earthquake. Victims were helped by an unprecedented level of federal temporary-housing rental assistance, but the fact that market rate units were available diffused what could have been a significant housing crisis had the rental market been tighter.

Was repair and reconstruction financing an issue? For apartments, yes; for single-family homes, no. The same economic slowdown that provided available units for disaster victims put owners of damaged units in difficult financial straits. Before the earthquake, owners of the large modern apartment complexes had high vacancy rates and many had negative cash flows. Without insurance, and disqualified from SBA loans because of their size and ownership structure, many of these units would never have been repaired without a concerted effort by city housing officials and local lenders anxious to avoid foreclosures.[1] The Ghost Town apartment owners were able to make repairs because lenders were willing to forgive and/or refinance mortgages to allow for city-sponsored loans.

By contrast, owners of older, smaller apartment buildings (with fewer than ten units) renting to moderate- and low-income renters were financially better off because their units were typically fully occupied, and because they were able to qualify for SBA loans. Still, only one-quarter of these owners took advantage of SBA financing. The majority of owners of multifamily structures had to rely on personal finances to make repairs (Comerio, with HR&A 1996). Ironically, the generous government programs that provided rental assistance to victims may have discouraged owners of damaged buildings from quick repairs. In a soft market, as tenants found other units, owners saw little prospect of drawing tenants back and no prospect of increasing rents to cover the cost of repairs.

Although damage to single-family homes was massively underreported in the damage assessments, a higher-than-average portion (40 to 60 percent) of San Fernando Valley home owners carried earthquake insurance, and almost all of them made claims. Three-quarters of the $12 billion expended for repairs on single-family homes came from insurance claims (Comerio, Landis, and Firpo 1996). In this case, the unexpected volume of minor damage in single-family homes became the tail that wagged the dog. Two years later, attention focused on the high cost of insured losses and away from the difficulties in financing repairs to the multifamily structures.

FLOODS, FIRES, AND OTHER AMERICAN DISASTERS

The midwestern floods of 1993 did not create serious rehousing or rebuilding problems. In part this was because the impacted population was distributed over a very large geographic area. Most flood victims returned to their homes once the waters receded, and only a very small number required alternative housing. Further, repair and reconstruction financing was not a major problem, because most victims were covered by private or federal flood insurance. Similarly, in California, fires in Oakland in 1991, Malibu in 1993, and Santa Barbara in 1994 each affected about three thousand single-family homes. While the losses were concentrated and dramatic, the number of victims in need of alternative housing was small, and in urban areas normal market rate vacancies could easily absorb them. And, since fire insurance is required as part of a home mortgage, virtually all had insurance that provided assistance for temporary living expenses and reconstruction financing.

MEXICO CITY

Here, the worst damage was concentrated in two modern high-rise housing developments and in housing in two wards of the old city—Cuauhtemoc and V. Carranza, home to poor but well-established working-class families. Was there a short-term alternative housing problem? Yes. At a minimum some thirty thousand to fifty thousand people were left homeless. More than thirty-seven hundred residential buildings were destroyed; according to government reports, 76,000 units were lost, although housing units were never counted in the damage survey. Estimates by newspaper reports and community activists placed both the number of people left homeless and the number of units lost at nearly double the official estimates. With a housing deficit of 30 percent before the earthquake, it was clear that no alternative shelter was available.

Was there a recovery financing problem? Clearly, there could have been. Owners of dilapidated properties had no financial incentive to rebuild housing for minimal rents; there was no insurance or other financial safety net for owners or tenants. However, the Mexican government, supported by a World Bank loan and concessions in the national debt restructuring that was occurring at the same time, decided to rebuild many of the damaged structures on site in order to preserve the social fabric and improve the economic circumstances of victims by subsidizing their purchase of the new units. This decision was made in part because the residents mobilized politically, and in part because Mexico was in a position to take advantage of financial aid from the World Bank and the International Monetary Fund.

Would there have been a housing crisis without the government-sponsored rebuilding program? In fact, the earthquake victims represented less than 1 percent of the population of Mexico City and only 6 percent of the population of the two wards most heavily impacted. Still, the intense concentration of housing damage affecting a largely stable working-class population clearly created the political perception of a housing crisis. At the same time, the damage was in the Federal District in the center of Mexico City. The district is Mexico City's administrative body. The mayor and the city government are closely tied to federal government ministries, a situation that makes the city government unlike any other in the world. Under these circumstances, it is not surprising that the government of Mexico was motivated to act quickly, decisively, and generously to avert a housing and perhaps a political crisis within Mexico City.

KOBE, JAPAN

The shallow inland earthquake, officially called the Southern Hyogo or the Great Hanshin Earthquake, was a major disaster for Kobe City. Was there a short-term housing problem? Yes. The displaced population lived in public shelters for months, using public bathing units, saunas, and golf club facilities for hygiene. In May 1995, four months after the earthquake, thirty-eight thousand people were still living in public shelters. Some 26,000 units in various public housing projects had been secured for victims, and construction had begun on 48,000 temporary housing units. One year after the event, there were still two thousand people living in shelters, renamed "waiting centers." The government announced a three-year plan to build 125,000 units, of which 64,000 would be publicly owned rental units, but two years after the event, financing and the construction schedule remained uncertain.

Is there a recovery finance problem? In all likelihood, yes. Earthquake insurance and government assistance for privately owned buildings are extremely limited. Most reports indicate that the funds needed for reconstruction will have to be raised by government bonds and that the government is likely to spread the reconstruction expenditures over a period of years to avoid flooding the bond market.

For all practical purposes, Japanese residential property owners must rely on private sources of financing to make repairs. In addition, private rebuilding has been stalled by publicly mandated redevelopment programs, implying that housing in the heavily damaged wards of central Kobe will not be rebuilt for at least ten years. By that time, most of the displaced victims will have permanently resettled outside the city. At that point, the concept of "recovery" from the disaster will have little meaning. As vacant sites are bought and sold in a new market, recovery will be measured in terms of redevelopment and growth, not in terms of repaired housing units or resettled households.

INDICATORS OF URBAN CRISIS

Overall, the concentration and intensity of units lost, in combination with the vacancy rate, are critical indicators of the need for temporary shelter. The type of housing lost (single family versus multifamily, as well as its age and condition), the degree of damage, and the state of the housing market, together with the social and economic status of the residents, are critical indicators of the capacity to rebuild. It is these factors, and not the number of units damaged or the insured value of single-family housing losses, that indicate the real nature of disaster housing losses and whether, in fact, the natural disaster has caused a housing crisis, impeding a community's ability to recover.

To understand what constitutes a housing crisis after a natural disaster, it is useful to compare disasters and to investigate the housing market circumstances particular to the locale in which the event has taken place. Of the four recent American disasters, only one had a real sheltering problem and only one had a real recovery financing problem. Loma Prieta, the disaster with the smallest number of housing units affected, proved in fact to be the only one to create a real housing crisis. Although Northridge had the greatest proportion of multifamily housing damaged, the high vacancy rate in the area and the increased public assistance made sheltering easier. After Loma Prieta, where 60 percent of the residential damage was in old, marginal buildings, and where the vacancy rate was less than 1 percent, there was no available alternative housing. As a result, temporary shelters became homeless shelters, and social service agencies were unprepared for the increased caseloads.

Similarly, the hurricanes created higher concentrations of damage, in terms of the higher proportion of damage in a localized area, and in terms of a greater percentage of uninhabitable damaged housing; but here again the vacancy rates in surrounding communities, along with the fact that many losses occurred in vacation developments (which did not create a housing demand), offset the dire need for alternative shelter. Also, given the job losses as a result of the destruction of the air force base and damage to local agriculture, combined with the long time frame (in months) required to restore local services, it is not surprising that many chose to leave the area rather than seek alternative shelter. After Loma Prieta, the critical concentrations were not only physical but social. Loma Prieta victims were clearly the oldest, the poorest, the most transient of those affected by any of the disasters. Hugo, Andrew, and Northridge largely affected working- and middle-class suburban families, a population with strong ties to their community and strong reasons to reestablish their homes and communities.

The most disturbing and surprising indicator of a potential housing crisis is the relationship of private insurance payments to recovery. The matter appears straightforward on the surface: more insurance equals quicker recovery. The affordable housing stock damaged by Loma Prieta had the least insurance and the least financial capacity to recover. In both hurricanes, where the damage was primarily concentrated in single-family homes, insurance payments clearly contributed to the speed of the repairs.

After Northridge the official damage assessments based on inspections suggested that the majority of residential damage was concentrated in apartment units, not single-family homes. Then, two years after the event, researchers and state officials were surprised by the high volume of insurance and federal disaster program payments to home owners. Why is the number of single-family insurance claims that followed Northridge comparable to those that followed Andrew, when Andrew clearly impacted a predominance of single-family homes and the Northridge damage was perceived to be largely in apartment structures? Were middle-class home owners better at "extracting their due" from insurance? Did insurance companies overpay? Were there fraudulent claims? Were the policies appropriate for the risk? These questions are critical because residential insurance claims typically drive the valuation of disaster losses.

The post-Northridge recovery situation was complicated by the local and federal governments' reliance on safety inspection data as an accurate representation of damage. While the count of significantly damaged apartments and single-family homes was reasonably complete, the data in the tabulation of nonstructural damage were far less reliable. In previous disasters, inspections may also have underassessed minor damage, but those households simply relied on personal resources to make repairs. Their losses were never tallied in insurance claims or government payments. In the Northridge impact area, a higher-than-average percentage of home owners had insurance, and the claim rates (defined as the number of claims divided by the number of policies) exceeded 50 percent as far as 20 kilometers away from the fault rupture (Comerio, Landis, and Firpo 1996).

This mismatch between damage estimates and damage claims may not be unique to the Los Angeles case. Comparing the insurance payouts to the damage estimates after Hugo, Andrew, and even Loma Prieta, the number of claims appears to be consistently three to four times the number of housing units counted as significantly damaged, and more than double the total number of single-family units affected. See table 36. This suggests that the majority of funding for postdisaster rebuilding goes to insured households, regardless of the level of damage. Thus, unlike in the Mexico City program, the millions of dollars paid for recovery are not necessarily spent to repair the worst damage. In future urban disasters, when recovery capital is severely limited because insurers have limited their coverage or left the market entirely, and federal agencies offer limited assistance, American disaster recovery will resemble the Kobe experience.

WHAT IF A TRULY LARGE DISASTER STRIKES AN AMERICAN CITY?

The housing losses sustained in recent hurricanes and earthquakes clearly demonstrate the vulnerability of an urban housing stock, even in moderate-intensity suburban disasters. What would happen if a magnitude 7.0 or greater earthquake hit the center of Los Angeles or the San Francisco Bay Area or Memphis or St. Louis or Seattle? What would happen if the eye of a category 5 hurricane crossed the center of Miami or New Orleans or another eastern seaboard city? What would happen if the disaster took place during working hours or commute hours, when families were away from their homes, when children were in school? Would the impact of losses be on the scale of those in the Mexico City or Kobe earthquakes? See figure 67.

To estimate the potential for a housing crisis triggered by a natural disaster, it is useful to look at the damage estimates for a magnitude 7.0 Hayward fault scenario earthquake (EERI 1996b) in the San Francisco Bay Area and compare these to previous losses in American disasters and urban housing losses in Mexico City and Kobe. Despite the differences in urban development patterns and construction methods, the Mexico City and Kobe experiences exemplify a scale of housing loss comparable to what could be expected in American urban centers. In addition, the combined differences in recovery strategies provide a benchmark for measuring the impact of disasters on cities and particularly on housing. Because the housing losses in these two international examples are comparable in scale to a Hayward scenario earthquake, the recovery prob-

TABLE 37

COMPARISON OF HOUSING LOSS AND RECOVERY IN MEXICO CITY AND KOBE, AND ESTIMATES FOR RESULTS OF MAGNITUDE 7.0 EARTHQUAKE IN SAN FRANCISCO BAY AREA

	Mexico City September 1985 Magnitude 8.1	Kobe January 1995 Magnitude 7.2	Hayward Fault In the Next 30 Years Magnitude 7.0
Deaths	7,000	6,000	~ 4,000
Total Damage Value (Billions)	$12.5	$150	~ $40–50
Housing Loss	33% value	50% value	50% value
	64% buildings	99% buildings	~ 90% buildings
Housing Units Lost	76,000	400,000	88–100,000
Total Units Damaged	180,000	600,000	300–400,000[a]
Multifamily	100%	30%	80%
Uninhabitable	50%	50%	Minimum of 25%
Vacancy Rate	>1%	>1%	>4%
Concentration	200 city blocks in 2 wards of the Federal District	24 neighborhoods central Kobe (5 x 20 km)	20–25 neighborhoods in Oakland, Berkeley, Richmond, Hayward
Recovery Short Term	50,000 units temporary housing	48,000 units temporary housing	50,000 temporary units needed
Long Term	46,000 new units; 42,000 repaired with government funding and completed in 2 years; 7,400 units repaired by NGOs	Redevelopment plan delays private repairs; plans for 125,000 units but no public financing or construction begun 2 years after[b]	30% of single family with earthquake insurance; limited public finance (especially for multifamily)

SOURCE: Comerio in EERI 1996b.

[a] If minor damage to single-family homes is comparable to the Northridge experience, the total number of damaged units could be as high as 1 million.

[b] Unpublished government reports from 1997 indicate that the government has begun construction on some public housing and purchased some units from private builders in order to provide rental units for the occupants of temporary housing. The number of units provided is estimated to be between 20,000 and 30,000.

Figure 67. Twister in Miami, 1997. Earthquakes and hurricanes are not the only threat to urban areas, although they typically account for the greatest damage. This tornado whirled through downtown Miami, shattering the glass facades of several buildings. (© *The Miami Herald*/Arthur Harvey)

lems encountered furnish lessons for future urban disasters in the United States. See table 37.

A PROBABLE SCENARIO OF LOSS IN THE SAN FRANCISCO BAY REGION

The Hayward fault lies in a northeast-southwest direction through the hills east of the San Francisco Bay. The fault runs through one of the oldest, most densely populated urban areas of California, crossing large jurisdictions such as San Jose and Oakland and a myriad smaller ones such as Hayward, Berkeley, and Richmond. The San Francisco Bay region is considered to be one of the more seismically active regions in the world. During the past 160 years, local faults have produced a dozen moderate-to-large magnitude (i.e., magnitude greater than 6) earthquakes within

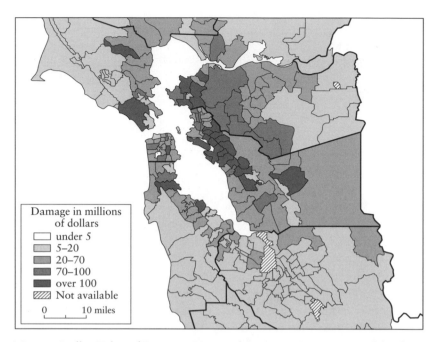

Map 9. Dollar Value of Damage, Hayward Scenario. Computer models of a magnitude 7.0 earthquake on the Hayward fault suggest that severe damage to wood-frame buildings would result in the loss of a hundred thousand units and cause property damage worth $10 billion. (Mary C. Comerio)

the bay region, and seismologists estimate a 67 percent probability of one or more large earthquakes occurring in the region within the next thirty years (Egan 1995; Schwartz 1994; WGCEP 1990).

In 1995, for a presentation at its annual meeting, the Earthquake Engineering Research Institute asked a group of experts to prepare a reasonable estimate of the impact of a magnitude 7.0 earthquake on the northern segment of the Hayward fault. This work was published by EERI in 1996, and it included estimates of loss to utility infrastructure, roads, bridges, buildings, and housing. Using EQE International's computer model, EQE HAZARD™, Ron Hamburger estimated that damage to building structures would be valued at approximately $16 billion, of which $10 billion would be the value of damage to wood-frame residential buildings. Estimates made by the Association of Bay Area Governments (Perkins 1996) put the number of red- and yellow-tagged (e.g., uninhabitable) dwelling units at about one hundred thousand, two-thirds of which would be in Alameda County. These two estimates cover only

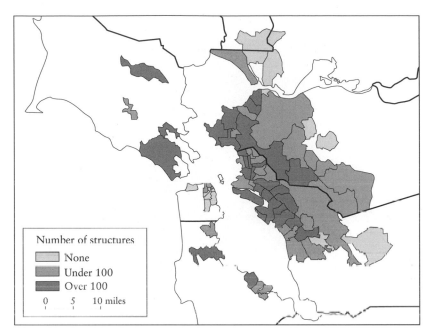

Map 10. Red-Tagged Wooden Structures, Hayward Scenario. Damage from a Hayward event would be concentrated in the communities between the bay and the hills to the east, including Richmond, Berkeley, Oakland, Hayward, and San Leandro. (Mary C. Comerio)

the most severely damaged buildings and housing units and do not include damage to building contents, window breakage, stucco cracking, or other minor damage. That is, this estimate of one hundred thousand units damaged and $10 billion in losses represents only the most serious damage—at best, one-quarter of the full extent of residential losses. See maps 9 and 10.

As was the case in Northridge, the damage will be concentrated in twenty to twenty-five neighborhoods in the narrow strip between the East Bay Hills and the San Francisco Bay, from the cities of Vallejo and Richmond on the north, through Berkeley and Oakland, to Hayward, San Leandro, and San Jose in the south. In the event of a magnitude 7.0 earthquake, the area is likely to see some two hundred thousand people in need of alternative shelter. Will it be available? In all likelihood, no. Housing conditions in the Bay Area work against both short- and long-term sheltering. In the areas with the highest potential damage, the housing stock is old, with more than 30 percent of it pre-1940, and 60 percent built between the 1940s and the 1970s. The stock is predominantly mul-

Figure 68. Typical Mix of Housing, Oakland. East Bay Area housing is a mix of older single-family houses and small apartments. (Mary C. Comerio)

tifamily and vacancy rates are typically lower than 4 percent. See figures 68 and 69. The population is ethnically diverse, and incomes are modest. Rents are low, relative to other parts of the Bay Area, but still consume an average of 40 to 50 percent of income.

Engineers estimate that there will be significant damage to roads, bridges, and other infrastructure. In addition, the topography of hills and bay will further limit access to neighboring communities. These transportation problems, combined with dramatic income and property value disparities, will make it difficult for victims to find alternative accommodations in neighboring cities. Tent cities or temporary shelters will certainly be needed.

In the long term, recovery financing will also be an issue. At the time of this writing, 30 to 40 percent of home owners have earthquake insurance, but that may decline. After the Northridge experience, insurance companies threatened to leave the state unless a mandate to offer earthquake insurance to every home owner was dropped. As a compromise, the legislature approved a plan to replace traditional insurance policies with a state-managed insurance fund offering "mini" earthquake insurance policies. These policies resemble Japanese earthquake insurance in that they only cover damage to the structure itself, and not to appurtenant structures such as garages or swimming pools. The deductible is

Figure 69. Typical Modern Multifamily Housing, Berkeley. Many apartments were built in the 1960s and 1970s on infill sites throughout the East Bay Area. In order to accommodate parking, there are few structural supports at the lower level. (Mary C. Comerio)

15 percent on the structure coverage, and there are minimal allowances for contents and additional living expenses. On average such policies cost twice as much as previous policies, for less insurance coverage.

Thus, in a future Hayward fault earthquake, fewer home owners will have access to insurance funds for recovery financing. Owners of multi-family structures may have a demand for their units but may not be able to finance repairs even with increased rents. Only owners of the least damaged buildings will be in a position to borrow limited funds for repairs. In the past, federal assistance for privately owned buildings was never available for more than one-quarter of the total cost of repairs, and it is not clear that future administrations will continue to offer subsidies for housing repairs, as happened in Los Angeles. The problem will be compounded by the fact that the damage will occur not in a single city but in eight or ten smaller jurisdictions lacking the political clout to garner the degree of federal attention claimed by a city like Los Angeles.

COMPARING THE BAY AREA TO MEXICO CITY AND KOBE

Can the circumstances in Mexico City or Kobe be repeated in California? Will the death toll be as high? Will Americans live in tents and

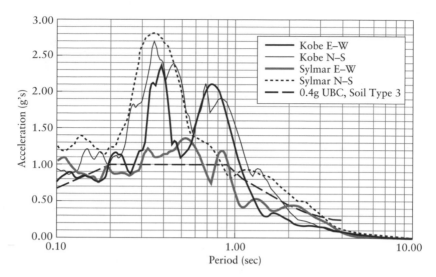

Figure 70. Building Code Design Levels Compared to Actual Forces. The Uniform Building Code requires buildings to be designed to withstand .4 g of acceleration, but recorded ground motions in recent earthquakes have been much higher. (EQE International, Inc.)

trailers on public land for two to three years or more while housing is rebuilt? While the building conditions that caused the heavy damage in both Mexico City and Kobe are unique, the similarities between the geological, seismological, and land use characteristics of Kobe and the area east of the San Francisco Bay are striking. In both areas, cities lie nestled along a narrow strip of land between mountains and bay. Both areas have high densities of residential, commercial, and industrial buildings in a wide range of ages and structural types. In both areas, the fault runs near important transportation and lifeline corridors. The strength of recorded shaking in the Kobe earthquake was about the same as that in Northridge (see figure 70), and about the same as what is expected from a Hayward event (EQE 1995a).

However, most of the deaths in Mexico City and Kobe were caused by collapsing residential structures. In both cases, the greatest loss of life occurred in the oldest, most densely populated wards of each city, in the early morning hours, in older buildings with little lateral resistance. The population density of Cuauhtemoc is nine times that of Los Angeles or Oakland, and the Nagata ward is four times as dense as the latter two (see table 38). In these cases, casualties were not simply a result of the earthquake's intensity, but of population density, building construction,

TABLE 38

POPULATION AND HOUSING DENSITY IN MEXICO CITY, KOBE, LOS ANGELES, AND THE SAN FRANCISCO BAY AREA COMPARED WITH HIGH-DAMAGE AREAS

City or Built-Up Area	Rank (by Population)	Population (Millions)	Area in Square Kilometers	Population Density (Persons per Square Kilometers)
Tokyo	1	28.4	2,820	10,070
Mexico City	2	24.0	1,351	17,746
Osaka/Kobe/Kyoto	6	14.0	1,282	10,920
Metro Los Angeles	16	10.4	2,874	3,618
Metro San Francisco	46	4.1	1,108	3,700
High-Damage Areas				
Cuauhtemoc (Mexico City)	Not applicable	.815	33.1	24,622
Nagata (Kobe)	Not applicable	.130	11.5	11,375
Oakland (Scenario)	Not applicable	.373	145.0	2,572

SOURCES: Bureau of the Census 1993; UNPF 1988; UNCRD 1995; Japan National Census 1995.

and time. American cities are considerably less dense, and typical wood-frame construction is more resilient and less likely to collapse. For these reasons, casualties in a Hayward scenario earthquake may not reach into the thousands as a function of residential collapse, but various other factors such as the time of day will contribute to the degree of hazard and the number of casualties.

Mexico City's lake bed and Kobe's alluvial soils and islands built of reclaimed land made these cities particularly vulnerable. Clearly, soil conditions along the San Francisco Bay are comparable to soil conditions in Kobe, but not all of the areas that would be affected by a Hayward event are on soft soils. The Oakland port, bay bridges, freeways, public transit, and other lifelines built on poor soils may sustain damage similar to that of their counterparts in Kobe. Such losses would have significant financial impacts, contribute to larger economic disruption, and undergo slow recovery.

While there are more similarities than differences in the structural performance of buildings in both Mexico City and Kobe, there are important differences, particularly in the residential stock. The residential stock in California is not as vulnerable as the *viviendas* destroyed in Mexico City or the traditional heavy-roofed, open-plan, wood structures in Japan. However, the Northridge earthquake demonstrated that severe and costly damage will occur in modern residential structures. Despite significantly lower densities, most of the housing stock is about twenty-five years old, and more than half is in multifamily structures with "tuck-under" parking that creates a collapse-prone soft first story.[2] Damage to this housing stock could easily render one hundred thousand units uninhabitable, and as many as 1 million homes could sustain cracked glass, plaster, and stucco siding. Without the capacity to rehouse displaced victims and finance repairs, a moderate-to-large Hayward earthquake could certainly create both a short-term and a long-term housing crisis in the San Francisco Bay Area.

The urban housing losses in Mexico City and Kobe may not be perfect comparative models, because American cities simply do not have such dense populations or the same high number of hazardous buildings. The physical losses in future American urban disasters are likely to be comparable to those in the Northridge earthquake or Hurricane Andrew, or three or four times as high if concentrated in an urban rather than a suburban environment. However, the economic impact of such loss on residential owners may be more like that in Kobe than either Mexico City, Northridge, or Andrew, because the federal government is unlikely to provide massive reconstruction subsidies, and private insurance is less likely to cover the full cost of repairs, even for single-family dwellings. In terms of alternative shelter and financing for recovery, the next American disaster could easily resemble Kobe. Thousands will be forced to relocate outside the city. The old, the poor, and all those without private resources will wait for years in temporary shelters, or they will be forced to leave the area. Redevelopment plans will take years to realize, as owners struggle to assemble funds for repairs and local governments struggle to manage the planning and permissions process. The quality of existing rental housing will deteriorate from incomplete repairs and overcrowding, and the capacity to replace housing for low- and moderate-income owners and renters will be virtually nonexistent. The housing crisis will be real.

CRITICAL FACTORS IN EVALUATING DISASTER LOSSES AND IMPROVING DISASTER RECOVERY POLICY

With each succeeding American urban disaster, individuals and local governments have demanded increased federal assistance. With each succeeding disaster, researchers have documented the losses and attempted to understand the nuances of economic recovery. With each succeeding disaster, private banks and insurance companies, as well as federal disaster assistance agencies, have become increasingly wary of potential exposure in future urban disasters. Thus, while residents in disaster-prone areas take false comfort in the apparent availability of public and private funds and the speed of recovery in past disasters, the financial community and the government are looking for mechanisms to limit future disaster costs.

Despite rapid strides to improve a federal disaster relief policy conceived in an era when storms and tornadoes never affected more than three thousand households, the federal government cannot afford to function as the "national 911," or as the national insurance policy. At the same time, private insurers shocked by their experiences in Florida and Southern California are working to leave those markets and/or to seriously limit their exposure. State and local governments are caught in between. What should the government do? How does government draw the line between public and private responsibility for losses? How do lenders provide financing and insurance for residential buildings in disaster-prone regions?

Disaster policy in both the public and private sectors is stuck because standard measures for analyzing and understanding disaster losses, and particularly housing losses, are no longer relevant in an increasingly urbanized environment. To develop policies that protect the urban community from a housing crisis, we need to move away from the limited government assistance model, where government and insurance fully compensate a subset of victims (i.e., home owners) for the full value of their losses. We need to move toward strategies that lead to loss prevention and balance public and private responsibility. A number of factors integral to the evaluation of the true nature of the disaster loss are also critical to the development of a more strategic, crisis-averse set of policies. These include building conditions, social conditions, financial conditions, and institutional conditions before, as well as after, a national disaster.

BUILDING FACTORS: HOW SAFE IS SAFE ENOUGH

The building stock in the Loma Prieta earthquake was the oldest of all the housing damaged in the four disasters. In that case, the age of the damaged stock was indicative of the economic stature of its inhabitants as well as the degree of hazard the buildings posed. Engineers knew that unreinforced masonry buildings and buildings with soft first stories were vulnerable in earthquakes, and programs had been instituted in the state of California to address these hazards. Unfortunately, Loma Prieta happened before many of the buildings could be upgraded.

By contrast, engineers, researchers, and local residents were surprised by the degree to which wood-frame buildings built in the past thirty years suffered extensive and costly damage in the earthquakes and the hurricanes. After both Hurricane Hugo and Hurricane Andrew, engineers argued that much of the damage could have been avoided. Local building codes did not require sufficient hurricane ties in roofs, construction was shoddy, and owners did not bother to shutter or board windows before the storms. What resulted was a good deal of expensive, nonstructural water damage that could have been avoided.

Similarly, the Northridge earthquake, centered in a modern suburban environment, revealed that building codes, clearly intended as a minimum standard, do their job in protecting life but do not prevent extensive and expensive property damage. The lesson from the four recent American disasters is that newer buildings built with mediocre code requirements will suffer a degree of economic damage similar to that suffered by older buildings built with limited seismic and hurricane protection requirements. While newer buildings may be safe from collapse, they are not going to offer residents protection from expensive repairs. The problem cannot be addressed by simply changing the building code for new construction. Even if codes and new-building performance were improved, new buildings are never more than 1 to 2 percent of the overall housing stock available. Nearly all of the population will continue to live in damage-vulnerable buildings.

There is a great deal of analytic research on the performance of engineered structures, from steel-frame high rises to concrete parking garages. What is needed is the same type of systematic evaluation of specific damage in various types of wood-frame single-family and multifamily structures. Such data can be used to understand the prevalence of certain building failures and the costs associated with those failures: that is, to understand the extent to which housing damage will lead to a housing crisis after a disaster. Such data can also be used to improve computer models employed in estimating future damages, and to develop realistic solutions to hazard mitigation and realistic incentives for owners to improve their homes, apartments, and condominiums before disaster strikes again.

After the Northridge earthquake, engineers and government officials followed the traditional assumption that the losses were concentrated near the earthquake's epicenter, so inspections were focused on an area within a ten-to-fifteen-kilometer radius. Although the heaviest damage was within twenty kilometers of the fault rupture and was concentrated in neighborhoods in the San Fernando Valley, consistently high levels of damage were in fact found as far as fifty to sixty kilometers from the fault rupture.

The discounting of widespread minor damage is endemic to the process of safety inspections and has led to a history of misrepresenting the full extent of earthquake and hurricane damage. As a result, it is difficult for owners of residential property to grasp the potential for losses in future disasters. In addition, it is impossible for individuals to plan for hazard mitigation in their homes, as it is impossible for a community to make hazard mitigation policy, without a clear understanding of the real costs and the real risks. A better accounting of specific damage conditions in specific housing types from past disasters will be necessary to develop effective mitigation policies and to improve postdisaster housing services.

FINANCIAL FACTORS: PUBLIC AND PRIVATE
RESOURCES AVAILABLE FOR RESPONSE AND RECOVERY

Sheltering victims is a critical part of disaster response. Whether a disaster causes a sheltering crisis depends heavily on the kind of housing damaged and the housing market in the local area. For this reason, the public resources needed for sheltering after disasters cannot be locked into specific preplanned programs. The needs are too varied and too locally specific.

After Loma Prieta, federal disaster and housing officials were blind to the homelessness created by the earthquake, and long-term sheltering was a problem left to the Red Cross and local nonprofits. After Andrew, Florida officials were slow to recognize the full extent of the damage and wasted days before calling on the military to establish tent cities until longer-term arrangements could be made. After Northridge, federal officials overreacted to the sight of people sleeping in parks and pushed to erect tent camps and distribute an unprecedented amount of temporary housing assistance. In each case, local and federal decision makers did not look at the damage in light of the local housing market conditions. Clearly, it would help to have a variety of contingency sheltering programs in place, to be activated in stages depending on the types of damage and the alternative housing available in the private market.

Once victims are temporarily rehoused, recovery is essentially a capitalization problem. As with sheltering, the local economy and the local housing market will play a significant role, as will the extent to which the housing lost was covered by insurance. Although the great majority of homes significantly damaged in Hurricane Andrew were valued below the county median and the occupants were largely low- and moderate-income families, the fact that more than 95 percent had insurance virtually guaranteed that single-family home recovery finance would not be a major problem.

After the Northridge earthquake, local housing officials were deeply concerned that apartment owners without insurance and without market incentives would simply abandon their properties. While a strict supply-side economist would argue that these apartments were unnecessary in a soft housing market, the city was afraid that the influx of vandalism, gang activity, drugs, and so on into neighborhoods with concentrated damage could exacerbate a downward spiral of declining property values and force out neighbors with undamaged property. Here, the city took a proactive role in securing federal funds to finance recovery of multifamily homes, advocating the social and financial health of the larger community.

After any urban disaster, the availability of sheltering and recovery finance will depend on the type of housing affected and the market at the time of the disaster, and so the need for public assistance will depend entirely on the local circumstances. Given the variation among the four recent large urban disasters, the narrowly targeted home-owner loan programs offered by the federal government seem redundant in light of private insurance. At the same time, the lack of specific programs for recovery for owners of multifamily structures opens the door to a serious urban housing crisis in the event of a disaster in which a large number of renters are displaced in a tight rental market.

INSTITUTIONAL AND POLITICAL
FACTORS SHAPING PUBLIC RESPONSE

Quite separate from the amount and type of housing damaged, and from the local market conditions, urban disasters are not created equal. Loma Prieta came only one month after Hurricane Hugo, trying the capacity of federal emergency response personnel. Because of the directionality of the earthquake and the soil conditions, Loma Prieta damaged housing in four different cities. While the damage was concentrated in affordable housing, the overall number appeared insignificant in a metro-politan region. In addition, Loma Prieta struck in a largely liberal, largely democratic stronghold. There was little political incentive for President George Bush to offer federal aid, and the losses, measured in traditional terms, did not appear to justify an extraordinary effort.

The dramatic loss of housing in Hurricane Andrew in 1992 occurred as President Bush was seeking reelection. The president's promise to re-build Homestead Air Force Base in an era of national base closures, along with the generous outpouring of federal aid, was clearly designed to boost his standing in Florida. Similarly, in 1994 President Bill Clinton had just seen his package of economic recovery assistance for Southern Califor-nia rebuffed by Congress. The Northridge earthquake provided an ex-cellent opportunity for an infusion of federal funds to jump-start the lo-cal economy. Here too there was an unprecedented outpouring of federal support for disaster recovery in the hopes of engendering some political support.

While the politicization of disasters is nothing new, the nationaliza-tion of disasters through media attention grew after Loma Prieta. The national media was already in San Francisco when the earthquake oc-curred just minutes before the start of a World Series baseball game. The earthquake became national news for days, when only a month before, the coverage of Hurricane Hugo was treated as a strictly local event. Given that both Miami and Los Angeles are high-profile cities with pow-erful media centers, it is not surprising that their disasters captured the national attention. Unfortunately, the attention and the assistance given to these cities has raised expectations in cities across the nation.

Cities cannot count on perfect political timing or dramatic news cov-erage to define a disaster's impact or to influence public opinion and pub-lic assistance. Every urban area needs to take stock of the institutional and political opportunities that are part of disaster recovery, and the bar-riers to disaster recovery, as part of its general planning. Understanding these factors will influence the strategies for recovery and decrease the likelihood of a natural disaster becoming a housing or urban crisis.

SOCIAL FACTORS:
DEMOGRAPHICS OF THE AFFECTED POPULATION

Who loses housing is as important as what kind of housing is lost. It is axiomatic that the rich will fare better than the poor, that home owners will fare better than renters, that stable, employed families with social and religious support networks will fare better than those who are single, marginally employed, elderly, transient, without kinships, and without a social safety net. The more important issue is why a city should care. Should a city simply rely on market mechanisms to adjust to disasters, assuming that victims will leave the area if housing is unavailable and that others will replace them in future developments?

After Loma Prieta, elderly residents of Santa Cruz were largely dispersed to surrounding communities. In San Francisco and Oakland, some of the victims stayed in homeless shelters, and others dispersed. While the earthquake triggered a personal crisis for each victim, the housing crisis was felt communitywide. Not only did low-income individuals lose their housing, but the communities lost the capacity to provide shelter in one critical segment of the market. After Northridge, 130,000 households received federal assistance to secure alternative shelter. Most middle-class victims found vacant apartments nearby, because the economic downturn had created high housing vacancies. But what if that earthquake had happened in the mid-1980s, when the Los Angeles economy was booming and vacancy rates were below 3 percent? What would have been the impact on local employment if victims had been forced to leave the area for lack of housing?

The balance between housing and jobs, as well as the availability of housing in a range of prices, is critical to the stability of any urban community. Disasters can destroy that delicate social balance in a matter of seconds. The notion that the market will adjust is flawed, because the market is flawed in the best of times. Although the private market provides 98 percent of American housing units, the notion that the market adjusts toward equilibrium does not work well in urban areas, particularly for low-income renters (Smith-Heimer 1992). Similarly, the post-disaster housing market hinders the reconstruction of low- and moderate-income rental housing primarily because the units are occupied by lower-income households and the owners cannot raise rents to cover rebuilding costs (Comerio, Landis, and Rofé 1994). Clearly, an understanding of the housing market and population demographics in disaster-vulnerable urban areas will be necessary to develop both mitigation and recovery planning.

In general, the ability to integrate information on building and social conditions in a community with housing market information and information on available insurance, government programs, and private finance, as well as political-institutional realities, will provide a more realistic picture of the nature of disaster loss, an understanding of the degree to which the loss has created an urban crisis, and an ability to move toward realistic recovery strategies in a shorter time frame.

The devastating disasters of the 1970s and early 1980s (in China, Latin America, Italy, etc.) forced the United Nations, the World Bank, and charitable nongovernmental organizations to rethink their disaster aid and recovery assistance policies. The experiences of relief organizations around the globe led to a reexamination of disaster aid and to proposals to make it more useful and appropriate (Anderson and Woodrow 1989; Geipel 1982; Kreimer and Munasinghe 1991; Aysan and Davis 1992). Researchers found that most disaster aid was aimed at meeting the immediate need for food, medicine, blankets, temporary shelters, and so on, but often promoted dependence and increased vulnerability by supplying inappropriate technology unsuited for local environmental and social conditions. New policies are designed to use disaster aid in ways that support social and economic development rather than impede it.

Similarly, the urban disasters of the last decade in the United States, Mexico, and Kobe are forcing governments, insurance companies, and financial institutions to rethink how losses are assessed and how relief and recovery aid are administered. Recent urban disasters have made it clear that housing is the single greatest component of all losses, in terms of economic value and in terms of buildings damaged. As a result, the potential for a major housing crisis exists if there is no mechanism to provide alternative housing for victims, or if there is no capacity to finance within a reasonable time frame the repair or reconstruction of units lost.

However, recent experience has also demonstrated that not every natural disaster in an urban area causes a housing crisis. Because the scale of metropolitan areas is large and housing resources are varied, one can no longer measure the magnitude of the disaster in terms of units affected or victims displaced. Instead, it is important to look at the loss in relation to existing housing resources and conditions in the housing market. If the number of units lost or rendered uninhabitable is very large, but it represents only a small percentage of a particular housing type in a soft market, finding alternative housing may not pose a significant problem. But when the number lost represents a majority of housing types in a limited price range, then shelter will be a critical issue, even if the number is small.

Determining the degree to which losses are concentrated in particular economic or social groups (i.e., the geography and demography of the loss) will provide a better understanding of the capacity to finance recovery and the need for special intervention. The degree to which cities, governments, and financial communities are prepared to cope with future urban disasters depends on their capacity to understand locally specific factors that affect the evaluation of loss and recovery policies. These include (1) an understanding of building conditions in the damaged as well as the undamaged building stock, (2) an understanding of the limitations on public and private resources for relief and recovery, (3) an understanding of the social and economic circumstances of the population affected by the disaster, and (4) and an understanding of the political factors that will shape public response in general and in locally specific terms.

But ultimately, what every disaster planner, what every city official, what every citizen wants to know is, "Can it happen here?" Can American and European cities expect the devastating losses experienced in Mexico City and Kobe? The answer is yes and no. Certainly, the financial and physical losses that accompanied Andrew and Northridge are a fraction of what could result from a slightly larger disaster, one slightly closer to the urban core. Certainly, the older sections of European cities have building conditions and population densities that mirror those in Mexico City or Kobe. But to answer the question "Will there be a crisis here?" cities need to take stock of what they have, in human and physical terms.

Planning must be based on a realistic assessment of local conditions, but must also include contingencies for the vagaries of the economic climate, the housing market, and the politics of the times. There is no simple numerical index whereby disasters can be measured to indicate the degree of crisis in the physical infrastructure of a city. Instead, planners must first understand which variables matter, and then they must have a variety of plans prepared, based on varying damage conditions and varying circumstances in the marketplace. At the time a disaster occurs, planners can choose the response and recovery plan that most closely resembles actual conditions.

The next chapter will describe the evolution of disaster policy in the United States and discuss the issues and problems inherent in the current system. Chapter 6 will offer a strategy for rethinking disaster assistance and recovery policies.

CHAPTER 5

Current Policies, Current Problems

The contemporary American model for providing disaster relief and recovery assistance is a mixture of charity, federal programs, and private
insurance which has developed by the accretion of legislation and common practice. Prior to World War II the Red Cross provided emergency
relief to disaster victims throughout the country, but federal government
assistance was generally limited to specific appropriations designated for
financial assistance to local governments on a case-by-case basis. After
the war, federal involvement in disaster assistance grew from policies on
aid to local governments, to policies governing aid to individuals for private losses.

With each succeeding disaster, the government programs expanded and
changed, but they had always been developed in the context of providing a "safety net" that paralleled but did not substitute for charitable relief or private insurance for the repair of damaged buildings. This system of assistance has worked reasonably well for the majority of garden-
variety disasters, such as storms, small floods, wildfires, and so on, of
which there are thirty to forty annually. Typically in these cases, the
number of victims is usually small (fewer than two thousand to three
thousand households) and the dollar value of losses is relatively insignificant (less than $1 to $2 billion). The large urban disasters in the
United States in recent years tested the existing policies and demonstrated the limitations and inefficiencies in the current model for disaster
assistance.

This chapter reviews the evolution of disaster response and recovery programs, including descriptions of the agencies involved and the standard procedures undertaken by local, state, and federal governments. Using examples from recent cases, the chapter makes a case for distinguishing between emergency relief and recovery (i.e., rebuilding) activities, and it details the problems with public assistance and private insurance. The American system of funding disaster repairs is compared to policies developed in Mexico City and Kobe, and the chapter concludes with an assessment of current trends.

THE EVOLUTION OF DISASTER RESPONSE AND RECOVERY PROGRAMS

The first organized aid for disaster victims began with the American Red Cross (ARC) when the founder, Clara Barton, organized the distribution of food and relief supplies after an 1881 disaster. Since then, the ARC has continued to be the primary agent of emergency disaster relief. In 1900, Congress granted the ARC a charter authorizing the organization to carry out a system of national and international peacetime efforts to bring people relief from the sufferings of pestilence, famine, fires, floods, and other national calamities (U.S. Congress 1995).

The programs and policies that have evolved in the United States over the course of a century are clearly the product of the county's experience— and lack of experience—with certain types of disasters. During this century, there have been few great disasters, and the most devastating disasters have been caused by floods (Smith and Reed 1990). On a number of occasions since 1917, Congress has enacted flood control legislation to protect private property. Congress has also enacted a variety of disaster relief acts—from the formation of the Disaster Loan Corporation in 1939 to the 1988 Stafford Act—based largely on flood experience (May and Williams 1986).

A series of floods in the 1920s and 1930s, combined with the 1933 Long Beach, California, earthquake, led to the first attempt to go beyond disaster relief and provide some rebuilding assistance to home owners (Mittler 1992; 1996).[1] Before the 1950s, however, relief was largely humanitarian, a function of individual donations and efforts by organized charities.

After the Ohio River flood inundated Evansville, Indiana, in January and February 1937, the Red Cross provided funds to sixty-seven hundred families for building repairs and household goods, while the federal Disaster Loan Corporation provided only 202 loans. Despite the good intentions of Congress to act on behalf of flood victims, the government was more comfortable with procedures that kept disaster assistance in the hands of private charities. The government was called upon to act only when the scale of the disaster was beyond the capacity of the Red Cross.

Beginning in 1950, Congress established a federal role in supplementing state and private disaster relief efforts in instances when state and local areas were deemed by the president to be unable to cope with the disaster at hand. According to R. T. Sylves, "The first law to establish a disaster relief program that broke the single incident cycle was the Federal Disaster Act of 1950 (U.S. Congress 1950). It embodied the basic philosophy of disaster relief and laid the foundation for federal and state cost sharing in disaster assistance" (1995). This act, combined with the Civil Defense Act of 1950 (which specifically assigned responsibility for preparedness to states and localities), laid the groundwork for government to provide assistance, usually to support infrastructure repair or replacement.

Individual victims of disasters were not covered by these laws—they were expected to rely on private charities like the Red Cross—but over time the statutes were amended to include assistance to private citizens and businesses. For example, after the 1951 Midwest flood in Kansas, Oklahoma, and Missouri, President Harry Truman (a Missouri native) promoted the Disaster Relief Act. Although the act followed the precedent that federal disaster assistance should supplement state, local, and charitable assistance, it also provided funds for temporary housing for victims (Mittler 1996). President Dwight Eisenhower created the Small Business Administration in 1953 to administer disaster relief loans to home owners and businesses and made it permanent in 1955 (replacing the Depression-era Reconstruction Finance Corporation).

Since then, each administration has added agencies or programs to address specific needs in response to the problems encountered in affected localities after specific disasters. The most significant of the many disaster program additions for citizens were the provisions for refinancing of federal home loans in 1966 and expanded food programs and unemployment assistance in 1969 (U.S. Congress 1995).

Over the years, two trends emerged: the cost and effectiveness of structural flood controls were called into question, and federal outlays for disaster assistance increased dramatically. As Peter May and Walter Williams noted, "From the early 1950s until the early 1970s, the outlay for fed-

eral disaster grants and loans increased by a factor of nearly ten times
the growth of the value of disaster losses" (1986, 8).

As a result, Congress began to look for alternative disaster management programs, including national flood insurance and mandates for state
and local hazard-mitigation plans. Unfortunately, these require a level
of cooperation among states, localities, and individuals that is not always forthcoming. For example, building code enforcement and land use
planning—potential tools to promote mitigation—are generally under
the control of local governments, where mitigation efforts usually conflict with development goals.

The criticism of federal agencies involved in both preparedness and
relief, combined with a renewed emphasis on preparedness for nuclear
attack, led to the creation of the Federal Emergency Management Agency
(FEMA) by executive order of President Jimmy Carter in 1979. FEMA
served to reorganize many duplicative agencies and programs existing
before and after the 1974 Federal Disaster Relief Act (U.S. Congress
1974). At the same time, the three emergency management operations
with the largest federal budgets—the Small Business Administration and
Farmer's Home Administration recovery loan programs, and the flood
prevention activities of the Army Corps of Engineers—were not moved
to the newly created agency.

FEMA was a small agency stitched together from units in the Department of Defense, Department of Commerce, Housing and Urban Development, and General Services Administration. President Ronald Rea-
gan saddled it with the responsibility for developing plans for nuclear
attack, and over the years Congress and various presidents introduced
legislation and executive orders to mandate that it undertake a vast ar-
ray of emergency planning, response, and recovery missions (May and
Williams 1986).[2]

The new FEMA reflected the concept of comprehensive emergency
management developed in the late 1970s to encompass the four phases
of disaster management: preparedness, mitigation, response, and recovery. While preparedness and mitigation reflected the obvious need to
lessen the cost of relief, the last phase, recovery, reflected the growth of
programs designed to help local governments, businesses, and citizens
return to "normal." Effectively, that translated into funding to return
damaged buildings to predisaster conditions. Recovery assistance for private losses was justified by the notion that victims were returning to a
predisaster condition, not benefiting from the disaster with improvements
to their homes and businesses.

The 1988 Robert T. Stafford Disaster Relief and Emergency Assistance Amendments (U.S. Congress 1988) reorganized emergency management legislation and provided the principal authority for the president to act and authorize assistance in all four phases. While preparedness assistance is made available independent of a specific event, funding for other activities is established as part of the federal disaster declaration, including grants to individuals for temporary housing, and grants to state and local governments as well as private nonprofits for repair, reconstruction, and mitigation. The Stafford Act gave direction to FEMA, but it did not streamline previous legislation or the activities of other federal agencies.

The Civil Defense Act still covers preparedness planning, the Coastal Zone Barrier Act addresses mitigation issues, the Army Corps of Engineers is in charge of flood control, the Small Business Administration makes loans to businesses and home owners, and the U.S. Department of Agriculture provides emergency loans to agricultural producers. In addition, the federal government operates two disaster insurance programs, the National Flood Insurance Program and the Federal Crop Insurance Program (U.S. Congress 1995).

Thus, the federal role in disaster assistance has expanded greatly since the 1950s. During the 1970s and particularly since the establishment of FEMA in 1979, the authority to provide federal assistance for various types of disasters has evolved into a set of standard operating procedures for both federal agencies and local and state government recipients. Recent urban events have brought changes in the way disaster response agencies perform their assigned responsibilities and have forced programmatic innovations. Because agencies tend to carry forward "lessons learned" from one disaster to the next, the overall system of emergency response is generally improving. However, disasters are unique in time and place, and a solution to a sheltering problem in one disaster may in fact exacerbate the problem in another.

AGENCY ROLES

The various functions involved in disaster response and recovery are shared by a patchwork of state and federal agencies. Depending on the circumstances of any given disaster, a large variety of federal and state agencies will become involved. These may include the Corps of Engineers providing emergency water supplies, the Department of Agriculture distributing food and food stamps, the Department of Transportation repairing highways and bridges, the armed forces, the Departments of Energy, Labor, Justice, and Education, and the Veterans Administration, as well as others providing specialized services.

For the housing needs of private citizens after a disaster, the key government agencies are FEMA, SBA, more recently, HUD, and, to a limited extent, state housing and emergency service agencies. Although each agency typically has multiple areas of responsibility, the brief descriptions below focus on those functions and programs concerning individuals who have lost housing (see table 39).

THE AMERICAN RED CROSS

The American Red Cross is the first relief provider in emergencies of all scales, from individual home fires to earthquakes and floods. Its role is to provide care and shelter to persons dislocated from their homes by disaster. Its policy is to provide services as long as an emergency exists. Although operations are governed by national guidelines, decisions regarding what constitutes an adequate response and decisions regarding resource deployment are all made locally, and they depend on the experience and expertise of the local chapter.

The ARC generally assumes that about one-quarter to one-third of the population affected by a disaster will need some form of temporary shelter, usually organized in schools and public buildings. Tent camps are used as a last resort, because of the difficulties in terms of management and disease control. Other victims will typically deal with their housing needs individually with the help of friends, relatives, and private resources. Victims in shelters will be relocated as soon as possible to motels, rental units, or other forms of temporary shelter. In all cases, the Red Cross is focused on immediate shelter needs, not the replacement of losses.

THE FEDERAL EMERGENCY MANAGEMENT AGENCY

Although FEMA's primary role was intended to be that of coordinator of all emergency management—from preparedness to the provision of funds for repairing public buildings and infrastructure—provision of private assistance to individual disaster victims has dominated public perception of FEMA's role and raison d'être. While FEMA actually administers only a handful of individual assistance programs, the agency is responsible for coordination of all state and federal agencies involved

TABLE 39

SUMMARY OF POSTDISASTER RESIDENTIAL RECOVERY AND REBUILDING AGENCIES AND PROGRAMS

Phase	Agency	Program	Target Group	Funding and Time Limits
Emergency Response	American Red Cross and other charitable organizations	Emergency mass care shelters	Anyone requiring assistance	30 days
	U.S Department of Defense	Emergency mass care shelters	Large unhoused populations	As needed
Relief	Federal Emergency Management Agency	1. Temporary housing program	1. Short-term rental assistance to displaced renters	3 months' rental assistance
		2. Additional living expense program	2. Rental and/or mortgage assistance to displaced home owners	18 months' rental and mortgage assistance
		3. Minimum home repair program	3. Home owners with immediately repairable homes	$10,000 per unit
	U.S. Department of Housing and Urban Development	Section 8 rental vouchers	Low-income renters	18 months (with possible extensions)
Recovery	State Disaster Response	Individual and family grant program	Home owners and renters covering replacement of real and personal property	$12,200 total, 75/25% match with state
	U.S Small Business Administration	1. Home-owner disaster loan program	Home owners with damaged homes	Loan maximum of $200,000 depending on borrower and property creditworthiness
		2. Renter disaster loan program	Renters with losses	
		3. Individual business disaster loan program	Damaged businesses	Loan maximum of $1.5 million, depending on ability to repay the loan
	U.S. Department of Housing and Urban Development	CDBG, HOME (by special appropriation)	Low-income single-family owners / Apartment owners	Lender of last resort
	California Department of Housing and Community Development	CALDAP-Owner	Low-income single-family owners	Lender of last resort
		CALDAP-Rental	Apartment owners	Lender of last resort

SOURCE: Comerio, Landis, and Rofé 1994.

in disaster assistance. Individuals can apply for FEMA assistance through teleregistration and for other federal and state assistance at local Disaster Application Centers (DACs). In California, the establishment and staffing of DACs is coordinated between FEMA and the Governor's Office of Emergency Services. In other states with less active emergency management programs, FEMA takes the lead. At the DACs, individuals can find information on federal programs, as well as help from state and local social service agencies for mental health counseling, the recovery of veterans' benefits, Social Security, Medicare, and so on.

FEMA also provides temporary housing assistance for victims, based on agency staff inspections of damage to property. This includes rental assistance to displaced tenants for up to three months, rental assistance for displaced home owners for up to eighteen months, as well as additional living expenses and temporary mortgage payments if the victims have lost their jobs and/or incomes as well as their homes. FEMA also has two other focused grant programs: the Minimal Home Repair program provides up to $10,000 for quick repairs that will keep the individuals in their homes (and out of sheltering programs), and the Individual and Family Grant program, which matches federal and state funds up to $12,200 for replacement and repair of real and personal property. In fact, the IFG program is administered by the state and is only available if funds from other programs do not cover an individual's losses. Typical grants in both programs range between $2,000 and $3,000 and are largely used to compensate victims for minor repairs and/or personal property losses.

SMALL BUSINESS ADMINISTRATION

Much of the federal funding for residential postdisaster reconstruction is provided by the SBA's Disaster Loan Program. This program offers low-interest loans to individuals and businesses to repair or replace damaged homes and places of business within (or adjacent to) a federally declared disaster area. SBA loans cover only that portion of the loss not insured. In 1989, loan limits (including mitigation) were $144,000 for individual properties and $500,000 for businesses. In 1994, these limits were raised to $288,000 for homes and $1,500,000 for rental properties and businesses. Loans are ultimately based on the creditworthiness of the borrower.

SBA representatives are stationed at the local Disaster Application Centers to explain loan programs and procedures. Depending on the nature of the disaster, the SBA may conduct workshops with groups of home owners and/or business owners. Although the application deadline is typically sixty days after the federal declaration of disaster, in large disasters the deadline has been extended as much as one year. Once the application is in process, the SBA verifies the losses using its own inspectors. Applications are taken on a first come, first serve basis and can take several months to gain final approval.

THE DEPARTMENT OF HOUSING AND URBAN DEVELOPMENT

Created in 1965, the Department of Housing and Urban Development has not technically been part of the disaster response agency network. However, various programs within HUD have been called upon over the years to assist in the provision of temporary or permanent housing after disasters. More important, HUD is the focus for supply-side affordable-housing assistance programs such as the Community Development Block Grant (CDBG) program and the HOME Investment Partnerships program, which provide block grants for construction of new and renovation of existing affordable housing through local governments.

In addition, HUD has furnished a demand-side affordable housing assistance program since 1974. The Section 8 Rental Housing Voucher pays qualified households an allowance equal to the difference between local apartment rents and 30 percent of their income. Although HUD provides the funding for these allocations, they are administered by local housing authorities. HUD is responsible for maintaining the nation's public housing, and the agency includes the Federal Housing Administration, which provides loan guarantees for many private mortgages. In recent disasters, HUD has been called upon to use the Section 8 program for temporary housing assistance, and the CDBG and HOME programs to provide funds to local governments to assist in the rebuilding efforts. Since the Northridge earthquake, HUD staff are now included in FEMA's network of disaster response agencies.

STATE OFFICES OF EMERGENCY SERVICE AND HOUSING

In every state, an Office of Emergency Services is responsible for various aspects of emergency response, preparedness, and planning. In a state like California, the Governor's Office of Emergency Services (OES) is professionally staffed, and the office serves as FEMA's agent within the state. In other areas, FEMA works directly with the state governor's office. In a California disaster, OES operates as the center of the command and control unit, reestablishing communications and coordinating mutual aid assistance. The OES negotiates with federal agencies on behalf of the state and coordinates the emergency-related work of other agencies.

Other state government agencies are sometimes brought into the disaster response team, depending on the nature of the losses. A Department of Housing and Community Development (HCD), the state-level equivalent of HUD, typically is involved in state grants to urban and rural affordable housing programs. For example, in California, after the Whittier earthquake in 1987, the state HCD administered an experimental program known as the State Earthquake Rehabilitation Assistance Program. In 1989, after Loma Prieta, another housing assistance program was designed to provide loans and grants to home owners and apartment owners who were not covered by SBA loans or FEMA grants.

This new program, the California Disaster Assistance Program (CALDAP), was unique in that awards were not made on a competitive basis but according to eligibility; and that awards were not specifically targeted to low-income populations but were based on rejection from other disaster assistance programs. While CALDAP was designed to be a "lender of last resort" for residential disaster repairs, it was designed to be funded from state surplus. When that surplus ended and voters did not approve bond issues to finance the program, the program was effectively terminated and now exists in name only.

A STANDARD DISASTER SCENARIO

In the event of any disaster, large or small, each individual local government affected by the disaster initially responds and takes responsibility for directing emergency activities. When the emergency is large enough to exhaust its resources, the local government requests assistance through a system of mutual aid, typically coordinated at the state level. The mutual aid system is tiered, with local government first turning for assistance to neighboring jurisdictions, then to the county, region, or state.

If the state's resources are not sufficient to respond to the emergency requests of the local jurisdictions, the governor requests assistance from the Federal Emergency Management Agency.[3] FEMA can immediately respond to the state's request without a federal disaster declaration, through preexisting memorandums of understanding.[4] At this phase, FEMA can respond by coordinating assistance from other federal agen-

cies. Although the above description assumes a linear pattern of information exchange, this hierarchy of response is naturally an interactive
process. Federal and state agencies may be forewarned of an impending
hurricane by weather reports or may know of an earthquake through
the news media before official requests for assistance are made.

EMERGENCY RESPONSE PHASE

The emergency response phase includes fire suppression; emergency protective measures such as stabilization of structures; emergency medical response; flood control; hazardous materials cleanup; and provision of emergency relief services such as furnishing food, shelter, and health care on
an as-needed basis. Depending on the disaster, the emergency response
phase can be as short as twenty-four hours or as long as two to three weeks.

When a local government becomes aware that there has been an emergency within its jurisdiction, the local government requests mutual aid
for needed personnel and equipment from adjacent jurisdictions as its
own fire, police, and medical emergency departments begin to respond.
The larger the disaster, the harder it is to assess the extent of the damage because transportation and communication facilities are likely to be
impaired. Often, disaster intelligence is gathered from the reports of news
media using the equipment they have in the field or news helicopters de-
ployed for the purpose of gathering images and information for broadcast. Local governments send out their own reconnaissance equipment
or rely on mutual aid to provide the service. If, as was the case with the
Northridge earthquake, the disaster is at night or, as with the Loma Prieta earthquake, darkness falls shortly after the event, this form of communication is limited.

At the same time that government response activities commence, the
Red Cross, traditionally the first relief organization on the scene, provides medical assistance, food, and water and begins the process of sheltering the victims left homeless by the disaster. In a small disaster such as
a localized storm, tornado, or small earthquake, this may consist of lo-
cating unaffected rental housing and providing vouchers for one month's
rent. In a larger disaster, the ARC will open emergency shelters for disaster victims in the affected areas. If the ARC's resources are taxed, the
state and/or FEMA will request the assistance of the National Guard and
the Department of Defense. After Hurricane Andrew, the army built tent
camps to house victims, and after the Northridge earthquake the National
Guard provided shelters, which were staffed by the Salvation Army.

In the wake of a large disaster in which it appears that local resources are overwhelmed, the state disaster management agency requests a gubernatorial Declaration of a State of Emergency and advises the governor to request a Presidential Declaration of Disaster. Some disasters, when deemed "catastrophic," are declared even before a gubernatorial request is received by the White House. In most instances, the state is asked to prove that the disaster is beyond its capacity to respond, but the exact criteria that governed the need for a presidential declaration are imprecise and the decision to grant a presidential declaration for small or marginal disasters such as snowstorms, beach erosion, and crop failures is political and subjective.

When the president declares an area a disaster, federal programs are made available to local governments, state agencies, and disaster victims, and to voluntary agencies active in disasters.[5] In addition, the presidential declaration requires the formation of a Disaster Field Office (DFO), operated, in cooperation with the state, by FEMA, which coordinates all federal agencies involved in disaster response and recovery.

Within twenty-four hours of the disaster, many activities occur simultaneously: emergency response, including fire fighting, emergency medical assistance, search and rescue, public policing, and inspections of essential facilities; mass sheltering and feeding; commencement of plans to move from the response to the relief phase; and commencement of plans to open the DFO. By then, the local government also has conducted "windshield surveys" of buildings with damage visible from the street in order to assess the extent and distribution of damage.

THE RELIEF PHASE

In the relief phase, debris is cleared and normal public services are restored. Depending on the disaster, the relief phase can range in duration from a few days to several months. For disaster victims who have lost housing, the transitional phase between sleeping on cots in an emergency shelter and rebuilding their homes (or finding alternative housing) is often known "temporary sheltering."

The length of the relief phase depends on many factors, including the size of the event and the distribution of damage. In a small and concentrated disaster, the phase may be as brief as one week. Relief in this type of disaster might include finding rental housing for victims of a localized flood while their homes are cleaned and repaired. A moderate disaster may require more time because rental housing is not readily available, as when a forest fire affects an entire rural community, or the population affected is more difficult to house.

In a large, complex disaster with a great number of victims with diverse needs, the relief phase can last up to six months. Whereas emergency response supplies shelter and food to people who have lost housing, the relief phase provides temporary housing, which may consist of federal assistance for rentals in local apartments or hotel rooms, or mobile homes and camper trailers, if no alternative housing is available in the area. Temporary housing, in contrast to shelters, implies a certain quality of living, where one can have privacy and security, cook, go to work, send children to school, and so on (BAREPP 1992a).

Simultaneously, a less visible portion of the public process is developing as agencies begin to send advance teams to the area to plan their relief and recovery activities, while still gathering information on the extent and distribution of the damage.[6] This assessment includes making decisions about the scale of response that may be appropriate in terms of staff and equipment, and the timing of the deployment of these resources. Meeting with political officials is also a part of the process. Historically, the Department of Housing and Urban Development became involved if there was a need for housing recovery programs. Because of the scale of housing losses in recent disasters, however, HUD has entered the field during the relief phase and has begun to respond earlier.

A critical component in the first seventy-two hours is the utilization of the Post-Disaster Safety Assessment Plan. The program is designed to help local governments determine if buildings are safe to be occupied. While various state agencies are responsible for inspecting public facilities from schools to hospitals to freeways and bridges, private buildings are inspected by local government building officials or by a deputized volunteer engineer or architect. Once an estimate of the extent and severity of the damage has been made through the windshield survey started in the first twenty-four hours, the structures needing detailed safety assessments are prioritized, with essential facilities given the highest priority and single-family homes the lowest.

In a small disaster, the local government may elect to first conduct rapid evaluations of building damage, posting apparently safe and obviously unsafe structures, and designating others for further evaluation. In a large disaster such as the Northridge earthquake, the entire inventory of buildings will be rapidly assessed, and only buildings whose conditions are uncertain will receive further evaluation. Building owners are responsible for any evaluations beyond the initial safety assessment. In some cases, if a building poses a threat to the general population, the local government will condemn and demolish the building. If the building is demolished within thirty days of the presidential declaration, FEMA can partially reimburse the city for this expense as an emergency protective measure.

Generally, within seventy-two hours of a presidentially declared disaster FEMA begins staffing several teleregistration centers around the country in preparation for the onslaught of applicants for federal aid. Teleregistration is used during any disaster where phone service is available to the victims. Prior to the development of the teleregistration system, FEMA relied on Disaster Application Centers (DACs) to process requests for government assistance. DACs are still used, but they have been criticized recently because victims are often confused about what is available at the center. DACs are supposed to provide victims with access to a variety of government agencies involved in recovery programs (such as loans and grants for repair and replacement of homes and personal property), but because DACs are opened while agencies are still in the response and relief phases, victims come to them expecting to find food, water, and emergency shelter, as well as cash for home repairs. For political reasons, DACs have been opened more quickly, raising victims' expectations for assistance with a full range of services.

In order to distinguish between relief and recovery assistance, FEMA changed the name from Disaster Assistance Centers to Disaster Application Centers after the Loma Prieta earthquake. The Disaster Application Centers do, in fact, house the providers of some emergency services, such as mental health counseling and rental housing assistance, but the expectations of anxious victims run much higher, and often long lines form for services not available on site.

In recent disasters in California, the state has requested that FEMA rely on the teleregistration program alone to avoid the politics of DAC placement and the misunderstandings that arise when DACs are opened too soon after an event. However, DACs are still valuable and will continue to be used in disasters, especially if phone service is interrupted or if the damage is localized and assistance can be adapted to the particular situation.

If the disaster has a relatively small impact on housing, the Red Cross and FEMA typically begin to move people from emergency shelter to temporary housing in the first seventy-two hours. The process of housing people temporarily also includes moving those who, for any number of reasons, did not locate in the shelters during the emergency response phase. These people may have sheltered themselves in their cars or in makeshift tents in front yards or have gathered with others in parking lots or open spaces near their homes. The temporary housing phase may include rehousing disaster victims in available vacant housing in the private market, housing them in tent cities on vacant land, housing them in mobile homes provided by FEMA, or creating long-term shelters in public facilities such as schools or ships. In addition, victims often find temporary housing by moving in with relatives and friends who were not affected by the event.

Funding for temporary housing typically includes FEMA grants for rent and mortgage assistance. In large disasters traditional housing aid such as HUD's Section 8 rental vouchers is used to assist low-income victims. During the relief phase, some permanent housing services are performed as displaced renters are permanently moved into existing permanent rental housing, if it is available.

THE RECOVERY PHASE

During the recovery phase, owners of public and private property repair or replace their damaged buildings. This phase can take as little as few months or as long as ten years, especially when the concept of disaster "recovery" is defined as a return to "normalcy" or a return to what existed prior to the disaster. The repair of public facilities can take years, because the process requires the local government to negotiate with FEMA for recovery funds. In the private sector, however, the normal economics of the real estate market usually take over within two years, and most decisions to repair or rebuild housing, as well as commercial and industrial facilities, are driven by market factors, not by an artificial goal of returning to predisaster circumstances.

The recovery phase and the relief phase often overlap. See figure 71. Much of the government agency planning that goes on in the relief phase influences the development of the recovery phase. FEMA distinguishes between private and public recovery, labeling assistance to individuals "human services" and assistance to public agencies "infrastructure." Some states refer to the two forms of recovery as "individual" and "public" assistance.

Public Sector Assistance for Public Property   Although the focus of this book is housing recovery, it will be useful to briefly describe the public property recovery process, if only to illuminate the structure of existing government recovery-assistance programs. The Stafford Act spec-

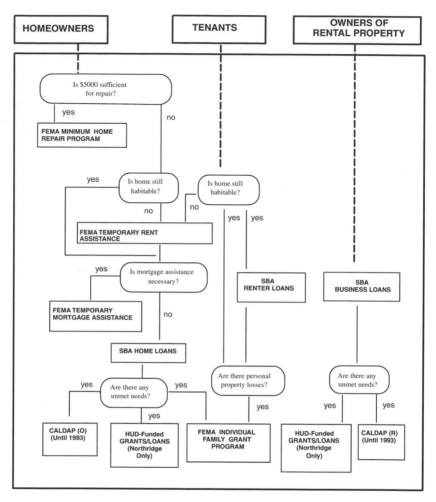

Figure 71. Public Disaster Recovery Assistance Programs. The majority of assistance is targeted to owners of single-family homes. (Mary C. Comerio)

ifies that 75 percent of the cost of repairing qualified damaged state and local property be borne by the federal government. Of the remaining 25 percent, each state pays the full amount for state properties and may elect to pay some portion of the damage to local government property. The process of reimbursement for public damage takes much longer than public assistance for the repair of private damage. Local governments must submit a damage survey report (DSR), which must be approved by state and FEMA officials. The damage evaluation and the construction cost estimates are usually a source of contention. Local governments typically want funds for the best possible design, while federal officials, charged with the job of managing all disaster expenditures, view most design proposals with skepticism. This leads to prolonged negotiations between the state, FEMA, and the local government, and delays in the repair and rebuilding of public property.

Public property eligible for reimbursement includes buildings, road systems, and public utility systems and equipment. Debris clearance and protective measures are also included.[7] Nonprofit organizations that provide government services such as housing, health care, and education are also eligible to submit DSRs for damage to their facilities and for relocation expenses. FEMA also reimburses state and local governments and qualified nonprofits for emergency services rendered during the emergency response and relief phases.[8]

Public Sector Assistance for Private Property   In a federally declared disaster, any individual who has sustained damage as a result of the disaster can apply for disaster assistance. All victims requesting assistance fill out the same application form. Applications are taken at DACs or sent by mail as part of the teleregistration process. The form of the assistance granted depends on the financial situation of the applicant, the amount and type of damage sustained, and the tenure type. Whether they are renters or home owners, individuals or families, people can get temporary housing assistance and funds for medical supplies as well as eyeglasses and other personal possessions lost in a disaster. After the initial application is taken, the victim must apply to some of the programs individually because each program offers a different kind of assistance and requires additional information from the applicant.

Once a home owner has applied for assistance, the home is inspected by FEMA inspectors and an estimate is prepared to document the cost of repairs needed before the residence may be safely reinhabited, as well as the total cost of repairs for all eligible damage.[9] Those homes that could be made habitable with less than five thousand dollars (raised to ten thousand dollars during the Northridge earthquake) are given a Minimal Home Repair Grant. This program is designed to quickly move people out of temporary housing and back into their homes. These funds are targeted to restore habitability and are not necessarily sufficient to bring homes back to their prequake condition. In this circumstance, FEMA funds will allow residents to live in their houses while applying for other funds to complete the repairs. For example, a home with chimney damage could be red tagged and unsafe for occupancy. The MHR grant would pay for the removal or repair of the chimney and for other work, up to the maximum allowed. This program is available to all home owners, regardless of income, and does not fund repairs covered under the home owner's insurance policy.

If the FEMA inspection determines that the building will need more than the maximum allowance to make it safe for occupancy, the application for disaster assistance is forwarded to the Small Business Administration Disaster Assistance Program and the applicant is given a check for two to three months' worth of temporary housing. In addition to rent checks, the federal government supplies home owners with mortgage assistance. If the application is forwarded to the SBA and the person decides to apply, another inspection is conducted. The SBA gives loans to home-owning victims in several circumstances: to those living in their damaged homes who are in need of more repair funds than they were granted by MHR or their insurance companies; those in temporary housing who are in need of repair funds; those who have sufficient earthquake insurance but need to make up the deductible amount; and those who have insurance but whose policy does not cover all sustained damages. If home owners can demonstrate the ability to repay the loan, they are allowed to borrow—since the Northridge earthquake—up to two hundred thousand dollars for home repair and forty thousand dollars for replacement of personal property (up from one hundred thousand dollars and twenty thousand dollars, respectively, reflecting higher-priced markets).[10] SBA loans are limited to the amount of damage only and do not cover additions or improvements. This program does not fund repairs covered under the home owner's insurance policy.

Renters whose units are inspected and deemed uninhabitable are given temporary housing checks for three months' rent, if rental housing is available within forty kilometers of their original residence. If no rental units are available for rental housing victims or displaced home owners, FEMA is required to provide mobile homes for temporary housing. Renters are also eligible for SBA loans for real property loss from a disaster. The amount of the loan is determined by the owner's loss and ability to repay. For both home owners and renters the Individual Family Grant program can provide up to ten thousand dollars[11] for replacement of real and personal property lost in the disaster, as well as medical and funeral expenses. In fact, a typical award is much lower than the maximum, usually between two to three thousand dollars for personal items not covered by SBA. Hurricane Iniki furnished an exception, where full IFG grants were used to replace roofs blown off by the high winds. Some states theoretically offer a supplementary IFG program that allows an additional ten thousand dollars for needs unmet by the federal program, but these programs are rarely used. The IFG programs do not fund any repairs covered by home owners' insurance.

Owners of commercial or residential rental properties are also eligible for SBA business loans, up to five hundred thousand dollars (raised to $1.5 million during Northridge to reflect realistic construction costs). These low-interest loans are based on the owners' ability to repay. The SBA requires that any applications for disaster assistance be submitted within sixty days of the presidential declaration. In large, complex disasters, the SBA has extended the application period to one year.

Public Sector Assistance Using Nonemergency Programs   In a large disaster, the federal government also utilizes nonemergency programs for special housing assistance. The Community Development Block Grant Program and HOME Investment Partnership Program, administered by HUD, were used after Andrew and Northridge to assist local governments in making loans to owners of multifamily apartments and to low-income home owners who do not qualify for other disaster rebuilding assistance. In addition, HUD has supplied emergency Section 8 rental vouchers to local governments to make up the gap between the cost of lost affordable housing and the rental housing available in the market.

Private Sector Assistance to Home Owners and Renters   The private sector typically plays the largest role in assisting disaster victims in their recovery. Property casualty insurance and private lenders provide a substantial proportion of the funds for rebuilding residential properties. Home owners with the right insurance coverage can make claims to cover a major portion of their repair costs. Banks can grant forbearance to borrowers in order to avoid foreclosure proceedings or they can provide loans for repairs. In addition, nonprofits, individuals, and corporations often provide special assistance to low-income populations and communities. And the Mennonites and other religious groups regularly offer free construction labor to assist in postdisaster rebuilding efforts.

Home-owner insurance policies typically cover fire, theft, vandalism, personal injury, and storms, but not natural hazards such as landslides, floods, and earthquakes.[12] In different parts of the country the types of coverage under home-owner policies vary. In some places tornadoes, storm damage, and even volcanic eruptions are covered, while in others they are not. Floods and earthquakes, however, are not typically covered, except by special riders.[13] Renters can purchase earthquake riders to cover their possessions. Condominium owners can buy policies that insure contents as well, and they have access to earthquake insurance through their home owners' association. As of January 1, 1985, California law required all insurance carriers selling home-owner policies in the state to offer earthquake insurance, thus making policies more available to home owners.[14]

In California, prior to Loma Prieta, earthquake insurance cost two hundred dollars per year for one hundred thousand dollars' worth of coverage with a 10 percent deductible. Less than 30 percent of home owners in the state carried it. On a house valued at two hundred thousand dollars, the insurance premium was four hundred dollars per year with a deductible as high as twenty thousand dollars (Roth 1996). The majority of homes affected by Loma Prieta did not sustain a level of damage requiring twenty thousand dollars' worth of repair. This high deductible was seen as a disincentive to purchasing earthquake insurance. Home owners either believe that their house will be spared catastrophic damage, or that in the event of major damage to their home, the government will provide assistance.

After Loma Prieta, which occurred in 1989, the state attempted to solve the two biggest problems of private insurance: high deductibles and the lack of insurance coverage. To solve the problem of high deductibles, the state developed the California Residential Earthquake Recovery (CRER) Fund, which offered nonmandatory, low-cost insurance to meet a deductible gap of up to fifteen thousand dollars. This insurance was offered through companies selling home owners' insurance in California at the time of policy renewal. Problems arose for the CRER Fund when it became clear that the revenue generated from consumers was inadequate to meet the expected losses, that reinsurance costs were higher than expected, and that revenue bonds were unworkable as a source of financing. Legislators introduced several bills to try to correct the funding problems, but the insurance commissioner supported the repeal of the California Residential Recovery Act. At the time, consumer groups and insurance companies were supporting national all-hazards insurance legislation, and the CRER Fund was repealed (Isenberg et al. 1992).

In the period between Loma Prieta and Northridge, more people in big cities purchased earthquake insurance, and the number of home owners with earthquake coverage in San Francisco and Los Angeles climbed to 40 percent. Because of the high price of housing in these markets and because of the number of policies sold, the risk to insurance companies increased significantly. The Northridge earthquake cost insurers an estimated $9.7 billion for residential claims ($12.5 billion in total claims). Afterward, insurers argued that earthquakes were uninsurable in California, and, in many cases, companies suspended the sale of home owners' insurance and/or raised earthquake premiums substantially. At the same time that some insurance companies withdrew from the state, efforts were being made nationally to require earthquake insurance with second mortgages (U.S. Congress 1995).

Because earthquake insurance became more difficult for consumers to purchase, the state offered minimal earthquake coverage through a state-managed Fair Access to Insurance Requirements (FAIR) plan to home owners who could not find coverage in the private market. In an effort to limit the liability of insurance companies while making earthquake insurance available to California home owners, the state reduced the required coverage that insurance companies were mandated to offer to a "miniplan," which covers only the house (no appurtenant structures). The deductible is 15 percent of the structure coverage, contents are covered only up to five thousand dollars, and additional living expenses are limited to fifteen hundred dollars. On average, this form of earthquake insurance costs three hundred to four hundred dollars per hundred thousand dollars. A policy on a two hundred thousand–dollar home ranges between six hundred and eight hundred dollars per year, with a thirty thousand–dollar deductible.

In an attempt to create a more permanent solution to the problem of residential earthquake insurance, the California legislature passed a bill, signed into law by the governor in September 1996, creating the California Earthquake Authority. The Authority created a $10.5 billion tax-exempt fund with moneys from private and public sources to provide the equivalent of the miniplan insurance policy to owners of homes, mobile homes, and condominiums, as well as to renters. At the time of this writing, the program was in the early stages of implementation, and newspaper accounts cautioned home owners that such insurance was not for everyone, given the high deductible and the capped coverage (Louis 1996).

Florida faced a similar situation when a there was short-term crisis in the availability of property insurance. After Hurricane Andrew, consumers in South Florida were unable to purchase property insurance, and many feared their existing policies would be canceled or not renewed. The state of Florida estimated that as many as five hundred thousand households would be unable to protect their assets. The state created the

Florida Residential Property and Casualty Joint Underwriting Association (RPC-JUA) in early 1993 to provide alternative coverage for consumers who could not find home owners' insurance in the market (Florida Department of Insurance 1993a). In addition, the state put a moratorium on cancellation of home-owner policies.

Although intended as a temporary solution, the state-run underwriting association became a permanent part of insurance in Florida. The JUA underpriced insurance with the goal of keeping prices "affordable" in South Florida. In fact, the insurance offered was so underpriced that home owners not at risk of losing private insurance canceled policies to join the JUA. The result was that the JUA rapidly became the second largest underwriter of home-owner policies in the state, with more than two-thirds of its exposure concentrated in five coastal counties with a very high risk of hurricane damage. Ironically, because the JUA was undercapitalized, the risk exposure was greater, creating another incentive for private insurers to leave the state, since any such carriers doing business in Florida were liable for JUA deficits, in proportion to market share.

At the same time, home owners in safer inland and northern counties who continued to pay market rates for private insurance had higher costs than coastal residents and were in fact subsidizing higher-risk coastal properties. State insurance regulators did not allow the results of hurricane computer simulation models to be used in the rate hearings, so the politics of insurance regulation prevented rational market pricing. Together, the underpricing of policies by the JUA and the homogenizing of private insurance rates across the state provided a dual subsidy of rates in the highest-risk regions (West 1996).

While Florida attempted to find a solution to sharing the risks posed by hurricane claims, Carol Taylor West said that the state's actions were in fact "a textbook example of public policy gone awry both with respect to attempting to stem market adjustments to real risk differentials and with respect to losing sight of the legitimate role of the government in regulation. Indeed, the clear lesson of the Florida insurance experience is simply to let the regional redistribution occur" (1996, 8).

Ultimately, pressures applied by the private insurance companies affect federal and state government polices. If home owners in high-risk areas lose access to disaster insurance, they will increasingly depend on government programs already stretched to capacity.

In summary, the public programs, private charities, and private insurance that provide for the needs of local governments and private citizens after a disaster are inextricably linked in policy as well as in actual service delivery. The tangle of government and private programs that have evolved since the 1950s has been and continues to be focused on the provision of emergency relief services to all disaster victims, and financial assistance for the recovery of losses to middle-class owners of single-family homes. Nothing in the 1988 Disaster Response Plan prepared government officials and volunteers for the housing problems that would emerge in the large urban disasters that began in 1989.

With each successive event, the federal agencies attempted to expand existing programs and services to meet the unusual problems created by urban disasters. The result has been to increase expenditures in temporary housing and home owner loans, without addressing the fundamental division between the needs of home owners and the needs of rental-housing owners. At the same time, each succeeding disaster has raised the insurance industry's awareness of its concentrated risk and led to a retreat from markets with natural hazards, particularly Florida and California.

THE EXPANSION OF AGENCY MISSIONS AND ROLES

In the five-year period between 1989 and 1994, five U.S. disasters caused $75 billion in damages, half of which was in residential structures. Four of those five disasters were concentrated in the suburbs of major metropolitan areas. Federal and state emergency management professionals tried to learn from mistakes in previous disasters, but between the big disasters there were dozens of smaller ones. California alone had thirteen federally declared disasters in the five years since Loma Prieta, including earthquakes, floods, fires, pestilence, and civil unrest.

There was little time for analysis and review of policies and programs. Instead, learning took the form of trying to answer the questions "What can we do to avoid the problems of the last disaster?" and "What worked well in the last disaster and can we do it again?" Under unprecedented pressure, federal and state disaster agency personnel did what they had always done, which was to rely on a standard operating procedure and tinker with the rules to accommodate the circumstances. The growth of programs and services developed in various federal agencies since the 1950s was semiconsolidated in FEMA in 1979. But every few years, a new disaster demonstrated a particular local need. That need would be met with a new program or special funds. Each time, the programs would be carried forward to the next event. Thus, in the period between 1989 and 1994, in the heat of the political spotlight focused on them, agencies and programs simply continued to expand and add or redirect services.

The most significant programmatic improvements came in the area of emergency response. In California, emergency communication problems after Loma Prieta and the Oakland Hills fire resulted in the development of statewide satellite communications and standardized emergency response procedures. The inequities and problems in sheltering after Loma Prieta and Andrew led to a review of procedures by charitable and government agencies. Red Cross workers, state agency staffs, and volunteers received training in cultural sensitivity, foreign languages, and specialized services for poor and minority victims. Mayors, police chiefs, and other key local department heads in areas unaffected by a disaster were trained to assist their counterparts in impacted areas. At FEMA, regulations were changed to allow federal agencies to take action on catastrophic disasters before states officially requested help. See table 40.

The housing recovery problems after Hugo and Loma Prieta were met with the standard range of federal, state, and local programmatic responses, even though the scale of housing loss was new. In South Carolina, there were a large number of houses damaged but most were covered by insurance, and the government aid process did not pose insurmountable problems. In California, however, home owners who had earthquake insurance were shocked by the ten to fifteen thousand–dollar deductibles on their policies, but most (70 percent) had no earthquake insurance and were forced to rely solely on government programs for rebuilding loans and grants. Home owners were frustrated by the complex maze of alternative programs, each requiring that applicants be rejected by one program before they could work through another application and inspection process, with different rules and regulations. The process was bewildering as well as time consuming. As one local housing official observed, "Middle-class people are not used to standing in endless lines to get a government handout."

The report *Post-Disaster Residential Rebuilding* (Comerio, Landis, and Rofé 1994) described the pitfalls for low-income home owners and detailed the process that "creditworthy" home owners endured to obtain housing assistance. Although much of the federal funding for private rebuilding comes in the form of low-interest loans from the Small Business Administration, a number of other programs are designed for special circumstances, such as grants for repair of minimal damage or help for owners that makes up the difference between the actual losses and what is covered by insurance or allowed by SBA. In fact, this host of piecemeal

TABLE 40

SUMMARY OF AGENCY INITIATIVES AND INNOVATIONS

Disaster	Agency	Innovation (key innovations in boldface)
Loma Prieta Earthquake	Federal Emergency Management Agency (FEMA)	Settled $23 M lawsuit brought by Alameda Legal Aid to provide affordable housing
		Developed historic building memorandum of understanding
	Small Business Administration (SBA)	**Simplified application forms**
	American Red Cross	Supported long-term homeless shelters
	California Office of Emergency Services (OES)	Developed **Operational Area Satellite Information System (OASIS)**
	California Department of Insurance (DOI)	Developed CRER program
	California Department of Housing and Community Development (HCD)	Developed **California Disaster Loan Program (CALDAP)** as lender of last resort
	City of San Francisco	Used media to get national attention and funding for reconstruction
	City of San Francisco	Created redevelopment district for rebuilding affordable housing
Oakland Hills Fire	FEMA	Wanted to open DAC earlier than in previous disasters
	OES	Proposed Senate Bill 1841 to coordinate mutual aid and develop the **Standardized Emergency Management System (SEMS)**
	City of Oakland	Developed concept of one-stop service to replace DAC
Cape Mendocino Earthquake	FEMA	Allowed **mitigation as part of Minimum Home Repair Program**
	OES/FEMA	Created a repair guide to be disseminated to all affected jurisdictions
Lander/Big Bear Earthquake	OES/USGS/CDMG/EERI	Convened disaster clearinghouse for intelligence

TABLE 40 (continued)

Disaster	Agency	Innovation (key innovations in boldface)
Northridge Earthquake	FEMA	**Developed teleregistration**
	FEMA	**Mailed temporary housing checks to registered victims in zip codes with highest level of ground shaking**
	FEMA	**Developed and implemented recovery channel concept**
	FEMA	**Opened DACs early with more agencies in them**
	FEMA	**Opened several earthquake service centers as DACs closed**
	HUD	Funded nonprofit to develop Section 8 apartment availability list
	HUD	**Assigned special Section 8 rental vouchers for disaster relief**
	HUD	Allowed the use of CBDG and HOME funds for recovery
	Fannie Mae	Required condominiums to have earthquake insurance in order to receive funds
	SBA	Raised limits on home and business loans
	SBA	Upgraded computer and loan processing equipment and procedures
	OES	Convened housing task force
	OES	**Developed Emergency Managers Mutual Aid (EMMA) program**
	OES	Conducted research on affected populations and funded further research
	OES	Proactively sought FEMA assistance for specialized services for local governments and special populations
	HCD/OES	Mobile home repair program
	HCD	Proposed alternative financing strategies
	DOI	**Developed concept of California Earthquake Authority (CEA)**
	City of Los Angeles	Proactively sought HUD recovery funding
	City of Los Angeles	Actively pursued expanded rebuilding role for Los Angeles Department of Housing
	City of Los Angeles	Sought FEMA funding for fencing and security patrols in Ghost Towns

SOURCE: Comerio, Landis, and Firpo 1996.

programs (originally intended to fill gaps) creates confusion, red tape, and delays for applicants.

The first critical housing issue raised by the 1989 disasters was that damage to large numbers of housing units spotlighted the inefficiency in the multiagency, multiprogram system of delivering housing assistance. The second housing recovery issue was the lack of assistance for the large number of low-rent, multifamily apartments and hotels. In no previous disaster did the federal government have to deal with damage to a large number of multifamily housing units. SBA business loans were available to owners of rental housing, but neither the private owners nor the non-profit affordable housing agencies who owned the apartments and hotels damaged by Loma Prieta or Hugo qualified for SBA loans. Further, the issue was complicated by the fact that the earthquake's effect on affordable housing in the Bay Area was a tiny fraction of the larger problem of affordable housing faced by nearly ever major city in America.

After Loma Prieta, California created a new loan fund, CALDAP, to meet the needs of both home owners and apartment owners who fell through the cracks of federal funding. Unfortunately, the program was slow to get off the ground, in part because it was difficult to run a disaster loan program in a traditional state agency dedicated to affordable housing programs. As a result, the state borrowed rules from federal disaster programs, which were complex and inflexible. The most important reason for the program's ultimate failure, however, is that CALDAP's funding was based on state surplus moneys, which were not available in later disasters (Comerio, Landis, and Rofé 1994).

The Loma Prieta experience raised the federal consciousness about housing loss in disasters, and, as in other programmatic areas, disaster housing services expanded through the use of existing agencies and programs. After Hurricane Andrew, a variety of existing disaster programs was combined with traditional housing assistance programs to help the victims in south Dade County. FEMA provided over thirty-six hundred mobile homes and travel trailers to disaster victims. The county, in conjunction with the U.S. Department of Agriculture, developed a mobile home park for migrant farm workers within ninety days of the storm. HUD made eight thousand Section 8 rental vouchers available for disaster victims and provided reconstruction loan funds for housing to the county through the acceleration of Community Development Block Grant and HOME Investment Partnership funds.

Hurricane Andrew, Hurricane Iniki, and Typhoon Omar (which hit Guam on August 28, 1992) were the first disasters for which Congress passed a supplemental appropriation bill. Enacted in July 1993, it authorized $85 million specifically for "the repair, renovation, or other community development activities affecting structures damaged or destroyed . . . in the areas impacted by these disasters" (U.S. Congress 1995, 108). One month later, Congress authorized another $450 million for the same purpose for the midwestern flood and for other disasters as defined by the secretary of HUD.

It is not surprising, then, that within hours of the Northridge earthquake, Henry Cisneros, secretary of Housing and Urban Development, was on an airplane to Los Angeles, ready to offer the resources of HUD to assist with the problems of temporary shelter and reconstruction of damaged housing. The combined resources of FEMA and HUD quickly rehoused displaced residents of all income levels. There were still no special disaster programs for repair of multifamily housing, and most apartment owners faced certain rejection by SBA loan programs. HUD filled a significant gap with $300 million in CDBG and HOME allocations, but the larger issue of financing for housing recovery has yet to be resolved.

The entry of nondisaster agencies like HUD into the disaster arena, along with the continued expansion of disaster agencies into new areas, has been an attempt to solve the new problems posed by large-scale disasters in urban areas. Unfortunately, these expanding roles also smack of mission creep, leading conservative members of Congress from states outside the earthquake and hurricane belt to question the federal role in disaster assistance. Politics aside, the recent experience with large urban disasters makes it important to revisit government policies concerning use of public assistance to help individuals recover from their losses in disasters.

Disaster assistance programs have grown and developed over time, in much the same manner that building codes have undergone regular updates and revisions because of new information and new technologies. As with the building codes, new sections amend existing rules, and over time the intent and logic of the regulations become hard to follow; at some point, it becomes critical to rewrite the code. Similarly, federal disaster recovery programs need to be reviewed, not only in terms of their efficiency and equity but also in terms of their original policy intent.

RISING EXPECTATIONS

In the wake of coping with the appropriateness of agency roles and programs in recent disasters, there was another important question on the minds of most disaster agency professionals: "What can we do to avoid the bad press we received in the last disaster?" The Loma Prieta earth-quake was a big-time news event, in part because the national media were already in San Francisco for the World Series, and in part because the damage to the Cypress freeway and the Marina district was particularly dramatic and therefore photogenic. With the introduction of twenty-four-hour cable TV news, Loma Prieta moved disasters into the same category as wars (and, later, murder trials); that is, disasters became ongoing events requiring serial coverage with regular updates. Television personalizes disaster, and after Loma Prieta, local politicians took advantage of the medium to make their case for affordable housing assistance.

This was not lost on other local governments. Witness the head of Dade County's Emergency Management Office tearfully telling the TV cam-eras, "Where in the hell is the cavalry? . . . I'd like [President George Bush] to follow up on the commitments he made." Never mind that Florida officials had not only not asked for military assistance, they specifically said they didn't want any (Garvin 1993). The constant broadcasting and updating of disaster footage (the CNN-ization of disasters) intensified the politicization of disasters light-years beyond the ordinary dimensions of pork-barreling and drove it into a new realm. For every unchallenged tirade against the federal government for failure to deliver more services, the federal agencies tried to improve their tattered images by offering more dollars and more services than ever before.

In the fall of 1992, facing reelection, President Bush promised Florida voters $480 million to rebuild Homestead Air Force Base (which Hur-ricane Andrew had leveled), despite the closure of military bases around the country. The president made good on pledges to pay 100 percent of Florida's cleanup costs (instead of the customary federal share of 75 per-cent), and promised to pay 100 percent of the costs for Louisiana (also an Andrew victim) and Hawaii (struck by Hurricane Iniki a few weeks later) when those states sought similar relief. When Senator Fritz Hollings complained, South Carolina was retroactively included. Only in North-ern California, where Bush was unlikely to receive additional votes, were funds allocated less generously.

Conservative commentators at the time decried the federal largesse, lambasted FEMA, and suggested that the Pentagon be converted into a giant national 911 (Garvin 1993). In fact, the black humor was a mask for a much more serious concern: that the federal attempt to be all things to all disaster victims was leading us to become a nation of whiners and con artists, out to fleece the federal government. Every city, every county, every state, every individual was a *victim*, deserving compensation and restitution, as if the hurricane/earthquake/storm/flood was *somebody's fault*.

In times of disaster, individuals and governments have become dependent and demanding. CNN and other broadcast organizations have done more than fuel the politicization of disaster aid: their coverage has fundamentally changed disaster response. Gone is the notion that a federal declaration of disaster signifies that state and local resources are overwhelmed. With TV cameras rolling, the federal government is first on the scene and the deep pockets are immediately opened. Given that scenario, state and local politicians assume the role of lobbyists seeking funds for their constituents, instead of partners in the response and recovery efforts.

Big-city politicians can rely on preexisting relationships with congressional delegates and federal agencies, while smaller cities stand in line for assistance through state agency contacts with Washington bureaucrats. When the mayors of Miami or Los Angeles want certain kinds of assistance, they contact whoever is on their Rolodex, not who is on the disaster recovery organization chart. Local governments set the example that individuals follow: they are lining up for entitlements they never knew they had, expecting and demanding help for everything imaginable.

The notions of kinship and self-reliance as critical components of disaster recovery are lost by private individuals as well as those within the establishment. Despite spontaneous acts of bravery and kindness in emergencies, middle-class Americans and local governments have lost track of the age-old tradition of depending on friends, relatives, and neighbors in the short term and using their own initiative in the process of cleaning up the mess and repairing the damage of disasters. The federal funds designed to assist "victims in need" have been transformed into entitlement programs for aggressive individuals and governments. Constant TV broadcasting of disasters has forced the federal government to promise more and more assistance, and the visibility of those promises has built unrealistic expectations.

THE INSURANCE PROBLEM

Just as the disasters concentrated between 1989 and 1994 focused attention on the role of government in disaster response and recovery, they also focused attention on the role of private insurance in disaster recovery. See figure 72. Earlier in the century the government faced the problem of having insurers leave the market because of the repeated

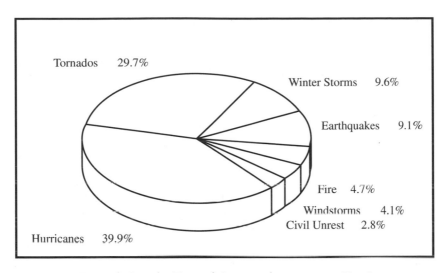

Figure 72. Property Loss by Type of Catastrophe, 1984–93. Hurricanes caused nearly 40 percent of nonflood, insured property losses. (American Insurance Services Group)

losses from floods, which accounted for 70 to 80 percent of all disasters in the United States.

As discussed above, the federal government first attempted to address flood loss through a program of structural flood control measures (dams, seawalls, levees, etc.) begun in the 1920s. The first federal flood insurance was instituted in 1956, followed by the National Flood Insurance Program (NFIP) in 1968 (Mittler 1992). The flood insurance program was designed to serve as an alternative to disaster relief, because private insurance companies have not been covering flood losses since the 1930s. Participation was tied to local mitigation efforts, and many communities and individuals did not participate. Currently, about 20 percent of home owners living in eligible floodplains have flood coverage under the NFIP (ISO 1994), which, despite its limitations and problems as a government program, insures private home owners against flood losses.

At the time of the midwestern flood in 1993, only 20 to 30 percent of insurable buildings were covered by federal flood insurance, and communities choosing not to participate in the NFIP received substantial disaster assistance, despite regulations to the contrary (Interagency Floodplain Management Review Committee 1994). Since then, the flood insurance program has been reorganized, but problems remain. The federal government has a great deal of difficulty enforcing participation in a national insurance program. State and local governments retain control of land use and development regulations, and these governments are more likely to defer to real estate interests than enforce safe building policies and require insurance participation. At the same time, the federal government has an extremely difficult time refusing aid to citizens in a disaster, even when those same citizens ignored insurance requirements. In a time of crisis, the government cannot afford to look miserly.

Given this experience, a national multihazard insurance program has faced an uphill battle. Many fear that a government-sponsored disaster insurance, in essence a federal safety net, would de facto condone poor building practices. Others are concerned that non-disaster-prone states would refuse to participate in spreading the risk, believing they would never receive their share of the benefits. Thus, the insurance crisis faced by Californians and Floridians is not likely to be solved by a federal program.

At the time of Loma Prieta, only 20 percent of California residents had earthquake insurance. Although the average was closer to 30 percent in urban coastal areas and less inland, it is important to ask why so many households in high-hazard areas were uninsured (Roth 1996). For more than fifty years in California, the disasters were small, few, and infrequent, and home owners simply did not buy earthquake insurance. The reasons varied, but generally included these:

1. Home owners did not think "it" would happen to them.

2. Home owners perceived the premiums and deductibles as too high.

3. Banks did not require earthquake insurance.

4. Insurers did not market coverage, because it appeared underpriced relative to potential losses.

5. Home owners assumed that the federal government would come to their aid (Palm and Hodgson 1992).

As a result, despite the fact that California required insurance companies to offer earthquake insurance in 1985, purchases of policies increased very slowly. Following the 1989 Loma Prieta earthquake, approximately $560 million in insurance was paid to home owners and renters, $400 million of which was based directly on earthquake policies. Despite the value of the residential damage, there were only twenty-six thousand claimants, who collected an average of fifteen thousand dollars on their earthquake policies (Comerio, Landis, and Rofé 1994; Steinbrugge and Roth 1994).

Loma Prieta exposed consumers' problems with earthquake insurance. The high deductible (10 percent) meant that owners had to finance the first ten to fifteen thousand dollars in damages themselves. In response, recognizing that the majority of residential damage is minor, the state government established the California Residential Earthquake Recovery Fund to provide low-cost insurance to cover the deductible gap but canceled it before its effectiveness or actuarial soundness could be fully tested.

With or without the CRER fund, Loma Prieta and other disasters raised consumer awareness, and more home owners began to purchase earthquake insurance, particularly in the urban coastal areas. At the same time, insurance companies had developed a number of concerns about the concentration of risks, reinsurance, and adequate pricing. Coastal cities were growing rapidly. Between 1960 and 1990, the population of the California coast increased 77 percent (ISO 1994); as more home owners purchased earthquake insurance, the companies' exposure increased, but their underwriting and premium structures had not changed to meet the risk potential.

The Oakland Hills fire made insurance companies recognize the value of potential real estate losses. Here was a case where three thousand homes were lost in one fire in an upper-middle-class residential area. The homes and their residents were generally older, and in some cases the basic home-owner policies did not reflect the replacement value of the homes. Still, after the fire, the state and media put tremendous pressure on the insurance companies to settle for more than policies were technically worth. In part, this was a component of a larger consumer backlash against rising auto insurance costs,[15] and in part, it was a push for humanitarian treatment of the disaster victims.

But even as insurers felt their product was underpriced and consumers found it overpriced, insurance companies faced a number of financial crises. Property insurance companies spread the risk of losses worldwide by a well-established network of reinsurance arrangements. However, in recent years as the demand for reinsurance has grown, the capacity has not. The stalwart of the industry, Lloyds of London, faced a bankruptcy crisis after numerous disasters in 1992. At the same time, a concentration among a few companies in the reinsurance industry has triggered rate increases and made reinsurance harder to obtain.

In California, the state requirement that insurers offer earthquake coverage with every home-owner policy forces another form of financial risk on the companies. Companies fear geographic concentrations of risk that could lead them to insolvency. Such fears are not unfounded. Hurricane Andrew's insured losses were $16.3 billion, and the Northridge earthquake losses were $12.5 billion. In both cases approximately two-thirds of the claims were made for residential losses.

Despite rapid increases in rates and deductibles in both states, insurance companies do not see the solution in higher rates alone. They would prefer to leave the market entirely. If they stay, they want to spread their risks. This could take a number of forms: in the financial market, insurers could expand recently devised schemes for trading risks with investors through options contracts and "Act of God" bonds.[16] Ultimately, insurers would like to create a tax-exempt risk pool specifically targeted for future disasters. Further, they would like state governments to uncouple catastrophe insurance from home owners' insurance, provide a state-backed reserve fund, and/or limit their exposure through minipolicies with capped payments for structure damages and minimal coverage for contents.

Insurers are caught between state government policies mandating that companies offer disaster insurance, and the need to make coverage affordable. Given the risks, full-replacement-value coverage typical of home owners' insurance would be extraordinarily expensive. Partial coverage limited to structural losses on the main dwelling is one solution to the problem of affordability, but it is one that is hard for consumers to understand. Consumers are willing to accept depreciated replacement value on cars, but not on their homes, in part because most have no comprehension of the magnitude of reserve funds that would be necessary to make every disaster victim whole, and in part because consumers simply do not understand home insurance, period.

Auto and home insurance is based on the principle of risk sharing, and it works because the industry knows from actuarial experience that a certain percentage of policyholders will have an accident or fire. Premiums are priced accordingly, and the payout to the claimant is part of the cost of business for the insurer. What drives premiums up are real costs that individual policyholders do not see. In auto insurance, for example, one in four drivers in California is uninsured (in Los Angeles, one in three is uninsured) and can receive compensation from an insured motorist in an accident. Fraudulent claims make up 25 percent of all payouts, and charges for pain and suffering drive up every settlement (Jaffee 1995). For home owners' insurance, there is often pressure on companies to pay full replacement costs, even if the owner carried only low-value, limited coverage.

Despite the growth of population and therefore the growth of exposure to risk, and despite the difficulties in educating consumers, insurance companies ought to be able to offer a variety of insurance products for disaster hazards. And they could price them appropriately if they had better technical information on hazards, soils, and building conditions, as well as some financial deregulation to improve operations. A current complaint of the insurance industry is that federal tax policy pushes it out of the disaster insurance market. Like other corporations, insurers are taxed on their annual profits, but disasters require that companies build a pool of funds over a period of years to have the reserves to pay for a catastrophic event. At present, such capital reserves make a company a target for takeover by another company, and it is costly to build the fund. Thus, the insurance market would be bolstered by a revision in the federal tax policy that would recognize the need for a special tax status for a multiyear disaster reserve.

CONFLICTING TRENDS

Government agencies at all levels have tried hard to respond to problems and issues that surface in each disaster. In fact, there have been numerous innovations, particularly in the area of emergency response, that have helped to provide timely shelter and services, along with insight and compassion, to all victims. At the same time, agencies have attempted to improve their procedures in expediting the process of moving victims from shelters to temporary rental housing, but in this area there has been a somewhat panicked response. Agencies have experimented with a whole variety of procedures, from zip code mailing of assistance checks to the use of Section 8 vouchers, without much analysis of what works or what is actually needed in any given circumstance.

The most intractable problem that has emerged is the inability to finance disaster reconstruction of residential buildings despite expanding government programs and attempts to rethink the insurance dilemma. The cost of government programs targeted to assisting individuals to recover from private property losses has increased exponentially. In the forty years between 1953 and 1993, the Small Business Administration approved approximately 1 million loans totaling $18.5 billion (U.S. Congress 1995). In one year after the Northridge earthquake, the SBA made ninety-nine thousand loans to owners of single-family homes, amounting to $2.4 billion, one-eighth of the value of the loans for the previous forty years (Comerio, Landis, and Firpo 1996).

The solution to the financing of disaster reconstruction for private property losses is not in expanded government assistance, nor is the solution solely in market-adjusted property values in the marketplace. Given the growth of urbanized areas, given expanded knowledge concerning hazards assessment, the whole concept of "recovery" needs to be reconsidered. In today's rapidly changing economy, the notion that public disaster assistance or insurance payments should restore buildings to pre-disaster conditions, under the guise of returning to "normal," is outdated and misguided.

Government assistance and private insurance need to be redirected to provide a variety of options for a variety of conditions in the residential marketplace. Home owners need viable disaster insurance with fair market choices regarding the degree of risk they are willing to assume and the costs they are willing to pay for differing levels of coverage. At the same time, the government needs to develop financial incentives for hazards mitigation. For example, California has failed to successfully legislate residential hazards mitigation, but some communities have found that tax incentives are a powerful motivator. The California legislature attempted to pass a bill in 1990 requiring that foundation anchors be installed in single-family homes at the point of sale, but the bill was vetoed by Governor Deukmejian.[17] Yet the city of Berkeley, California, allows residents to keep 50 percent of the real estate transfer tax if they seismically upgrade their houses. In a three-year period, some three thousand homes were seismically improved.

Similarly, several years ago, the insurance industry embarked on an attempt (known as the Building Code Effectiveness Grading Schedule) to evaluate construction quality through an evaluation of local building departments. This was begun in hurricane-prone regions after reports of substandard building practices in many suburban and rural areas. The program was instituted in California in 1997. But this is more regulation than incentive.

Finally, government assistance should target those whose losses outstrip their means, without bias toward one form of residential ownership over another, and assistance should recognize those who have made real efforts to protect their properties from hazard. The final chapter explores recommendations for a new approach to financing disaster reconstruction.

CHAPTER 6

Rethinking Urban Disaster Recovery Policy

In 1977, a group of social science disaster researchers published *Reconstruction following Disaster,* a book of detailed case studies on reconstruction issues resulting from housing and commercial losses, and an evaluation of the social impacts on cities and families (Haas, Kates, and Bowden). In this book, which was one of a small group of studies published since the late 1970s that reviewed American disaster recovery issues (see also Friesema et al. 1979; Rubin, Saperstein, and Barbee 1985; Bolin 1985; Bolin and Stanford 1993), Haas and his colleagues outlined the following seven basic policy questions that have become the fundamental basis for most disaster policy review by researchers and government disaster agency planners:

1. When should government use normal versus extraordinary decision-making mechanisms?
2. Should there be land use change?
3. Should there be building code change?
4. Should there be a concerted effort to improve the city (e.g., relocate transportation)?
5. Should there be compensation or special financial assistance for private property losses?
6. How should disaster-produced personal problems be handled

(e.g., the availability and cost of housing, employment adjustments, health and emotional problems)?

7.   How should increased local public expenditures be financed?

Of these issues, the first three have been carefully addressed in many federal and state response plans. The federal government has gone to extraordinary lengths to avoid conflict with states' rights and local police powers. The hierarchy of command in all emergency management is always local; the federal government and the armed forces will intercede only if requested to do so by the state. After criticism of the slow response to Hurricane Andrew, FEMA developed memorandums of understanding with states, allowing the agency to mobilize before a formal request for a disaster declaration is made, but the federal government remains cautious in order to avoid usurping a state's right to manage its own affairs.

Most researchers and emergency management professionals agree that land use changes are extremely difficult to implement in the aftermath of a disaster. While a newly vacant land area may appear to planners as an opportunity to improve urban design, planning procedures are viewed by citizens and businesses as impediments to the speed of repairs. Universally, disaster victims want a return to the status quo, as soon as possible. They do not want to be embroiled in negotiations with local governments that will slow their ability to make a decision about the disposition of their property. The Kobe experience bears this out. Government attempts to aggregate small lots and redesign some neighborhoods have constrained individual rebuilding efforts.

Similarly, citizens have resisted changes in building codes in the aftermath of disasters, but local governments often adopt stringent building code changes as part of their emergency procedures. This is not entirely abnormal, in that minor code revisions are regularly made on an annual basis and the three major national codes have a normal review process in which revisions are published and adopted every three years.

Issue four has often been hotly debated but tends to be resolved in the context of local circumstances. After the 1906 earthquake in San Francisco, for example, the proposal to widen streets and create a Beaux Arts city plan was abandoned in favor of expedient recovery. Similarly, the city of Oakland abandoned plans to widen streets and improve services after the 1991 fire in order to avoid a protracted planning process that would have involved negotiations with individual property owners. Rebuilding damaged highways after Northridge proved to be easier: the freeway damage was so localized that officials agreed that the only reasonable course of action was to rebuild the highways as they had previously existed. After Loma Prieta, however, the freeway damage affected two politically controversial structures in San Francisco, the Embarcadero and Central freeways, and the damage to the Oakland section of the Cypress structure was extensive. As a result, these transportation links underwent a lengthy planning and redesign process (Wachs and Kamel 1996). None had been finished as of this writing, more than eight years after the earthquake.[1]

The last three issues on the list have been under the purview of federal agencies and have been addressed more by the accretion of specialized programs devised in response to specific disasters than as a product of substantial policy debate. Most federal disaster agency officials would argue that there is need for federal assistance to citizens and local governments based on humanitarian values and a logic that seeks to spread risk and cost. At the same time, most federal officials are sensitive to the concern that no one should profit from disaster benefits. The result is a multilayered system of programs targeted to meet specialized needs, with bureaucratic checkpoints designed to prevent overcompensation and double-dipping.

This book is focused on understanding the problems of urban housing loss in disasters, and the ways in which individuals and communities are able to recover from those losses. This chapter revisits the policy questions concerning the public's role in compensating private property losses. In the past, the issue of funding assistance for privately owned building repairs has been lumped into the issue of how disaster-produced personal problems should be addressed. Victims had a number of housing needs—some more immediate, some more long term—but all were part of the range of human services that government made available in presidentially declared disasters. Essentially, American politicians proudly set forth the statement that Americans "took care of their own" in times of need. In fact, the degree to which the federal government provided assistance to disaster victims varied greatly from disaster to disaster, depending on who was in the White House at the time (Mittler 1996).

In the American experience with disasters since 1989, it is clear that a number of fundamental factors have changed: (1) the scale of future disaster losses and the cost of repairs will be similar to or greater than those experienced in Hurricane Andrew or the Northridge earthquake, given growth and development patterns; (2) the visibility of disasters through national news media will continue to politicize all disaster response efforts; (3) the federal government is now expected to be first on the scene with personnel, programs, and financial assistance; and (4) insurance companies are no longer offering full-coverage disaster insurance to home owners in earthquake- and hurricane-prone regions.

In view of these changes, there needs to be a rethinking of what recovery means, a comprehensive revision of the government's role in disaster recovery, and a more balanced and equitable set of policies and programs designed as construction finance tools. Essentially, the issues and problems that arise in the repairing and rebuilding of the built environment damaged in disasters should not be intertwined with the humanitarian services of government and volunteer agencies in the response and relief phases.

The term *recovery* has been used to encompass everything after the first seventy-two hours of emergency management. Government agencies now rush to provide a host of services, from mental-health-crisis counseling to temporary housing, at the same time that they are offering home owners applications for FEMA's Minimal Home Repair grants or SBA's disaster repair loans. It is important that relief functions, such as finding alternative housing for displaced residents, replacing lost medications and documents, and other stabilizing services, be complete before recovery activities—largely building inspections and construction financing—begin.

The main recovery problem appears to be one of capitalization: how to pay for repairs in private sector residential buildings. Financing repairs, however, is only one component of the problem. The capacity to recover from a disaster—that is, to repair and rebuild damaged buildings and infrastructure in a timely fashion—includes the need to reduce the cost of repairs in the first place, and the need to compel the populace in hazard-prone areas to recognize their risk and take precautions. The goal of any recovery policy should include a financing strategy, a mitigation plan, a preparedness program, and procedures to expedite the repair or replacement of damaged structures as quickly as possible, ideally within two years.

To accomplish these goals, government programs should be focused on providing real financial incentives for limiting damage before disasters occur, on preparedness, and on providing a climate in which private insurance can work. Essentially, the government should do what it does well in disasters—manage assistance in the postdisaster crisis—and it should leave the majority of construction financing to the insurance industry and the marketplace. The rationale for smarter and smaller government supports for disaster recovery is detailed below.

SEPARATING RELIEF AND RECOVERY

Since 1989, federal, state, and local disaster agencies have made serious attempts to address problems that have arisen in responding to disasters, and they have developed a host of procedural innovations. California built a satellite-linked information and response system to overcome communication problems in the first hours of an emergency, and it developed standards for mutual aid so that every jurisdiction in the state could coordinate fire fighting and rescue services. FEMA took steps to change regulations so that the agency could mobilize staff and prepare for assistance, even before state governments requested federal help, in order to avoid the kind of delays that took place in Florida after Hurricane Andrew.

Both the Red Cross and FEMA recognized that urban disasters posed unusual problems because of the diversity of populations that would be affected. Volunteers and staff with various language skills are now recruited and trained, local nonprofit service organizations are included in the disbursing of disaster aid and services, cable TV channels are used to broadcast information and updates, and service centers are used to provide help with housing, child care, and a host of social services. Although never perfect, the social services provided after the Northridge earthquake were markedly improved over those in earlier disasters.

Similarly, after the Loma Prieta experience, state and federal officials recognized the limitations of temporary housing assistance programs in large-scale disasters. It became clear that access to temporary housing was a crucial part of the response and relief efforts. Thus, after Hurricane Andrew cut a wide swath of destruction in southern Dade County, the federal government turned to its own nondisaster housing programs to provide emergency Section 8 Rental Housing Vouchers to victims who would clearly need to relocate for more than two or three months. After Northridge, FEMA attempted to expedite housing aid by sending temporary housing assistance checks to every household in the areas that, according to zip code, were the most heavily damaged, and the secretary of Housing and Urban Development was a participant in the response planning. Here again, Section 8 Rental Housing Vouchers were used alongside FEMA rental assistance to expedite the rehousing of thousands of displaced apartment dwellers.

After Northridge, two key policy changes were made in Washington: HUD was linked to FEMA's disaster response team with real-time disaster information, and the Federal Disaster Response Plan was revised and retitled the Federal Disaster Response *and Recovery* Plan. Unfortunately, it is precisely in the area of recovery that the least progress has been made.

If there is a federal disaster recovery policy, it is to reaffirm the American dream by helping home owners after a disaster make their way through a variety of small grant programs administered by FEMA and a loan program administered by the SBA. These federal recovery programs work best when they are needed least. After Hurricanes Hugo and Andrew and the Northridge earthquake, the federal programs functioned as a supplement to insurance for home owners but left the uninsured poor home owners and apartment owners, who could not qualify for SBA loans, without access to recovery financing. In the Loma Prieta and Northridge experience with damaged multifamily structures, financing depended on the establishment of alternative lending programs by state and local governments. After every disaster, low-income home owners without insurance relied on private charities for financing and rebuilding assistance. The first step in developing recovery policy is to segregate humanitarian relief (the immediate sheltering of disaster victims) from rebuilding programs.

There is no question that government agencies are critical to the organization and management of disaster response and relief efforts. Despite the criticisms FEMA has endured, this agency has made a concerted effort to professionalize and improve its services. If anything FEMA has been overwhelmed by its need to be all things to all people. As the representative of the federal government, in coordination with state emergency service functions, FEMA is the key link to federal support for emergency response and relief activities. In the aftermath of a large disaster, FEMA and HUD should continue to be key players in providing both the agency coordination and funding needed to help stabilize a shocked and disoriented population and to move victims from parks and hotels and Red Cross shelters into more permanent, albeit still temporary, housing.

All those who need food, water, eyeglasses, medicine, counseling, or a place to live ought to be able to get the help they need in one place. No matter how the volunteer agencies and government programs organize themselves behind the scenes, the relief goal should be to provide victims with short-term assistance for two to three months in order to give everyone a chance to actually assess the damage and determine longer-term housing and individual needs. The current rush to begin recovery within days of a disaster is a rush to satisfy media, not victims, and one that requires important and expensive financing decisions be made with very bad information.

It would be better for the immediate postdisaster focus to be on stabilizing and normalizing public and social services: that is, on restoring lifelines and transportation, and settling homeless victims in transitional housing. People with minor damage to habitable homes and apartments can simply wait until the emergency and transition periods are over before seeking assistance for repair funds. There is no need to clog DACs with applicants for grants or loans while some people are still sleeping in tents and public parks. In the interim, local and state agencies should do a thorough damage assessment in order to assess the real need for continued housing assistance and to develop specific recovery strategies.

Depending on the scale of the disaster and the availability of alternative housing, FEMA and HUD could decide if victims need longer-term temporary housing assistance, and what existing housing programs might best serve their needs. Owners of homes and apartments would have time to assess damages, begin insurance claims, and negotiate with lenders in a calmer period after victims are resettled—without the frustrations and delays that naturally occur when government staff are trying to cope with emergency needs as well as recovery needs.

Most important, the federal disaster agencies should get out of the construction lending business. Not only has the expansion of recovery assistance in recent years muddled the federal role in disaster relief and spread agencies too thin, the availability of federal recovery dollars for home owners has led the public into a false sense of security. Americans believe that mitigation is frivolous and insurance is unnecessary, because they believe Uncle Sam will be there to bail them out.

DEFINING THE RECOVERY PROBLEM

In simplest terms, the recovery problem is one of financing: how to pay for repairs to damaged buildings and infrastructure caused by hurricanes, earthquakes, floods, tornadoes, and other natural disasters. There is little disagreement on the role of the federal Department of Transportation in funding the repair of freeways and bridges, and there is little disagreement with the federal assistance to private utilities to expedite the repair of massive damage to lifelines. But over the past fifty years, American disaster policy has waffled on the role of the federal government in the provision of disaster recovery loans to private citizens for the repair of damage to private property. Help to home owners has seemed to be politically correct, but the help has always been tempered by caution, in the form of complex rules, regulations, and restrictions.

Recent disasters have clearly demonstrated that private sector damage, particularly to housing, represents the largest segment of the cost of recovery. Except in Loma Prieta where the high cost of repairs to transportation systems dominated the value of the losses, residential damage represents more than 50 percent of the losses in every major urban disaster. Thus, the disaster recovery problem is essentially a capitalization problem in a local housing market. Although recovery after disasters is perceived to be a function of government spending, in fact it is more closely related to the economics of the marketplace.

Different types of housing are valued for different reasons. Single-family houses are bought, sold, built—and, after a disaster, rebuilt—on the basis of their value as shelter, their location, and their profit potential (in terms of appreciation, tax savings, and cash flow). Rental property provides shelter and location to renters, but investors in rental housing are primarily interested in profit potential. Thus, home owners have an incentive to maintain and repair their property to the extent that it enhances cash flow or appreciation, while rental property owners' incentive to maintain and repair properties is tied to their ability to raise rents.

Condominium owners are somewhere in between, in that owners of individual units must defer to the will and the financial capacity of the condo association in making repair decisions. After a disaster, a single-family home owner's decision to repair or rebuild will depend on personal and financial concerns, while a condominium association behaves like a home owner constrained by dozens of partners with varying financial interests in the building. By contrast, a rental property owner will repair a damaged building only if rents can be raised to cover the additional expense, an unlikely situation except in a very tight rental market.

In almost every major disaster, there have been costly losses in insured single-family homes. Most of these homes were repaired or rebuilt, but not always by their original owners. In some cases, victims sold their lots, took their insurance settlements, and purchased homes elsewhere. Some with limited equity and limited insurance may have lost their investments and returned to the rental market. Others may have decided to stay, even if the insurance or government assistance was insufficient, because of their jobs or their attachments to the community. In every case, the employment status of the heads of households, individual family circumstances, and the residual value of the investment combined to influence the decision to make repairs or move on.

Unlike home owners, renters always moved on to other rental housing available in the marketplace, and the financing for the repair of multifamily housing (apartments and residential hotels) was virtually nonexistent. This was true in every disaster, but especially highly visible after Loma Prieta and Northridge. In 1989 in the Bay Area, 60 percent of the heavily damaged units were in older multifamily single-room-occupancy hotels and apartments serving an elderly, transient, and low-income population. For these low-rent buildings, repair costs were high and replacement costs were higher. The disaster exacerbated the problems of providing affordable housing in an urban market. The situation was different in a smaller submarket in the Marina district of San Francisco. Despite the earthquake damage, demand remained high for apartments in this fashionable area. After tenants left the damaged (and rent-controlled) buildings, owners privately financed the repairs and put their units back on the market at top prices.

In 1994 in Los Angeles, nearly four hundred thousand apartment units, housing a largely middle-class population, were damaged in the earthquake. The owners of these buildings were not necessarily better off than those holding low-rent properties after Loma Prieta. A recessionary economy in Southern California had left the rental market with a high vacancy rate, and many apartment owners had negative equity and negative cash flow before the earthquake. Given the soft market, tenants from damaged buildings easily found alternative rentals in undamaged buildings, and owners saw little prospect of drawing their tenants back and no prospect of raising rents to cover repair costs.

While it could be argued that in the short term no reinvestment in damaged apartments was necessary, there were many reasons that such investments provided a public good. Empty buildings generated no income for owners, leading to certain foreclosure and a lengthy legal process before any new owner could repair or rebuild the damaged structure. Neighborhoods with concentrated damage were empty of residents and quickly became the settings for crime, drug dealing, and prostitution, setting off a downward spiral of property values among the undamaged housing stock. For renters, a large and sudden reduction of low- and average-priced housing available in a community tightened the

market, driving up rents, and forcing out large families, the young, the
old, and the very poor, exactly those with the least capacity to cope with
disaster losses.

While private insurance has provided the major source of funding for
postdisaster rebuilding, this will not be true in future disasters. In the aftermath of Hurricane Andrew and the Northridge earthquake, insurers
have pressured state governments in Florida and California to participate in public-private disaster insurance programs with expensive premiums and limited coverage for home owners. These programs have removed the risk for insurers but left consumers with few options for
protecting their investments.

The insurance problem is twofold: disaster insurance must be affordable or home owners will not purchase it. At the same time, insurers must
be able to build substantial funds over multiple years to cover potential
losses and avoid bankruptcy. For most home owners, condominium owners, and all apartment owners, the cost of an earthquake or hurricane
policy rider is too high, the 10 to 15 percent deductible is untenable, and
the coverage does not necessarily protect their investment.

In the past, disaster polices offered standard insurance benefits for
unique natural hazards without accounting for the age or condition of
the structure. Thus, if insured an owner was reimbursed for the cost to
repair the damage and refinish affected surfaces or, in some cases, refinish all surfaces within the line of sight of the damage, with the amount
of reimbursement based on the cost of work by licensed contractors at
prevailing wage. Under such policies, earthquake or hurricane damage
was the best thing that could happen to owners of old, run-down houses.
They could patch the cracks themselves and pocket the difference, or they
could hire contractors and improve the quality of the houses. In all cases,
the cost of the repairs was high because it was based on new construction and new finish materials. Under the new policies, insurers cap the
total policy value and eliminate coverage for contents and appurtenant
structures.

For insurers, it has been difficult to actually price a disaster policy because of the limited actuarial data and the infrequency of events. At the
same time, insurers have been unwilling to distinguish disaster policies
from other insurance products for homes or automobiles, and their pricing structures have not reflected building-specific factors. More important, insurers cannot adequately spread the risk because of the limited
access to reinsurance and because tax laws prevent insurers from building private multiyear risk pools set aside for disasters. In California and

Florida, the insurance industry would prefer to leave the natural hazards market entirely but has compromised on state-managed risk pools. While these measures offer some protection for the industry, they do not address the larger issue of providing practical and affordable disaster insurance with all home-owner policies.

If finding the capital to finance repairs is the core of the recovery problem, then it seems logical that reducing the potential for damage is crucial to defining the problem and developing a solution. Since Northridge, the federal government has acknowledged that the need for capital is greater than what either the federal government or the insurance industry can provide under the current system. As a strategy, the Clinton administration and FEMA have taken the position that the cost of recovery must be reduced through hazards mitigation.

Mitigation includes structural improvements to existing structures as well as better land use planning and building codes for new construction. It is an important approach to reducing damages and therefore recovery costs, but mitigation alone does not solve the long-term need for capital to repair damages, nor does it address the disparity between funds available for single-family versus multifamily structures.

GOALS FOR A NEW DISASTER RECOVERY POLICY

An effective policy on disaster recovery would separate public and private sector issues and further separate single-family and multifamily housing from commercial, office, and industrial buildings. Each category needs special attention to the economic and social impacts of losses in a community and in that market. In the private sector the ideal outcomes of changes in policy are (1) less damage; (2) less expensive damage; (3) straightforward access to funding for repairs (or in some cases for demolition and rebuilding) through private insurance for home owners and owners of commercial structures; (4) government-backed loans for multifamily housing; and (5) an expedited recovery where residential owners can finance most damage repairs within two years.

MITIGATION

The best way to reduce the cost of postdisaster rebuilding is through mitigation. Numerous engineering reports have made it clear that much of the damage to wood-frame residential structures in hurricanes and earthquakes is preventable. In California, the cost of bolting houses to their foundations and bracing the cripple walls and chimneys averages three to five thousand dollars. While such measures will not prevent stucco and drywall cracks in buildings with no plywood underlayer, foundation bracing will prevent a substantial portion of the costly damage caused by earthquakes. Similarly, owners of frame homes in high-wind areas could add hurricane straps to roofs and shutters to windows in order to limit the interior water damage that results from unsecured roofing and exposed openings.

Mitigation is a benefit to insurance companies through lower payouts, to taxpayers through lower program costs, and, most important, to renters and home owners through reduced damage. However, in U.S. experience with disasters since Hugo and Loma Prieta, we have learned that in the private real estate market in general and the housing market in particular, owners who undertake mitigation are not rewarded with higher rents or higher resale values. At the same time, for a variety of political reasons, the public sector is unable and/or unwilling to require appropriate levels of hazard mitigation through retroactive planning and building regulations. Putting these together leads to the realization that mitigation will only be effective if supported by financial incentives.

FINANCE

The primary responsibility for funding private postdisaster reconstruction should rest with private insurers, and the goal of any disaster recovery policy should be to increase the utilization of private insurance. The more that can be done to fairly insure home owners, renters, and commercial property owners, the more efficient and expedient recovery will be. This is an argument made not out of admiration for the private insurance industry, but one that acknowledges the fact that, in practical terms, only the private insurance industry has access to the volume of capital required to finance postdisaster reconstruction. Act of God bonds and other capital market mechanisms that raise funds for alternative forms of reinsurance cover only a minuscule portion of the total capital needed and are insufficient to make up the reinsurance and/or underwriting gap that now exists.

For most people, the line between housing as an investment and housing as shelter is often blurred. Home owners in hazard-prone areas need to understand and make provisions for their exposure to risk, just as they make provisions to repair leaky roofs before the onset of the rainy season. However, recent disaster experience demonstrates that low-income home owners and the majority of apartment owners cannot afford disaster insurance. Here there is a role for the federal government to go beyond funding the reconstruction of public infrastructure and provide access to financing for repairs.

PREPAREDNESS

The concept of disaster preparedness has traditionally been focused on either a national or a personal "state of readiness." At the government scale, funds have been spent to improve storm warnings and emergency communications, and to improve the readiness of local, state, and federal emergency service personnel. On the individual level, California children learn to "duck and cover" and their families learn to keep three days' worth of water and food supplies on hand; Floridians learn to board up windows and heed evacuation warnings. In fact, governments and individuals need to be as prepared for the recovery phase of a disaster as they are for the emergency phase. For government, an important new preparedness role should be to assist the insurance industry in building both knowledge and its capacity to underwrite disaster policies.

Just as auto insurance and conventional home owners' insurance come in many different product forms, so too should disaster insurance. To develop such products, insurers first need to be able to build a pool of funds as reserves for the infrequent and unpredictable disaster claims. A critical step in this direction is for the Internal Revenue Service to allow current disaster reserves (against anticipated claims) to be taxed over multiple years.

Equally important, the government needs to sponsor and undertake applied research on disaster risk underwriting. The use of Geographic Information System mapping technologies and data collected on individual insurance claims and government assistance grants after recent disasters makes it possible to develop analytic models that predict with reasonable accuracy the likelihood and the magnitude of damage that will occur to particular buildings during a hurricane or earthquake, based on the building's age, design, construction quality, location, and soil conditions. It is particularly important that an independent public agency develop such models and disseminate the results, not only to improve underwriting capacity but also to maintain a degree of fairness in the assignment of risk categories to be used for pricing insurance.

SPEED

If recovery is viewed as repairing and replacing damaged buildings and infrastructure, rather than a return to some physical, psychological, political, or economic predisaster state, then speed is of the essence. Inevitably, major disasters change the physical and social fabric of cities in unalterable ways. As a result, governments as well as individuals attempt to make the best of what has happened and move forward. One individual rebuilding his or her house may want to make changes that he or she was contemplating even before the disaster struck, while another may use the opportunity to relocate. A city may target federal government funds for affordable housing or homeless services. A region may seize the opportunity to renew the infrastructure of the area.

It is within this context that individual and community decisions take place. These decisions are as much about rebuilding lives as they are about rebuilding the particular artifacts that sustain it. Yet it is precisely the capacity to access funding for the artifacts of life that make the reconfiguring of individual and community life possible. Housing and property decisions made within two years of a hurricane or earthquake bear a relationship to the disaster that forced such decisions. After two years, those same decisions are typically governed by personal circumstances (age, income, employment, children) and current market conditions. For these reasons, disaster recovery funds need to be tied to disaster-generated conditions and need to be made accessible in a timely fashion.

POLICY ALTERNATIVES:
PLANNING VERSUS MARKET SOLUTIONS

The difficulty in any disaster policy is the need to overcome the inertia in government and the private sector with regard to planning for postdisaster recovery. Although the federal government does regulate land use and building for environmental management (e.g., regulates development on wetlands, protects air and water quality, protects endangered species), it has been unwilling to impose land use controls in hazardous areas. Even with the establishment of national flood insurance, the federal government set minimum standards for hazards reduction as a condition for federal assistance, but it has never denied postdisaster assistance to noncomplying communities after a flood.

It is difficult for any level of government, or even a private lender, to require costly building improvements above and beyond the minimum life-safety standards for the purpose of protecting against damage from an event that may or may not happen within the next thirty years. The regulatory dilemma is not simply a disaster technology problem, it is endemic to the building and real estate industry. Developers seeking a competitive edge in commercial rents or home sales rail against local governments for imposing up-front fees for schools, transportation, and other community services. Home builders, a powerful political lobby at the local level, battle against any toughening of building standards. Whether the issue is impact-resistant windows in Florida, fireproof roofing in high-fire zones, hail-strength roofing in the Midwest, or lateral bracing of existing homes in California, builders resist changes. Builders have always fought code improvements, including simple and inexpensive features such as smoke detectors (Navaro 1996). They argue that people do not want the added safety features. Instead, builders believe that buyers want a cheaper home. Clearly, it is true that home owners keep their eye on the bottom line. Most are unwilling to add fifty dollars monthly to the cost of their mortgage, just as they are unwilling to spend the same amount for earthquake, hurricane, or flood insurance.

All safety regulations, embodied in building and land use controls, are a product of compromise between engineering knowledge and market demand. Thus, whether the issue is policy on new construction or mitigation to prevent costly disaster damage in existing buildings, mandatory requirements beyond the minimums for life safety face an uphill battle. One approach is to simply let the market resolve the dilemma after a disaster strikes. Those unwilling to protect their properties through mitigation or insurance should take the consequences, be it additional debt for repairs, loss of value, or foreclosure.

Given past experience with the flood insurance program, however, taxpayers should be wary of the apparently simple market approach. Taxpayers will end up paying for more emergency services, more temporary housing, and more specialized aid if building standards remain lax in high-hazard urban areas. Neither builders nor buyers want additional up-front costs; but at the same time, insurers are unwilling to underwrite disaster insurance in high-risk areas. How does a government make policy in the face of such resistance?

"DO NOTHING UNTIL IT HAPPENS" APPROACH

One alternative to unpopular demands for tougher standards and functioning insurance is for the government to develop a focused and realistic response and recovery strategy that includes capital for the replacement of uninhabitable units. Despite public perception that the federal government will bail out local jurisdictions and citizens in the event of a disaster, under current policy federal assistance is intended to supplement, not replace, local governments' and individuals' ability to provide for their own needs. With a targeted response and rebuilding strategy, the government would acknowledge that insurance and protective building regulation is too expensive as an annual cost, given that only a very small portion of homes and other buildings in any region might be severely damaged or destroyed by an earthquake or hurricane.

Following this logic, the government could argue that the savings accumulated by citizens and governments in all the areas—and for all the years—that no catastrophic disaster occurred would allow the government to fully assist a devastated locale with emergency and temporary housing as well as with funding subsidies for replacing and repairing damaged housing. This is essentially what happened in Mexico City, and it is the basis of the "cash infusion model" so often applied outside the United States. Despite efforts to improve construction quality in hazardous areas in developing countries with inexpensive and hand-crafted solutions such as bond beams and bamboo reinforcing, international aid agencies assume that when a major disaster strikes, they will finance the recovery. Here, the federal government would serve in a capacity similar to that of the World Bank or the United Nations in financing public and private rebuilding after a disaster.

Economically, the approach is rational and probably cost-effective. Politically, it is fraught with land mines. How would the government distinguish a catastrophic disaster triggering massive federal recovery intervention from the thirty to forty garden-variety events (floods, snowstorms, tornadoes, and little earthquakes and hurricanes) in which, presumably, it would limit assistance to funds for public infrastructure and emergency relief for citizens? Politicians have left the current policies intentionally vague in order to allow for special appropriations if they can convince their colleagues or make trades for support of other legislation. After spring floods inundated Grand Forks, North Dakota, in 1997, Congress was unable to pass legislation for the most basic disaster appropriations before the ten-day Memorial Day recess, because Republicans had attached so many spending riders that the president threatened to veto the legislation. How much more difficult would the process be if massive appropriations were at stake?

At the local level, would all the small cities like Santa Cruz, California; Charleston, South Carolina; or St. Petersburg, Florida, be comfortable trusting that the federal government would respond to the needs of their citizens in the same way that it would respond to the large powerhouse cities like Los Angeles, Miami, Boston, or New York? The ultimate question for local governments and citizens attracted to the "do nothing until it happens" model is whether they are willing to bet that the government will be there for them in the event that a serious disaster creates a housing crisis within their city.

Federal multihazard insurance is a version of the "do nothing until it happens" approach to disaster policy. Federal hazard insurance is a concept that insurance companies have promoted for years. Multihazard insurance would serve to spread disaster risk across the large pool of home owners in the nation, and it would use the federal treasury (instead of the private market) for reinsurance. In fact, it simply taxes home owners every year, so that those in disaster-prone regions can receive their individual cash infusion in the event of a disaster.

This home owner–to–home owner transfer at least creates a pool of disaster reserves, and it eliminates the need for distinction between ordinary and catastrophic disasters. On the down side, it only covers home owners in the insurance pool and leaves out anyone who cannot afford the insurance or anyone who lives in rental housing. Further, federal multihazard insurance faces two political hurdles: it too relies on the federal willingness to pay for catastrophic losses in the event that the insurance pool is insufficient, and it requires home owners in relatively safe regions to continue to subscribe to the insurance over time.

In any cash infusion model, there are technical as well as political problems. Most significant is the potential for seriously diminished standards of construction and maintenance. If an owner expects to receive government funds in the event of a disaster, there is no incentive to maintain or improve properties, particularly rental properties. The more dilapidated the property, the more easily damage occurs—and the greater the cost to the government for financing and the greater the benefit to the owner.

A MARKET APPROACH

If one takes the position that government should not be the general safety net for private property losses, then the policy debate is limited to whether the government should simply drop recovery funding programs or redirect funds to promote protection of property through mitigation, insurance, and/or saving for a rainy day. If the federal government simply stopped programs that provided repair and rebuilding funds to private individuals (SBA loans, FEMA Minimal Home Repair and Individual and Family Grants, HUD CDBG, and HOME special appropriations), agencies would save one-third of the total federal expenditure. For a Northridge-size disaster, that amounts to a savings of $4.5 billion of the $13.5 billion spent on disaster programs.

Would home owners and renters in high-hazard areas act differently if they did not expect to have access to federal recovery assistance? Probably not. Those who already have insurance would maintain it, and perhaps a very small percentage would seek some form of insurance, but most would simply put the car, the kids' orthodontia, and any number of personal expense payments before an investment in insurance, savings, or mitigation.

In the event of a disastrous earthquake or hurricane, many would lose their homes because damage made them uninhabitable or because the bank foreclosed for nonpayment of the mortgage. Home owners would compete with displaced renters for space in available rentals. Both poor and middle-class victims would have to choose between leaving an area and spending extended periods in some form of temporary housing until the market had time to catch up with demand.

The scenario of limited postdisaster housing, limited access to insurance, and extremely limited government assistance for privately owned property is not far-fetched. In fact, it is precisely the situation in Kobe, two years after the earthquake of 1995. In that case, the national government provided temporary shelter for one hundred thousand displaced victims and promised a construction program for 125,000 housing units, but the financing has yet to materialize.

For the national government, Kobe's housing problems are insignificant when compared to losses in a real estate market downturn. In fact, the commitment to provide a cash infusion for replacing Kobe's lost housing will have to compete with other pressing national and political needs. In the interim, property scavengers, with the capacity to buy and hold damaged homes and vacant lots, will profit from future development. Many former residents will leave the area, and many others will continue to live in damaged units, using their life savings to gradually repair and restore their properties.

A PLANNING APPROACH

If one accepts that the disaster recovery problem is at least partially a government responsibility, and if one accepts that the current withdrawal of private insurance companies from natural hazards coverage will adversely affect the capacity for recovery, two policy questions emerge: how can the federal government control costs under the present system of limited supplemental assistance for local governments and home owners; and how might the government refocus recovery spending to meet the needs of a broader spectrum of disaster victims?

In an administration policy paper prepared by James Lee Witt, director of FEMA, and Robert E. Rubin, secretary of the Department of the Treasury, and submitted to the vice-president in February 1995, federal officials acknowledge the interdependence between various levels of government, insurance, and business in providing financial protection to those living in disaster-prone areas. Officials also acknowledge the evidence that insurance markets are not functioning well and that real estate markets do not reflect expected disaster damage in pricing and land use decisions.

The policy paper essentially endorses the current federal policy of providing supplemental government assistance after disasters and proposes to save costs though proposals for loss prevention initiatives and better management of existing programs. The proposals to reduce losses include funding to enable communities to develop and adopt building codes and life-safety standards for wind and seismic risk, and the use of unexpended relief funds for rehabilitation of public buildings based on performance guidelines. These are minimalist approaches to mitigation, ones that essentially fund jurisdictions that have never had a building code in order to enable them to adopt one, and that support the upgrade of a handful of public buildings per year. However, as mitigation against future losses, the proposal will have no effect.

The paper also suggests means testing for FEMA grants and elimination of the subsidy (i.e., the low-interest rates) on SBA disaster loans. These are reasonable but minimal changes to existing programs, and they will not substantially reduce or limit federal expenditures after large disasters.

More significant are the two proposals that would require insurance for federally backed home loans and create a Treasury-based reinsurance fund of $25 to $50 billion. The first recommends that mortgages issued by federally related entities on newly constructed one-to-four-family structures be required to carry hazard insurance. This initiative, if undertaken for new construction and phased in for existing home sales, could have a powerful impact in promoting private insurance. To date, lenders have been unwilling to require disaster insurance on residential properties, because it was not required in the secondary market. Additionally, unless the requirement was a state or national standard, lenders felt their loans would not be competitive.

The second proposal, which recommends that the Treasury create national reinsurance pools to cover industry losses in single large events, is clearly an acknowledgment that one cannot require insurance unless it is possible to underwrite it. If such a pool could be created, it would certainly help to improve the availability of insurance, and perhaps it would provide an incentive to tackle the problems in pricing and accessibility of disaster insurance across a broad spectrum of the real estate market. Unfortunately, a federal reinsurance pool may simply provide a safeguard for current insurance practices without any inducement of reforms.

All together, the administration proposals would begin to make an inroad in the insurance crisis, but they would do very little to substantially address reductions in losses, reductions in costs for recovery, or financing for any form of housing other than single-family homes.

A STRATEGY FOR SHARED RESPONSIBILITY

To confront the housing and recovery problems exposed by recent urban disaster experiences requires an amalgam of planning and market-based approaches. Only government can compel individual property owners, through a combination of regulation and incentive, to improve building standards. Only government has the capacity to provide a true safety net for victims who, by virtue of low incomes or some form of market failure, cannot afford to purchase insurance. Conversely, only the private insurance market can guarantee that funds will be available for repairs, by virtue of a contract that underwrites a portion of the owner's risk in exchange for an annual fee. Finally, only a partnership between government disaster managers and the private insurance industry can provide the research and information necessary to develop fair and competitive insurance rates for the specialized hazards market.

RECOMMENDATION I

Create income tax incentives for hazards mitigation in housing and require insurers to offer discounts to policyholders who have undertaken significant mitigation.

Any substantial reduction of recovery costs will require a substantial reduction of existing risks. Saving postdisaster repair costs for individuals as well as for governments will require a serious commitment to mitigation through regulation and incentives to reduce losses.

All of the technical reports on damage to wood-frame single-family residential buildings in earthquakes as well as hurricanes make it clear that much of the damage could have been avoided through mitigation and preparation. Nonetheless, researchers, disaster preparedness professionals, and policymakers have not been able to educate the public or legislate action. Motivating a substantial number of home owners to take action is likely to require a direct financial inventive, in the form of a state or federal tax credit, capped at a reasonable amount and applicable in the year the mitigation work is completed.[2] This approach has been tried successfully on a small scale: Berkeley's real estate transfer tax rebate has prompted several thousand home owners to mitigate seismic hazards. In the few years that the program has existed, more than three thousand homes have been upgraded.

A federal or state income tax credit could offer home owners two thousand dollars per year and apartment owners two thousand dollars per unit per year as a tax deduction. Tax credits and deductions could carry over from year to year, subject to a total cap, such as ten thousand dollars over ten years. Although such a program might have a short-term negative effect, especially on state tax revenues, the benefits would include reduced exposure for state-run disaster insurance pools and lower costs for insurance. To better distribute the costs of training for agents and costs of inspection of individual properties, private insurers might be permitted to write multiyear policies, which would give the companies a more stable income stream and give the owners a guaranteed premium cost over several years.

A tax credit is a powerful incentive for mitigation, but it needs to be coupled with a clear message that no further federal assistance will be available for disaster repairs to single-family homes, and coupled with real choices among insurance policies and real price breaks for seismically improved structures. The stalemate in our present system of disaster recovery pits insurers against potential customers. The insurers cannot spread the risk of catastrophic loss if they are required to offer full coverage to everyone in high-risk states like California and Florida. At the same time, owners do not want to pay the high costs of full coverage when deductibles average between twenty and forty thousand dollars, especially if they believe the federal government will come to their aid. By the same logic, owners can easily ignore warnings to improve their property when they know that if something does happen, government will be there to help. To break the stalemate, the government needs to put financial impetus into its national mitigation strategy and help to develop the policies to make recovery financing work in the private sector.

RECOMMENDATION 2

Recovery should be reconceptualized as reconstruction financing, with federal government funds targeted for public sector rebuilding projects. Private sector recovery should be primarily managed through a variety of insurance products with a very limited set of public programs for promoting mitigation and specialized assistance in truly catastrophic events.

Finding mechanisms to fund repairs after a disaster requires a market that can deliver financing in an expedient, noncontroversial, and nonpolitical fashion. For most home owners, most commercial property owners, and some apartment owners, that market is private insurance. But insurance will only work if past perceptions as well as policy are changed—that is, if postdisaster government assistance for recovery is significantly curtailed.

The federal government cannot continue on the current trajectory of expanding recovery assistance programs to meet the expanding needs of the private sector in urban disasters. The proper role of public assistance lies in the public sector: aiding in the restoration of freeways, lifelines, ports, schools, hospitals, and public buildings in order to assist the affected community in stabilizing and recovering public services. Experience in recent large disasters has taught us that government aid for private sector recovery (largely housing) is very expensive and not particularly effective in reaching those hardest hit. Because the largest federal programs for private recovery (FEMA's Minimal Home Repair Grants and SBA's home repair loans) are targeted to assist home owners with limited damages, these programs are an absolute disincentive for all home owners to invest in mitigation or insurance.

If federal and state governments want to make mitigation central to a strategy for reducing losses in large urban disasters, the governments must recognize that mitigation will not work through regulation. Mitigation only works if there is a real financial incentive for property owners. To create such a climate, supported by real cash incentives, the federal government must take away the public safety net for damage repairs, and state governments must develop an environment in which private insurance can work. At the same time, it is important to recognize the difference between single-family and multifamily housing when designing both the incentives and the enforcement mechanisms.

Previous research has demonstrated that the financial characteristics of single-family housing—the combination of equity, tax benefits, and price appreciation—make home ownership profitable. As property values rise, owners can absorb significant postdisaster rebuilding costs—as much as 20 to 50 percent of the initial home value—and still make a reasonable profit on their investment (Comerio, Landis, and Rofé 1994). Thus, home owners have multiple private sector options for protecting their investment against disaster damage. The government does not need to provide reconstruction financing to home owners if the lending industry is properly evaluating the market value of home loans, and the insurance industry is able to offer a variety of insurance products.

By contrast, multifamily rental property depends on market rents for profitability, in both net operating income and resale value.[3] As such, any increased debt for repair of disaster damage will result in loss of profitability if rents cannot be increased accordingly. The implication is clear. There is little if any incentive for owners to rebuild damaged rental units, even with favorable financing terms. It is no surprise that successful repairs of apartments in Los Angeles typically required private lenders to "write down" (or forgive) a portion of the owner's original loan to accommodate the additional debt service on a SBA- or city-sponsored loan.

If apartment owners cannot afford repair loans after a disaster, it is axiomatic that they cannot afford mitigation loans before a disaster. This is a circumstance in which government can and should play a critical role in both mitigation and repair. First, it must be recognized that when multifamily rental housing is damaged there are two sets of victims, tenants and owners. Displaced tenants should be eligible for temporary housing assistance through FEMA's short-term programs or HUD's longer-term Section 8 programs, depending on the extent of damage and the market conditions in the area.

Like home owners, rental property owners need to take responsibility for recognizing their potential for risk and losses. At the same time, government should recognize the value of rental housing as a community resource, and the limits of private finance of both mitigation and repairs, and develop a safety certification and mitigation financing program. One mechanism could be a government mitigation loan program coupled with restrictions on access to recovery finance assistance.

Owners who believe their buildings were adequately built for the local hazards could apply to their local governments for a safety inspection. The certificate would remain valid for ten years, when another inspection would be required. If an earthquake or hurricane damaged the building during that time, the owner would be eligible to apply to the SBA for a low-interest business loan for repairs. If a building did not pass a safety inspection, the owner would be eligible to apply to HUD for a low-interest mitigation loan. If a building did not pass the safety inspection and the owner chose not to mitigate the hazards, the owner would not be eligible for any government assistance. Obviously, property owners could also choose insurance or other private market routes to protect against losses or pay for damage repairs

RECOMMENDATION 3

Government must work with private insurers to obtain the appropriate data and to develop the research capacity for improving hazards estimation, underwriting, and insurance products.

Finally, insurance, private lending, and government programs should be tied to building-specific conditions: location, soils, structure, design, construction quality, maintenance, and mitigation measures. To do this, government and industry must share and improve research on models for hazard and damage estimation, and develop a rating system for all buildings that reflects the building's age, construction materials and quality, and specific locational hazards such as adverse soil conditions and exposure to storm surge.

California has been a leader in working with the insurance industry to develop alternative insurance products to meet the needs of home owners and manage the risk. The California Residential Earthquake Recovery (CRER) fund was developed after the Loma Prieta earthquake in an attempt to create a policy to cover the first fifteen thousand dollars (the predeductible limit) in losses. The program was implemented with the hope that several years' worth of small payments by householders would build a fund to cover a large-scale disaster. The program was canceled within a year because it was actuarially unsound. In the interim, the program was extremely useful in funding repairs for owners of homes with minor damage following two small earthquakes, the Cape Mendocino and Landers–Big Bear earthquakes. While the funding structure of CRER was problematic, the concept of an insurance policy to cover a maximum of fifteen thousand dollars' worth of earthquake damage is a very attractive one.

Similarly the California Earthquake Authority (CEA), instituted in 1996–97, is an excellent attempt to provide earthquake policies to all home owners through a public-private fund. In this case, owners can buy a "mini" earthquake rider to their home-owner policy that will primarily cover damages to the main house but will not cover detached garages, swimming pools, garden walls, and other appurtenant structures. Coverage for loss of contents and additional living expenses is severely limited. If the CEA policy structure had been in effect at the time of the Northridge earthquake, the insurance industry would have paid out only $4 billion in residential claims, about 50 percent of the total actually paid (Firpo 1997).

Presumably an owner ought to be able to purchase additional coverage for contents and appurtenant structures at a price that reflects the value of the property and its risks (e.g., proximity to fault system, soil conditions, age of structure, etc.), but at the time of this writing, the industry appears to be focused on limiting access to most disaster-related products. The minipolicy has many disincentives for consumers. In addition to a 15 percent deductible, the policy does not guarantee full coverage if the fund is depleted in a large disaster. Further, state politicians intervened to flatten the highs and lows in the rate structure, so that policies do not accurately represent locational hazards or reflect building conditions or mitigation improvements.

Clearly, a price break on insurance combined with a tax credit would be a significant incentive for an owner to undertake preventive maintenance on a home. Then, the owner would be in a position to make an intelligent market choice on the amount of insurance to carry. A very conservative owner might want to buy a guaranteed replacement-cost, full-coverage policy; another might be satisfied to buy the front-end, zero-to-$15,000 minor-damage coverage, a minipolicy, and/or a separate contents policy. Someone in a slide zone adjacent to a major fault might not be able to purchase anything but the minipolicy because the risks are too high—and property values ought to reflect that risk. Conversely, someone in a low-risk zone, on good soil, with a well-built, seismically strengthened house might choose only the minor-damage coverage or none at all.

A similar tax credit model can be developed to recognize the difference between high-risk beachfront sites subject to storm surge, and safer inland locations. In addition, tax credits could be used for improved roof

construction, high-impact windows, shutters, and other hurricane mitigation features in communities from Florida to Boston and along the Gulf
Coast.

To date, insurance companies have maintained that they cannot adequately price disaster insurance because the events have been infrequent,
the risks high, and damage patterns uncertain. However, with the introduction of hazard mapping through the use of Geographic Information
System mapping technology, and the large-scale collection of damage data
in recent disasters, we now have the capacity to develop appropriate models for sophisticated risk maps—and intelligent insurance pricing. To accomplish this will require a concerted industry and government effort to
systematically rank buildings by their specific performance capacity (i.e.,
their ability to withstand ground shaking and wind loads as a result of
construction quality, soil conditions, and location) in order to build sound
actuarial profiles for housing and other building types.

The best model, and perhaps the best agency, for developing a government role in creating incentives for disaster insurance and mitigation
in the private housing market is the Federal Housing Administration
(FHA), a quasi-nongovernmental organization, often referred to as a
QUANGO. Established in the 1930s to provide government-underwrit-
ten home mortgage insurance, the FHA was also supposed to serve as a
demonstration to private insurers of the long-term profitability of insuring
homes. As part of its mandate, the FHA developed and published underwriting procedures that could be used by public and private insurers
alike to accurately assess insurance risk. Through these innovations the
FHA hoped to reduce the risk associated with mortgage lending, increase
the supply of mortgage capital, and ultimately reduce the cost of mortgage insurance. It was successful in all three of these efforts. Today, the
FHA is still in business but its role is much smaller and more indirect, as
the primary responsibility for mortgage insurance has devolved to a large,
competitive, and private mortgage insurance industry (Comerio, Landis,
and Firpo 1996).

Although Congress is now talking about privatizing the FHA entirely,
a new role for the agency might be to assist in developing a building
rating system as part of a requirement for federally backed mortgages.
This could provide the basis for a fair and actuarially sound building
rating system for private disaster insurance. It could also provide an incentive for individuals to improve their building ratings to lessen their
risk as well as their insurance costs. Alternatively, the agency could take
a more proactive role, mandating disaster insurance by adding ten to fifty

basis points (less than one half of one percent) to federally backed loans in high-hazard states.

Together, California and Florida make up nearly one-quarter of the market share of mortgage originations annually. Given that the FHA insures about 50 percent of all the mortgages in the United States, and given that annual mortgage originations account for about 10 percent of the housing in any given year (Housing and Urban Development 1996, 44–47), a large majority of the nation's housing could be insured against disaster losses within five to ten years.

There are many financial advantages to instituting federal or state requirements for disaster insurance tied to mortgage origination: (1) for consumers, national standards would provide good coverage at a relatively low rate, built into mortgage payments; (2) for lenders, the systematic application of an insurance fee across all mortgages would keep a level, competitive playing field; and (3) for state-managed insurance pools, tying insurance purchases to mortgage originations would guarantee sufficient participation and long-term financial capacity.

At the same time, there are disadvantages in the uneven application of the requirement to new mortgages. More important, there are enormous political obstacles to both ambitious and modest interventions in the complex world of mortgage finance, private insurance, and real estate taxes. Mortgage regulations, insurance regulations, and the tax code are extremely difficult to change. Each has a permanent corps of lobbyists dedicated to resisting change, or at least to trading particular benefits in one area for support for changes in another. Thus, instigating action on any changes to real estate finance, insurance regulation, and the tax code is an arduous process. Change in these politically sacrosanct territories for the sake of disaster policy is even harder to achieve, because the constituency is different with each disaster.

Ultimately, to develop a working private market for insuring and mitigating earthquake hazards will require political commitment. At the same time it will also require a technical commitment to research. Disaster management agencies at all levels of government have worked for years to develop sophisticated, professional emergency response techniques and processes. No equivalent level of investigation or analysis has gone into the task of coordinating and paying for postdisaster rebuilding.

We know from this and other research that the great majority of the damage from earthquakes and hurricanes is in wood-frame residential construction. We know that most of this damage is not life threatening.

We know that only a small percentage of the total damage leaves the dwelling uninhabitable. We know that the repair of so-called minor damage is incredibly expensive for individuals and for society. We know that individuals and government agencies have consistently underestimated the economic risk associated with urban disasters. We also know that we should not continue with our present models of government recovery assistance and single-product, all or nothing, disaster insurance. If we do, the next major urban disaster will be accompanied by unrecoverable financial and property losses.

Housing is a peculiar economic commodity—expensive, fixed in space, long lasting, and necessary for "normal" modern life. Because of this, large-scale damage in concentrations of urban housing resulting from natural disasters is both a public and private concern. Socially and politically, we have made a commitment to provide shelter for those made homeless in disasters, but economically we are uncertain how we are going to pay for it.

The policy solution requires separating emergency relief from recovery financing. Disaster policy needs to focus on programs that will effectively and substantially reduce damage in the existing housing stock. At the same time, disaster policy should maintain the federal government's role as a financier of public infrastructure and eliminate the government's role in financing recovery for private property, except for very low income home owners and renters. The best role for government in postdisaster recovery financing is as the underwriter of a working and healthy insurance market, so that in the event of a disaster, financing for repairs is both conventional and expedient.

Notes

CHAPTER 1

1. Measurements in this book are generally given in the metric system, as is the convention in earthquake engineering. In some cases, particularly with regard to hurricane wind speeds and storm surge levels, measurements are given in both metric and U.S. systems, since the latter is still the convention in weather information.

2. Scientists do not agree on whether the increase in violent hurricanes or destructive earthquakes is a function of change in global weather patterns or tectonic plate movements, or whether the increase in frequency is part of a larger random pattern.

CHAPTER 2

1. In Watsonville, there were tensions between white and Hispanic groups. At the time of the earthquake, the city was under court mandate to change local elections for city council from an at-large system to one of district elections.

2. The CALDAP program was funded by a state budget surplus from the 1980s. Such a surplus has not existed since the funds were dispersed in a tax refund by Governor George Deukmejian, and no new surplus fund was amassed in the 1990s.

3. Bay Area nonprofit housing organizations were pleased with the innovative gap-financing funds but frustrated by the knowledge that the Red Cross kept $20 million of the funds raised after Loma Prieta, as an endowment for other programs. Housing organizations believed that all the funds raised should have been spent in the Bay Area on recovery programs.

4. The high percentage of damage in multifamily units was estimated from

safety inspections conducted in the first weeks after the earthquake. More recent research (Comerio, Landis, and Firpo 1996) has reviewed insurance claims and suggested that minor damage in single-family homes was undercounted.

5. As in the Loma Prieta earthquake, building inspectors used colored tags to denote building conditions after evaluating the safety of structures. When the results are aggregated, the method provides a quick assessment of the overall quantity and severity of the damage. However, the damage data that postdisaster inspections generate are not always representative of the total damage picture. Within Los Angeles, for example, inspectors proactively performed at least cursory inspections of all buildings in certain heavily damaged areas. In other cities, inspectors performed building inspections only when called with damage reports by owners or tenants. This means that not all damage was included in the tallies, and the information was based on a quick inspection. While it may be nearly impossible to obtain accurate counts of the total damage, local governments do make an effort to estimate the true number of uninhabitable or risky housing units.

6. In sum, FEMA provided 119,000 families with two to three months of temporary housing assistance, and twelve thousand of the Section 8 vouchers were used for very low income families.

CHAPTER 3

1. The Soviet Union does not lack capable engineers, but the demands for state-sponsored buildings, particularly housing, since World War II have led to the development of concrete building construction systems that could be erected quickly. Because contractors were rewarded for speed not quality, precast floors were not connected to walls or frames, leaving buildings particularly vulnerable to seismic forces.

2. Even the official death toll represents an exceptionally heavy loss of life for the number of buildings that collapsed. On average nearly 10 people were killed for every collapsed building. By comparison, in the U.S. disasters only .1 person was killed per building collapse. The 1976 earthquake in China killed 1 person per building collapse, while the 1988 Armenian earthquake killed approximately 5 per building collapse (Coburn, Ohashi-Murakami, and Ohta 1987; Bilateral Technical Cooperation Project 1989). This unfortunate statistic provides an indication of the high occupancy of residential buildings in central Mexico City.

3. Approximately 50 percent of the value of the purchase price of the unit was subsidized by the government. The remaining payments made monthly by the new owners were designed to be between 20 and 30 percent of minimum wage, and the repayment period ranged from five to nine years.

4. Japan is divided into forty-seven prefectures, each with cities (shi), towns (cho), and villages (mura). Major cities are further divided into wards (ku). The Hanshin District is the general name for south Hyogo Prefecture and the Osaka plain. The major cities are Kobe and Osaka, with Kobe located about 450 kilometers southwest of Tokyo (UNCRD 1995).

5. In recent years, the number of nonwooden (i.e., reinforced concrete or steel)

residential structures has been growing as new condominiums have been built, but older wood structures still constitute the majority of the housing stock.

6. After World War II, surviving families who had lost housing in the bombings were allowed to inhabit any existing housing. Over time, families' rights to inhabit such housing without payment of rent became protected by the central government, and landlords seeking to redevelop such land had to buy out sitting squatters. Kobe's central wards are reputed to have housed a significant population of squatters.

7. In contrast to U.S. policies, the basic home owners' fire insurance does not cover fire following an earthquake. Any coverage for fire following an earthquake requires the earthquake endorsement.

8. The population of Hyogo-ken province is 5,403,000 and the population of Kobe City is 1,600,000. All of Japan has 123,587,000 people.

9. Although difficult to document, it has been reported that some of the funds appropriated for infrastructure repairs have been redirected toward the upgrading of freeways, bridges, and rail links in Tokyo.

10. This assumes that the owners have clear title to their lots. In many of the densely built areas, owners found that their deeds to the land were not clear, or that their preearthquake dwelling actually crossed over a neighbor's boundary.

CHAPTER 4

1. SBA loans are designed for small, individually owned businesses. Individual loans are capped at $1.5 million, and owners must provide recourse to personal assets to obtain a loan. Large apartment complexes are typically owned by limited partnerships or syndicates, and investors may have assets in numerous complexes. As such, the loan caps and the recourse clauses made these federal disaster loans unusable by owners of most large apartments.

2. Although generally American urban densities are low, there are pockets of very high density. For example, in Berkeley, California, just south of the University of California campus, in an area filled with student dormitories and fraternity houses, the population density is twelve thousand persons per square kilometer, equal to that in many areas of Kobe, Japan.

CHAPTER 5

1. This action was clearly influenced by the dire conditions imposed not only by the disaster but also by the economic conditions of the Great Depression.

2. The federal government has developed a number of plans specifying agency roles in disaster response. A Plan for Response to a Catastrophic Earthquake was in place when Hurricane Hugo struck. Afterward, FEMA updated the plan to include all natural disasters, retitling it the Natural Hazards Response Plan. This was updated and renamed the Federal Response Plan in 1992 as a result of the Gulf War and the need to include responses to domestic terrorism. In 1996, after the Northridge earthquake, the plan was under revision again; its new title is the Federal Response and Recovery Plan.

3. Although written policy on requests for disaster assistance use "exhaustion of resources" as a measure of need, most states take the attitude that they should do whatever they can to garner federal assistance.

4. Prior to Hurricane Andrew, FEMA could not respond until the president declared a disaster. The agency now mobilizes resources and staff while waiting for a state's official request.

5. Voluntary Organizations Active in Disasters (VOAD) is a national network of organizations (twenty-six full members and two associate members) that was formed after Hurricane Camille in 1969. The member organizations have territorial responsibilities before and after disasters. The primary mission puts a priority on disasters, and meetings provide a neutral forum in which information is exchanged between government and the member organizations. Many states have state-level VOADs as well. California has two, NorCal VOAD and SCVOAD in Northern and Southern California, respectively. Although VOADs already formally existed, the use of local agency networks to provide specialized services was developed in Northern California after Loma Prieta and in Southern California after the civil unrest in April 1992.

6. While FEMA and the state emergency management agency are typically associated with emergency response, the biggest portion of the responsibility for planning both relief and recovery in large disasters lies with the following federal agencies and their state counterparts: the Department of Agriculture, Department of Education, Department of Energy, Department of Health and Human Services, Department of Housing and Urban Development, Department of the Interior, Department of Justice, Department of the Treasury, Department of Transportation, Department of Veterans Affairs, Army Corps of Engineers, and Small Business Administration.

7. Protective measures include those used to keep damaged structures from threatening life and safety, property, health, and stream and drainage channels. Often, the federal government reimburses the cost to local government of demolishing both public and private property as a protective measure to reduce the risks to people, buildings, and infrastructure. In addition, bracing damaged buildings in danger of falling is also covered under protective measures. However, if a private property later needs to be demolished, the cost is borne by the owner. The city of Los Angeles obtained funds for the fencing and policing of the Ghost Towns through protective measures.

8. The Federal Register defines nonprofits eligible for reimbursement as those that provide health and safety services or essential services of a government nature. The Stafford Act defines them as private nonprofit educational, utility, emergency, medical, or rehabilitation facilities, or temporary or permanent custodial care facilities, or other private nonprofit facilities that provide essential services of a government nature to the general public, or facilities on Indian reservations as defined by the president. The relationship between the nonprofit and the government must be formalized by contract prior to the emergency activity. Because nonprofits are not eligible for state reimbursement, they receive a maximum of 75 percent of their costs from federal programs.

9. FEMA inspectors list damage to real and personal property that is eligible for Minimum Home Repair Grant and Individual and Family Grant funds,

described later in the text. Real property includes damage to the main structure and nonessential appurtenant structures, such as garages, garden walls, and swimming pools. Personal property eligible for replacement consists of clothing, furniture, automobiles, and appliances. However, if a household has two cars and one is destroyed, FEMA will not provide funds for replacing the lost vehicle. The same is true of appliances. If a household has two televisions or two microwaves and only one is destroyed, FEMA will not provide funds to replace it.

10. In addition to the loan for damages, SBA allows 20 percent above and beyond the damage amount for mitigation measures. Therefore, in Loma Prieta the maximum loan amount was $144,000, and in Northridge it was $288,000.

11. The state administers this program and must meet a 25 percent match. The standard maximum was raised to $12,200 in Northridge, and since then it has been raised to $12,900. This amount may change, depending on the disaster, and it is renegotiated by each state, each year.

12. The federal government offers a national program of flood insurance. The only other federal insurance offered is crop insurance. Since 1990 insurance companies have lobbied Congress for a national natural hazards insurance program, but to date no such program is under consideration.

13. At the time of Hurricane Andrew in 1992, hurricane damage was covered by home-owner policies. Following Andrew, insurance companies in Florida attempted to separate coverage for hurricanes from regular policies.

14. A settlement of a lawsuit brought after a 1980 landslide had destroyed a house in San Rafael, California, changed the liability of insurance companies. Although the insurance company argued that landslides were not covered by the home-owner policy, the owner successfully argued that construction defects contributed to the damage and the insurance company was forced to cover the loss. This concept of concurrent causation was used to force insurance companies to pay for residential losses in the 1983 Coalinga earthquake, and it led to the 1984 introduction of legislation that would exempt earthquakes from concurrent causation. As part of the legislation, insurers agreed to a mandate to offer separate earthquake insurance policies with home owners' insurance.

15. In November 1988, Californians passed Proposition 103, requiring insurers to roll back auto insurance premiums and giving oversight on rates to the elected insurance commissioner.

16. The Chicago Board of Trade has developed an index of insured catastrophe losses. Investors spread the risk by buying and selling options contracts based on this index. Act of God bonds are sold to investors with the promise of high interest rates in a specified period of time. If no disaster occurs in that period, the investor profits. If a disaster does occur, the investor loses the investment.

17. A much weaker bill requiring "disclosure" of seismic conditions at the point of sale was passed the next year. Had the original bill passed, about 25 percent of California's houses would have been upgraded within a five-year period.

CHAPTER 6

1. Completion of the Cypress freeway is expected in 1998. The Embarcadero freeway was demolished in 1990, but street improvements are not complete as

of this writing. Portions of the Central freeway were demolished in 1997, but rebuilding plans have been stalled by ballot initiatives and lawsuits.

2. An innovative government mitigation program involved the use of several FEMA programs—one designated for hazard mitigation, another for demolition of unsafe structures—combined with HUD CDBG funds to buy out residential properties in Illinois and Missouri in flood-prone areas along the Mississippi River. The effectiveness of the program was obvious when a 1995 flood hit many of the same areas inundated by the great flood of 1993. In Missouri alone, more than two thousand families were out of harm's way because of the buyout program.

3. Although condominiums are technically multifamily housing, their financial characteristics more closely resemble those of single-family housing. Their circumstance requires responsibility for insurance and mitigation on the part of individual owners, as well as on that of the association as the collective owner.

References

Ad Hoc Committee on Earthquake Recovery.
  1995.   *In the Wake of the Quake: Report to the Los Angeles City Council.* Los Angeles: City of Los Angeles Housing Department.
Alatec-Harris-TYM Consulting Group and Angel Lazaro and Associates.
  1993.   *Baguio and Dagupan, Urban Planning Project, Interim Report.* Vol. 1. Manila: Republic of the Philippines.
American Red Cross.
  1991.   *Meeting the Loma Prieta Challenge: An Interim Report of the Northern California Earthquake Relief and Preparedness Project.* Burlingame, Calif.: American Red Cross.
Anaya-Santoyo, J., and A. Rafael-Hernandez.
  1986.   *Programa de Reestructuracion de Barrio.* Mexico City: Departamento del Districto Federal, Direccion General de Reordenacion Urbana y Protection Ecologica, Direccion General de Renovacion Habitacional Popular, Delegacion: Cuahtemoc (Merced), Venustiano Carranza (Centro).
Anders, C. M., and J. Chao.
  1996.   Bay Area: Renters' Hell. *San Francisco Examiner and Chronicle,* 9 June, pp. A1, A8.
Anderson, M. B.
  1992.   Metropolitan Areas and Disaster Vulnerability: A Consideration for Developing Countries. In *Environmental Management and Urban Vulnerability,* edited by Alcira Kreimer and Mohan Munasinghe. World Bank Discussion Papers, no. 168. Washington, D.C.: World Bank.
Anderson, M. B., and P. J. Woodrow.
  1989.   *Rising from the Ashes: Development Strategies in Times of Disaster.* Boulder, Colo.: Westview Press.

Applied Technology Council.

1989.   *Field Manual: Post-Earthquake Safety Evaluation of Buildings.*
Report ATC-20–1. Redwood City, Calif.: Applied Technology
Council.

1989a.   *Procedures Post-Earthquake Safety Evaluation of Buildings.* Report ATC-20. Redwood City, Calif.: Applied Technology Council.

1991.   *Proceedings of the Workshop for Utilization of Research on Engineering and Socioeconomic Aspects of the 1985 Chile and Mexico Earthquakes.* Report ATC-30. Redwood City, Calif.: Applied
Technology Council.

Aritake, Masao, et al.

1986.   *Report on the Investigation of the Earthquake in Mexico September 19, 1985.* Tokyo: Tokyo Metropolitan Government.

Armillas-Gil, I.

1986.   *Planeacion para Revitalization del Centro Historico de la Ciu-
dad de Mexico, 21.01 Sismicidad en el Valle de Mexico, Identi-
ficacion de Danos en la zona Metropolitana Ocasionados por
Sismos.* Mexico City: Dipartamento del Districto Federal, Secretaria General de Obras, Programa de las Naciones Unidas Para
el Desarrollo, and Centro de Naciones Unidas Para los Asen-
tamientos Humano.

Arnold, C.

1990.   *Reconstruction after Earthquakes: Issues, Urban Design, and
Case Studies. Report to the National Science Foundation.* San Ma-
teo, Calif.: Building Systems Development.

Arnold C., and H. Lagorio.

1987.   Chinese City Starts Over after Quake: Totally Leveled, Tangshan
Is Replanned as Well as Rebuilt. *Architecture* 76 (7): 83–85.

Arthur Andersen and Co.

1994.   *South Dade Neighborhood Plan: Economic Development Program. Prepared for Metro Dade County.* Miami: Arthur Andersen and Co.

Asano, M.

1995.   Characteristics of the Southern Hyogo Earthquake, Damage to
Urban Facilities, and Data and Statistics, in Report on the South-
ern Hyogo Earthquake. *The Wheel Extended: Toyota Quarterly
Review,* no. 92 (July): 2–25.

Association of State Floodplain Managers.

1993.   *Cross Training: Light the Torch.* Special publication no. 29. Boulder: Natural Hazards Research and Application Information Center, University of Colorado.

Aysan, Y., and I. Davis, eds.

1992.   *Disaster and the Small Dwelling.* London: James and James.

Bay Area Economics and ARCH Research.

1993.   *The California Affordable Housing Cost Study: Comparison of
Market-Rate and Affordable Rental Projects.* San Francisco: Lo-
cal Initiatives Support Corporation and the California Tax Credit
Allocation Committee.

Bay Area Regional Earthquake Preparedness Project (BAREPP).

1990.   The Once and Future Quake: All about Loma Prieta. *Networks* 5 (1): 2–27.

1992.   *Findings and Recommendations: Symposium on Policy Issues in the Provision of Post Earthquake Shelter and Housing.* Oakland, Calif.: BAREPP, Governor's Office of Emergency Services, and the National Center for Earthquake Engineering Research.

1992a.   *Proceedings: Joint Symposium on Earthquake Hazards Management in Urban Areas.* Oakland, Calif.: BAREPP and Governor's Office of Emergency Services.

Berke, P. R., and T. Beatley.

1992.   *Planning for Earthquakes: Risk, Politics, and Policy.* Baltimore: Johns Hopkins University Press.

Berke, P. R., J. Kartez, and D. Wenger.

1993.   Recovery after Disaster: Achieving Sustainable Development, Mitigation, and Equity. *Disasters* (London) 17 (2): 93–109.

Berkeley, Charleston, and Dorchester Counties (BCD) Council of Government.

1990.   *Disaster Analysis and Recovery Tracking System (DARTS) Project Management Report.* Charleston, S.C.: BCD Council of Governments.

1990a.   *Mapping the 1990 Census, Berkeley County.* Vol. 1. Charleston, S.C.: BCD Council of Governments.

Berlin, G. L.

1980.   *Earthquakes and the Urban Environment.* Vols. 1–3. Boca Raton, Fla.: CRC Press.

Bertero, V.

1994.   The Nature of the Earthquake Problem; Occurrence of an Earthquake Disaster; and Control of Seismic Risks. Advanced Study in Earthquake Engineering Practice. In *Earthquake Engineering Research Center Short Course Proceedings.* Richmond, Calif.: Earthquake Engineering Research Center.

ed. 1989. *Lessons Learned from the 1985 Mexico Earthquake.* Publication no. 89–02. Richmond, Calif.: Earthquake Engineering Research Center.

Bilateral Technical Cooperation Project.

1989.   *Mitigation of Urban Seismic Risk: Actions to Reduce the Impact of Earthquakes on Highly Vulnerable Areas of Mexico City: First Year Report, April 1988–April 1989.* Cambridge, England: Bilateral Technical Cooperation Project between the Governments of Mexico and United Kingdom (Project team: Disaster Management Centre, Oxford Polytechnic, Cambridge Architectural Research, Ltd., and Departamento del Distrito Federal, Secretaria General de Obras, Direccion General de Reordenacion Urbana y Proteccion Ecologia).

Bolin, R.

1985.   Disasters and Long-Term Recovery Policy: A Focus on Housing and Families. *Policy Studies Review* 4 (4): 709–15.

Bolin, R. C., and L. M. Stanford.
    1991.   Shelter, Housing, and Recovery: A Comparison of U.S. Disasters.
                Disasters (London) 15 (1): 24–34.
    1993.   *Emergency Sheltering and Housing of Earthquake Victims: The
                Case of Santa Cruz County. The Loma Prieta, California, Earth-
                quake of October 17, 1989.* U.S. Geological Survey Professional
                Paper 1553-B. Washington, D.C.: GPO.
Bolton, P., E. Liebow, and J. Olson.
    1993.   Community Context and Uncertainty following a Damaging
                Earthquake: Low Income Latinos in Los Angeles. *Environmen-
                tal Professional* 15 (3): 240–47.
Booth, E. D., A. M. Chandler, P. K. C. Wong, and A. W. Coburn.
    1991.   *The Luzon, Philippines, Earthquake of 16 July 1990: A Field Re-
                port by Earthquake Engineering Field Investigation Team
                (EEFIT).* London: EEFIT.
Bourque, L., and L. Russell.
    1994.   *Resident Responses to the Loma Prieta Earthquake: A Summary
                Report.* Oakland, Calif.: Governor's Office of Emergency Ser-
                vices, Earthquake Program.
Boyd, B. M.
    1989.   The Way It Should Be Remembered. *New York Times Magazine,*
                19 November, pp. 44–45, 90–92.
Brown, J. M., and P. M. Gerhart.
    1989.   *Utilization of the Mortgage Finance and the Insurance Industries
                to Induce the Private Procurement of Earthquake Insurance: Pos-
                sible Anti-Trust Implications.* Working Paper no. 66. Boulder: In-
                stitute of Behavioral Science, University of Colorado.
Brown, P. L.
    1996.   Higher and Drier, Illinois Town Is Reborn. *New York Times,* 6
                May, pp. 1, 10.
Brushkin, E. J., and B. Daughtery.
    1989.   *Assessing the Effects of the 1989 Northern California Earthquake
                on Conventional Mortgage Pass Throughs.* New York: Mortgage
                Securities Research, Goldman, Sachs, and Co.
Building Research Institute.
    1996.   *A Survey Report for Building Damages Due to the 1995 Hyogo-
                Ken Nanbu Earthquake.* Ibaraki, Japan: Building Research In-
                stitute, Ministry of Construction.
Bureau of the Census, U.S.
    1990.   *American Housing Survey for the United States.* Washington,
                D.C.: Bureau of the Census.
    1993.   *Statistical Abstract of the U.S., 1993.* National Data Book, U.S.
                Department of Commerce, Economic and Statistics Administra-
                tion. Washington, D.C.: Bureau of the Census.
Burt, T.
    1986.   Questions Arise over Handling of Worldwide Aid. *Mexico City
                News,* 19 September, p. 14.

California Department of Insurance.
    1992.   *California Residential Earthquake Recovery Fund Program: History of Implementation, 1991–1992.* Sacramento: California Department of Insurance.

Cambridge Architectural Research.
    1995.   *Loss Estimation Model, Developed for Multi-hazard Conditions in Britain and Europe.* Cambridge, England: Cambridge Architectural Research.

Chen, Y., T. Kam-ling, F. Chen, Z. Gao, and Z. Chen, eds.
    1988.   *The Great Tangshan Earthquake of 1976: Anatomy of a Disaster.* Oxford: Pergamon Press.

Cisneros Sosa, A.
    1988.   Organizaciones Sociales en la Reconstruccion Habitacional de la Ciudad de Mexico. *Estud Demograficos y Urbanos* 3:339 52.

Coburn, A. W., and J. D. L. Leslie.
    1985.   *Dhamar Building Education Project: Project Assessment.* Yemen Arab Republic: Executive Office of the Supreme Council for Reconstruction.

Coburn, A. W., H. Ohashi-Murakami, and Y. Ohta.
    1987.   *Factors Affecting Fatalities and Injuries in Earthquakes. Internal Report for the Chair of Engineering Seismology and Earthquake Disaster Prevention Planning.* Hokkaido, Japan: Department of Architectural Engineering, Hokkaido University.

Coburn, A. W., and R. Spence.
    1992.   *Earthquake: Protection.* Chinchester, England: John Wiley and Sons.

Cochrane, H.
    1996.   Is Northridge a Model for Future Events: What Are the Economic Consequences with and without Insurance and Federal Assistance? In *Proceedings: Analyzing Economic Impacts and Recovery from Urban Earthquakes: Issues for Policy Makers.* Oakland, Calif.: Earthquake Engineering Research Institute.

Cohen, M.
    1983.   *Learning by Doing.* Washington, D.C.: World Bank.

Comartin, C. D., M. Greene, and S. K. Tubbesing, eds.
    1995.   *The Hyogo-ken-Nanbu Earthquake: Preliminary Reconnaissance Report.* Oakland, Calif.: Earthquake Engineering Research Institute.

Comerio, M. C.
    1992.   Hazards Mitigation and Housing Recovery: Watsonville and San Francisco One Year Later. In *Disasters and the Small Dwelling,* edited by Y. Aysan and I. Davis. London: James and James.
    1992a.   Impacts of the Los Angeles Retrofit Ordinance on Residential Buildings. *Earthquake Spectra* 8 (1): 79–94.
    1994.   Design Lessons in Residential Rehabilitation. *Earthquake Spectra* 10 (1): 43–64.
    1995.   *Northridge Housing Losses.* Oakland, Calif.: Governor's Office of Emergency Services.

1996.   The Legacy of Loma Prieta. *Urban Land* 55 (10): 59–61, 116.

Comerio, M. C., with Hamilton, Rabinovitz, and Alschuler, Inc. (Comerio with HR&A).

1996.   *The Impact of Housing Losses in the Northridge Earthquake: Recovery and Reconstruction Issues.* Final report on grant no. CMS 9416482 to the National Science Foundation. Berkeley: Center for Environmental Design Research, University of California.

Comerio, M. C., J. D. Landis, and C. J. Firpo.

1996.   *Residential Earthquake Recovery.* Berkeley: California Policy Seminar, University of California.

Comerio, M. C., J. D. Landis, and Y. Rofé.

1994.   Post Disaster Residential Rebuilding. Working paper no. 608. Berkeley: Institute of Urban and Regional Development, University of California.

Commerce (U.S. Department of).

1994.   *The Great Flood of 1993.* Washington, D.C.: National Oceanic Atmospheric Administration, National Weather Service Natural Disaster Survey Report.

Congressional Research Service, United States Library of Congress.

1992.   *A Descriptive Analysis of Federal Relief Insurance, and Loss Reduction Program for Natural Hazards, US House of Representatives: A Report Prepared Pursuant to the Request of the Committee on Banking, Finance, and Urban Affairs.* Washington, D.C.: Subcommittee on Policy Research and Insurance, 102nd Congress, 2nd Session, October 15, 1992, Committee Print 102–15.

Cook, R. A.

1993.   *Hurricane Andrew: Recommendations for Building Codes and Building Code Enforcement.* Tallahassee: Florida Dept. of Community Affairs, Division of Housing and Community Development.

Council of Economic Advisors, Office of the President.

1995.   *Economic Report of the President. Transmitted to Congress, February, Together with the Annual Report of the Council of Economic Advisors.* Reprinted without alteration. Lanham, Md.: Bernam.

County Supervisors Association of California.

1992.   Report of the County Supervisors Association of California, Earthquake Task Force Issues Summary, Loma Prieta Earthquake Unmet Needs Action Plan. *Earthquake Update* 4 (16): 1–8.

Cuny, F. C.

1983.   *Disasters and Development.* New York: Oxfam America, Oxford University Press.

Dacy, D. C., and H. Kunreuther.

1969.   *The Economics of Natural Disasters: Implications for Federal Policy.* New York: Free Press.

Degg, M. R.
 1989. Earthquake Hazard Assessment after Mexico (1985). *Disasters* (London) 13 (3): 237–46.

DeParle, J.
 1996. Slamming the Door: The Year That Housing Died. *New York Times Magazine,* 20 October, pp. 52–57, 68, 94.

Diacon, D.
 1992. Typhoon Resistant Housing in the Philippines: The Core Shelter Project. *Disasters* (London) 16 (3): 266–71.

 1992a. *Typhoon Resistant Housing in the Philippines—A Success Story.* Leicestershire, England: Building and Social Housing Foundation.

Dietz, D.
 1995. New Hope for San Francisco's Skid Row. *San Francisco Chronicle,* 24 July, pp. 1, 4.

Direccion General de Renovacion Habitacional Popular.
 1986. *Housing Reconstruction in the Federal District, Operational Program.* Mexico City: Departamento del Distrito Federal.

 1987. *Imagenes, Renovacion Habitacional Popular.* Mexico City: Departamento del Distrito Federal.

 1987a. *Reconstruction Program in Mexico City: Progress Report of the Program: A Synthesis, October 1985 March 1987.* Mexico City: Departamento del Distrito Federal.

Direccion General de Reordenacion Urbana y Proteccion Ecologica.
 1986. *Projecto de Normas de Conservacion para Zonas Patrimoniales.* Mexico City: Departamento del Distrito Federal.

Disaster Recovery.
 1992. The Wrath of Hurricane Andrew. *Disaster Recovery* 5 (4): 10 23.

Drabek, T. E.
 1986. *Human System Responses to Disaster.* New York: Springer Verlag.

Durkin, M., and J. Hopkins.
 1987. The San Salvador Earthquake of October 10, 1986—Architecture and Urban Planning. *Earthquake Spectra* 3 (3): 609–19.

Dynes R., E. Quarentelli, and D. Wenger.
 1990. *Individual and Organizational Response to the 1985 Mexico City Earthquake.* Disaster Research Center, Book and Monograph series, no. 24. Newark: University of Delaware.

Eadie, C.
 1996. *Kobe Eight Months After: Images of the "Interim City." EERI Special Earthquake Report.* Oakland, Calif.: Earthquake Engineering Research Institute.

Earthquake Engineering Research Institute (EERI).
 1988. The 1985 Mexico City Earthquake, Part A. *Earthquake Spectra* 4:3.
 1988a. The 1985 Mexico City Earthquake, Part B. *Earthquake Spectra* 4:4.
 1989. The 1985 Mexico City Earthquake, Part C. *Earthquake Spectra* 5:1.
 1990. Loma Prieta Earthquake Reconnaissance Report. *Earthquake Spectra* suppl., 6:2.

1995.   Northridge Earthquake Reconnaissance Report, Volume 1.
            Earthquake Spectra suppl. C, 11:1.
1996.   Northridge Earthquake Reconnaissance Report, Volume 2.
            Earthquake Spectra suppl. C, 11:4.
1996a.   *Public Policy and Building Safety.* Oakland, Calif.: EERI.
1996b.   *Scenario for a Magnitude 7.0 Earthquake on the Hayward Fault.*
            Oakland, Calif.: EERI.
Earthquake Engineering Research Institute (EERI) Ad Hoc Committee on Seis-
            mic Performance.
1994.   *Expected Seismic Performance of Buildings.* Oakland, Calif.:
            EERI.
Earthquake Reconstruction Programme, Formulation Mission to the Islamic Re-
            public of Iran.
1990.   *Mission Report and Technical Review of the Impact of the Earth-
            quake of 21 June 1990 in the Provinces of Gilan and Zanjan.*
            United Nations Development Programme, Office of the United
            Nations Disaster Relief Co-ordinator. New York: United Nations.
Echeverria, E.
1990.   Summary Paper: Mexico City Earthquake—Reconstruction, Re-
            search Mitigation. In *Proceedings of the Workshop for Utiliza-
            tion of Research on Engineering and Socioeconomic Aspects of
            the 1985 Chile and Mexico Earthquakes.* Report ATC-30. Red-
            wood City, Calif.: Applied Technology Council.
Edmondson, S. C.
1992.   Hurricane Andrew—Did It Have to Be This Bad? *Building Offi-
            cial and Code Administrator* 26:40–51.
Egan, J.
1995.   *Assessment of Site Specific Ground Motions and Liquifaction Re-
            lated Hazards. Civic Center Building, City of Berkeley.* San Fran-
            cisco: Geomatrix.
Eguchi, R. T., J. D. Goltz, C. E. Taylor, S. E. Chang, P. Flores, L. A. Johnson,
            H. A. Seligson, and N. C. Blais.
1996.   The Northridge Earthquake as an Economic Event: Direct Cap-
            ital Losses. In *Proceedings: Analyzing Economic Impacts and Re-
            covery from Urban Earthquakes: Issues for Policy Makers.* Oak-
            land, Calif.: Earthquake Engineering Research Institute.
El-Masri, S.
1989.   Displacement and Reconstruction: The Case of West Beirut—
            Lebanon. *Disasters* (London) 13 (4): 334–44.
EQE International.
1989.   *The October 17, 1989, Loma Prieta Earthquake.* San Francisco:
            EQE International.
1992.   *Hurricanes Andrew and Iniki, 1992.* San Francisco: EQE Inter-
            national.
1994.   *The January 17, 1994, Northridge, California, Earthquake: An
            EQE Summary Report.* San Francisco: EQE International.
1995.   *EPEDAT, Loss Estimation Model.* San Francisco: EQE Inter-
            national.

1995a.   *The January 17, 1995, Kobe Earthquake: An EQE Summary Re-
            port.* San Francisco: EQE International.

EQE International, Inc., and Geographical Information Systems Group of the
            Governor's Office of Emergency Services.

1995.   *The Northridge Earthquake of January 17, 1994: Preliminary Re-
            port of Data Collection and Analysis. Part A: Damage and In-
            ventory Data.* Irvine, Calif.: EQE International.

1997.   *The Northridge Earthquake of January 17, 1994: Report of Data
            Collection and Analysis, Part B: Analysis and Trends.* Irvine,
            Calif.: EQE International.

España, S. M.
1986.   *Programa Interno de Proteccion Civil para las Unidades Ad-
            ministrativas.* Mexico City: Secretaria de Educacion Publica, y
            Oficialia Mayor, Direccion General de Proteccion Civil y Emer-
            gencia Escolar.

Federal Emergency Management Agency (FEMA).
1989.   *Hurricane Hugo: Interagency Hazard Mitigation Team Report.*
            FEMA Report no. FEMA-843-DR-SC. Atlanta, Georgia.

1993.   *FEMA's Disaster Management Program: A Performance Audit
            after Hurricane Andrew.* H-01-93. Washington, D.C.: FEMA.

1993a.   *Interagency Hazard Mitigation Team Reports:* 1) 1993 Summer
            of Flood. Region V, FEMA 993-DR-MN. 2) State of Missouri,
            Region VII, FEMA-989, FEMA-995, FEMA-1006. 3) Region
            VIII, FEMA 1001 DR-ND. 4) South Dakota, Region VIII, FEMA
            999-DR-SD. 5) Kansas Region VII, FEMA 1000 DR KS. 6) Illi-
            nois, FEMA 997-DR-IL. 7) Wisconsin FEMA 994-DR-WI. 8) Ne-
            braska FEMA 998-DR-NE. Washington, D.C.: FEMA.

1993b.   *Building Performance: Hurricane Iniki in Hawaii.* Washington,
            D.C.: Federal Emergency Management Agency.

1993c.   *Hazard Mitigation Report and Addendum, Hurricane Iniki.*
            FEMA-961-DR-HI. Washington, D.C.: Federal Emergency Man-
            agement Agency.

1996.   *Status of the Northridge Earthquake Recovery—September 6,
            1996.* Pasadena, Calif.: FEMA, Northridge Long-Term Recov-
            ery Area Office.

Federal Emergency Management Agency (FEMA) and Governor's Office of Emer-
            gency Services (OES).
1996.   *DR-1008-CA, Situation Report, Applications and Assistance—
            September 6, 1996.* Pasadena, Calif.: FEMA/OES, Northridge
            Long-Term Recovery Area Office.

Federal Emergency Management Agency (FEMA), Office of Inspector General.
1992.   *Building Performance: Hurricane Andrew in Florida—Observa-
            tions, Recommendations, and Technical Guidance.* FIA 22. Wash-
            ington, D.C.: FEMA and the Federal Insurance Administration.

Ferrebee, A., and E. Terrazas.
1987.   Neighborhoods Rise from the Rubble: Mexico City's Remark-
            able Housing Reconstruction Program. *Architecture* 76 (7):
            78–82.

Firpo, C.
   1997.   *Northridge 2001: Earthquake Insurance Policy in California and the Cost of Future Earthquakes.* Working Paper no. 684. Berkeley: Institute of Urban and Regional Development, University of California.

Florida Department of Insurance.
   1993.   *Hurricane Andrew's Impact on Insurance in the State of Florida.* Tallahassee: Florida Department of Insurance.
   1993a.   *Recommendations on Improving Property Insurance Availability in Florida.* Tallahassee: Florida Department of Insurance.

Florida Governor's Disaster Planning and Response Committee.
   1993.   *Hurricane Andrew—Final Report.* Tallahassee: Florida Governor's Disaster Planning and Response Committee.

Fontaine Company, Inc.
   1991.   *An Analysis of the Damage and Effects of Hurricane Hugo and Status of the Recovery One Year Later.* Columbia: South Carolina Governor's Office, Division of Intergovernmental Relations.

Fratessa, P. F.
   1994.   Buildings. In *Practical Lessons from the Loma Prieta Earthquake Symposium Report,* 69–104. Washington, D.C.: Geotechnical Board and the Board on Natural Disasters of the National Research Council, National Academy Press.

Friedman, D.
   1986.   Analysts Say Economic Impact Mild. *Mexico City News,* 19 September, p. 11.

Friesema, H. P., J. Caporaso, G. Goldstein, R. Lineburry, and R. McCleary.
   1979.   *Aftermath: Communities after Natural Disasters.* Beverly Hills, Calif.: Sage Publications.

Fuentes, I.
   1986.   Three More Quake Damaged Buildings Destroyed. *Mexico City News,* 16 November, p. 4.

Fulton, W.
   1993.   In Los Angeles, the Healing Begins. *Planning* 59 (1): 21–28.

Funahashi, K.
   1995.   Damage Statistics in Hyogoken in Response to the Hanshin Earthquake Disaster. Pre-publication draft. Osaka, Japan: Department of Architectural Engineering, Osaka University.

Gaddis, W.
   1986.   A City Struggles to Rebuild. *Mexico City News,* 19 September, p. 3.

Galster, G., ed.
   1995.   *Reality and Research: Social Science and US Urban Policy since 1960.* Washington, D.C.: Urban Institute Press.

Galster, G., C. Herbig, J. Silver, and M. Valera.
   1995.   *Documentation of Los Angeles Earthquake Disaster Housing Assistance Policies and Procedures.* Report no. UI6488. Washington, D.C.: Urban Institute for the U.S. Department of Housing and Urban Development.

Garcia-Perez, H., et al.
   1986.   *Mexico: The September Earthquake, Its Consequences, Rehabilitation, and Reconstruction.* Mexico City: Departamento del Districto Federal, Direccion General de Reordenacion Urbana y Protection Ecologica, Direccion del Programa de Desarrollo Urbano.
Garvin, G.
   1993.   Reaping the Whirlwind. *Reason* 24 (January): 26–31.
Geipel, R.
   1982.   *Disaster and Reconstruction: The Friuli (Italy) Earthquakes of 1976.* London: George Allen and Unwin.
   1991.   *Long-Term Consequences of Disasters: The Reconstruction of Friuli, Italy, in Its International Context, 1976–1988.* New York: Springer Verlag.
Geis, D.
   1987.   Architectural/Urban Design Lessons from the 1985 Mexico City Earthquake. In *Research Progress Reports, 2nd US-Mexico Workshop on 1985 Mexico Earthquake Research, 5–7 November 1987.* Mexico City: EERI, NSF, Instituto de Ingenieria UNAM.
   ed. 1988.   *Architectural and Urban Design Lessons from the 1985 Mexico City Earthquake.* Washington, D.C.: AIA Council on Architectural Research.
Geis, D. F., and C. Arnold.
   1987.   Mexico City as Seismic Laboratory. *Architecture* 76 (7): 75–77.
General Accounting Office, U.S.
   1991.   *Disaster Assistance: Federal State and Local Responses to Natural Disasters Need Improvement.* GAO/RECD-91–43. Washington, D.C.: U.S. General Accounting Office.
   1992.   *Earthquake Recovery: Staffing and Other Improvements Made following Loma Prieta Earthquake.* GAO/RCED-92–141. San Francisco: U.S. General Accounting Office.
   1993.   *Disaster Management: Improving the Nation's Response to Catastrophic Disasters.* GAO/RCED-93–186. Washington, D.C.: U.S. General Accounting Office.
   1993a.   *Flood Insurance: Information on Various Aspects of the National Flood Insurance Program.* GAO/RCED-93–70. Washington, DC.: U.S. General Accounting Office.
   1994.   *Flood Insurance: Financial Resources May Not Be Sufficient to Meet Future Expected Losses.* GAO/RCED-94–80. Washington, D.C.: U.S. General Accounting Office.
Ghahraman, V. G., and M. K. Yegian.
   1993.   Reconstruction after 1988 Armenia and 1990 Iran Earthquakes: A Comparative Study. In *Proceedings [of the] 1993 National Earthquake Conference: Earthquake Hazard Reduction in the Central and Eastern United States: A Time for Examination and Action.* Memphis, Tenn.: Central United States Earthquake Consortium. 1: 501–9.

Glickman, N., M. J. Lahr, and E. R. Wyly.
    1996.   *State of the Nation's Cities.* Washington, D.C.: U.S. Department
                 of Housing and Urban Development.
Glittenberg, J.
    1985.   Social Upheaval and Recovery in Guatemala City after the 1976
                 Earthquake. In *Perspectives on Disaster Recovery,* edited by J.
                 Laube, 263–81. Norwalk, Va.: Appleton-Century-Crofts.
Gonzalez-Karg, S.
    1988.   Nonoalco Tlatelolco: A Human Experience. *Journal of Profes-
                 sional Issues in Engineering* 114 (4): 482–86.
Good, J. P., and S. Webster.
    1993.   *Housing Construction Programs in the Republic of Yemen fol-
                 lowing the 1892 Dhamar Earthquake.* Washington, D.C.: AID
                 Office of U.S. Foreign Disaster Assistance and Intertect Training
                 Services.
Goodnow, C.
    1986.   Remembering the Regis Hotel. *Mexico City News,* 19 September,
                 p. 12.
Governor's Office of Emergency Services (OES).
    1992.   *Post-Disaster Safety Assessment Plan.* Sacramento: Governor's
                 Office of Emergency Services.
    1994.   *Northridge Earthquake, January 17, 1994, Interim Report.*
                 Sacramento: Governor's Office of Emergency Services.
Greene, M.
    1993.   Housing Recovery and Reconstruction: Lessons from Recent Ur-
                 ban Earthquakes. In *Proceedings of the 3rd United States/Japan
                 Workshop on Urban Earthquake Hazard Reduction, Report 93-
                 B.* Oakland, Calif.: Earthquake Engineering Research Institute.
Greene, M., and J. Pantelic.
    1991.   Problems of Temporary and Permanent Housing following Earth-
                 quakes. In [*Proceedings of the*] *International Symposium of
                 Building Technology and Earthquake Hazard Mitigation.* Buffalo:
                 National Center for Earthquake Engineering Research, State Uni-
                 versity of New York.
Guarisco, T., B. Decker, and T. Monson.
    1992.   *Hurricane Andrew: A Diary of Destruction in S. Louisiana, Au-
                 gust 26, 1992.* Lubbock, Tex.: C. F. Boone Publishing.
Haas, J. E., R. W. Kates, and M. J. Bowden, eds.
    1977.   *Reconstruction following Disaster.* Cambridge: MIT Press.
Hamilton, Rabinovitz, and Alschuler, Inc. (HR&A).
    1994.   *1994 Rental Housing Study: Technical Report on Issues and
                 Policy Options.* Los Angeles: City of Los Angeles Housing
                 Department.
Hansen, G., and E. Condon.
    1989.   *Denial of Disaster.* San Francisco: Cameron and Co.
Hernandez Lopez, J.
    1985.   *Los Actores de la Reconstruction, Reconstruccion de Vivienda*

Popular, Sismos del 19 y 20 de Septiembre de 1985. Mexico City: Dipartamento del Distrito Federal, Direction General de Reordinacion Urbana y Protection Ecologia, SEDUE.

Hodges, S., and J. McCray-Goldsmith.

1994. Pulling Together or Pulling Apart: The Role of Government, NGO, and the Local Builder in Post-Disaster Housing Reconstruction. In *Conference Proceedings, Inter-American Conference on the Reduction of Natural Hazards.* Cartagena des Indias, Columbia: Sistema Nacional Para la Prevencion y Atencion de Desastres.

Hospital General Balbuena.

1989. *Programa Hospitalario en Caso de Desastre* and *Procedimiento de Evacuacion.* Mexico City: Distrito Federal

Housing and Urban Development, Region IX, U.S. Department of.

1990. *Proposed Earthquake Response by Region IX Housing and Urban Development.* San Francisco: Department of Housing and Urban Development.

1991. *Status of the Recovery from the Earthquake in San Francisco, Oakland, Santa Cruz, and Surrounding Areas.* San Francisco: Department of Housing and Urban Development.

Housing and Urban Development, U.S. Department of.

1974–75. *Cost Effective Housing Systems for Disaster Relief* Vols. 1–6. Washington, D.C.: GPO.

1993. *Assessment of Damage to Single Family Homes Caused by Hurricane Andrew and Iniki.* HUD PD&R 1432. Washington, D.C.: Department of Housing and Urban Development.

1995. *Preparing for the "Big One": Saving Lives through Earthquake Mitigation in Los Angeles, California.* Washington, D.C.: Department of Housing and Urban Development, Office of Policy Development and Research.

1996. *The Mortgage Market Statistical Annual for 1996.* Washington, D.C.: Department of Housing and Urban Development.

Housing Foundation of the Islamic Republic of Iran.

1990. *Housing Reconstruction of the Areas Devastated by the June 21st 1990 Earthquake in Iran: Plan Program and Budget.* Tehran: Housing Foundation of the Islamic Republic of Iran.

Housner, G. W.

1990. *Competing against Time.* Sacramento: Governor's Board of Inquiry.

Housner, G. W., et al.

1994. *The Continuing Challenge: The Northridge Earthquake of January 17, 1994.* Sacramento: California Department of Transportation.

Hyogo Cultural Center.

1996. *The Kobe Region Today: Report to the Kobe Region Earthquake Response Task Force Meeting, January 17, 1996.* Seattle: Hyogo Cultural Center.

Institute of Public Administration.

1995. *Report of the International Advisory Team for Rebuilding the Kansai Region after the Hanshin-Awaji Earthquake.* New York: Institute for Public Administration.

Insurance Institute for Property Loss Reduction (IIPLR).

1995. *Coastal Exposure and Community Protection: Hurricane Andrew's Legacy.* Boston: Insurance Institute for Property Loss Reduction.

Insurance Services Office, Inc. (ISO).

1994. *Catastrophes: Insurance Issues Surrounding the Northridge Earthquake and Other Natural Disasters.* New York: ISO Insurance Series.

Interagency Floodplain Management Review Committee.

1994. *Sharing the Challenge: Floodplain Management into the 21st Century.* Washington, D.C.: Executive Office of the President.

Intertect.

1986. *Assessment Report: Estimated Damages in the Housing Sector Caused by the October 1986 San Salvador Earthquake and Suggested Reconstruction Strategies.* Washington, D.C.: Office of U.S. Foreign Disaster Assistance, Agency for International Development.

Isenberg, P., et al.

1992. [*History of AB 2409*] *Repeal of State Earthquake Insurance Program.* Sacramento: California State Assembly.

Jaffee, D. W.

1995. The California Insurance Crisis: Earthquake, Homeowner, Auto. In *Proceedings, Policy Advisory Board Annual Meeting, 14 October.* Berkeley: Fisher Center for Real Estate and Urban Economics, University of California.

Japan National Census.

1995. *Japan National Census: Hyogo Prefecture.* Tokyo: Department of the Census.

Japanese NGO Forum.

1996. *Japan NGO Country Report.* Toshima-ku. Tokyo: Japanese NGO Forum for Habitat II.

Kagami, H., K. Kuge, B. K. Bhartia, and S. Sakai.

1994. *Reconnaissance Report on the 30 September Earthquake in the State of Mahrashtra, India: Research Report on Natural Disasters.* Tokyo: Japanese Ministry of Education, Science, and Culture.

Karplus, W.

1992. *The Heavens Are Falling: The Scientific Prediction of Catastrophes in Our Time.* New York: Plenum Press.

Kosowatz, J. J.

1990. Armenia Struggles to Rebuild. *Engineering News Record* 225 (4): 27–30.

Kreimer, A.

1977.   Reconstruction Planning on Shaky Ground: Learning from Recent Disaster Experiences. In *Proceedings: International Conference on Disaster Area Housing; Istanbul, September 4–10, 1977,* edited by Oktay Ural. 5.1–5.19. Istanbul, Turkey: World Bank.

1991.   Reconstruction after Earthquakes: Sustainability and Development. *Earthquake Spectra* 7 (1): 97–106.

Kreimer, A., and M. Munasinghe, eds.

1991.   *Managing Natural Disasters and the Environment.* Washington, D.C.: Environmental Policy and Research Division, World Bank.

Kristof, N. D.

1995.   The Quake That Hurt Kobe Helps Its Gangs Get Richer. *New York Times,* 6 June, pp. A1, A4.

Kroll, C.

1990.   Economic Impacts of the Loma Prieta Earthquake: A Focus on Small Business. In *The Socioeconomic Impacts of Disasters: Report and Summary of Proceedings, Fourth International Research and Training Seminar on Regional Development Planning for Disaster Prevention.* Washington, D.C.: World Bank, with the U.N. Center for Regional Development, Nagoya, Japan.

Kultenbrouwer, P.

1986.   The Collapse of Nuevo Leon: Survivors Demand Answers. *Mexico City News,* 19 September, p. 8.

1986a.   Deputies Advocate Further Land Expropriation. *Mexico City News,* 19 September, p. 4.

Kunreuther, H.

1973.   *Recovery from Natural Disasters: Insurance or Federal Aid.* Washington, D.C.: American Enterprise Institute for Public Policy Research.

1978.   *Disaster Insurance Protection: Public Policy Lessons.* New York: Wiley.

Ladinski, V. B.

1995.   Development and Conservation Aspects of Urban Regeneration in Seismic Prone Areas: A Case Study. In *Development through Conservation: Toward Shaping World Cities, 22–24 March 1995.* York, England: Institute of Advanced Architectural Studies, University of York.

Lagorio, H. J.

1990.   *Earthquakes: An Architect's Guide to Nonstructural Seismic Hazards.* New York: John Wiley and Sons.

Landis, J., and D. Simpson.

1992.   *Policy Lessons from the Loma Prieta Earthquake and the Oakland Firestorm.* Draft working paper. Berkeley: Institute of Urban and Regional Development, University of California.

Levin, H.

1978.   *You Can Build It.* Berkeley: Center for Environmental Design Research, University of California.

Levy, L. J., and L. M. Toulmin.
    1993.   *Improving Disaster Planning and Response Efforts: Lessons
                  from Hurricane Andrew and Iniki.* McLean, Va.: Booz-Allen and
                  Hamilton.
Los Angeles Housing Department.
    1995.   *Rebuilding Communities: Recovery from the Northridge Earth-
                  quake, January 17, 1984.* Los Angeles: Housing Department.
Louis, A. M.
    1996.   New Era of Quake Insurance. *San Francisco Chronicle,* 22 De-
                  cember, pp. B1, B3.
Mader, G. G.
    1994.   Recovery Mitigation and Planning. In *Practical Lessons from the
                  Loma Prieta Earthquake: Report from a Symposium Sponsored
                  by the Geotechnical Board and the Board on Natural Disasters
                  of the National Research Council,* 69–104. Washington, D.C.:
                  National Academy Press.
May, P., and W. Williams.
    1986.   *Disaster Policy Implementation: Managing Programs under
                  Shared Governance.* New York: Plenum Press.
McDonald, J.
    1993.   *Hurricane Andrew and Iniki.* San Francisco: EQE International.
Mendez, L. L.
    1986.   Assistance for the Mexico Earthquake Victims. *Disasters* (Lon-
                  don) 10 (1): 25–26.
Mesa, B.
    1993.   When the Wind Dies Down. *Planning* 59 (1): 10–14.
Metropolitan Dade County Planning Department.
    1992.   *Hurricane Andrew: Impact Area Profile.* Miami, Fla.: Metro-
                  politan Dade County Planning Department, Research Division.
    1993.   *Population Estimates and Projections, Post Hurricane Andrew.*
                  Miami, Fla.: Metropolitan Dade County Planning Department,
                  Research Division.
    1994.   *Housing and Population Recovery Post Hurricane Andrew.* Mi-
                  ami, Fla.: Metropolitan Dade County Planning Department, Re-
                  search Division.
Mexico City News.
    1986.   Mayor Tells Legislators Rebuilding Program Broke, 23 September,
                  p. 4.
    1986a.   Morelos Neighbors Pitch In to Restore Homes, 19 September,
                  p. 12.
    1986b.   Red Cross: 100,000 Mexicans Still Homeless, 19 September, p. 6.
Miami Herald.
    1992.   What Went Wrong: Miami Herald Special Report, 20 December.
Middleton, D.
    1996.   Rehousing after a Disaster: EQC and Risk Management. *Tephra*
                  (Ministry of Civil Defence, Wellington, N.Z.) 15 (1): 32–35.
Miller, H. C.
    1990.   *Hurricane Hugo: Learning from South Carolina.* Washington,

D.C.: United States Department of Commerce, NOAA National Ocean Service, Office of Ocean and Coastal Resources Management.

Miraftab, F.
1995.   A Misfit between Policy and People: The Search for Housing by Female Headed Households in Guadalajara, Mexico. Ph.D. diss., Department of Architecture, University of California at Berkeley.

Missouri Emergency Management Agency.
1995.   *Out of Harm's Way: The Missouri Buyout Program.* Jefferson City: Missouri Emergency Management Agency.

Mittler, E.
1989.   *Natural Hazard Policy Setting: Identifying Supporters and Opponents of Nonstructural Hazards Mitigation.* Program on Environment and Behavior, monograph no. 48. Boulder: Institute of Behavioral Science, University of Colorado.
1992.   *A Fiscal Responsibility Analysis of a National Earthquake Insurance Program.* Boston: The Earthquake Project, National Committee on Property Insurance.
1996.   Disaster Recovery Policies. In *The Northridge Earthquake "Ghost Towns": Final Report to the National Science Foundation,* edited by R. A. Stallings. Los Angeles: School of Public Administration, University of Southern California.

Moehle, J. P., et al.
1994.   *Preliminary Report on the Seismological and Engineering Aspects of the January 17 1994, Northridge Earthquake.* Report 94-01. Berkeley: Earthquake Engineering Research Center, University of California.

Monday, J. L.
1992.   *Learning from Hurricane Hugo: Implications for Public Policy.* Washington, D.C.: Association of State Floodplain Managers, Inc. (ASFPM), and Federal Emergency Management Agency.

Moore, M.
1993.   Quake Rebuilding Efforts Clash with Lifestyle of Indian Villagers. Washington Post, 11 December.

Mullen, J.
1986.   D.F. Rebuilding High on MMH Priority List. *Mexico City News,* 19 September, p. 1.

Murozaki, Y.
1989.   A Study on the Process for Disaster Recovery in Cities. In *Proceedings: Ninth World Conference on Earthquake Engineering (9WCEE).* Vol. 8, Paper SK-2, pp. 1037–42. Tokyo: Organizing Committee, Japan Association for Earthquake Disaster Prevention.

National Academy of Public Administration (NAPA).
1993.   *Coping with Catastrophe: Building an Emergency Management System to Meet People's Needs in Natural and Manmade Disasters.* Washington, D.C.: NAPA.

National Association of Home Builders (NAHB) Research Center.

1992.   *Estimated Cost of Compliance with 1991 Building Code Seismic Requirements: Final Report.* Oak Brook, Ill.: Insurance Research Council.

1993.   *Assessment of Damage to Single Family Homes Caused by Hurricanes Andrew and Iniki.* Upper Marlboro, Md.: NAHB Research Center.

1994.   *Assessment of Damage to Residential Buildings Caused by the Northridge Earthquake.* Washington, D.C.: NAHB Research Center and the United States Department of Housing and Urban Development.

National Committee on Property Insurance.

1992.   Natural Disaster Loss Reduction. *Update* 1 (1): 1–4.

National Economic and Development Authority.

1990.   *Reconstruction and Development Program.* Manila: Republic of the Philippines.

National Institute of Building Standards (NIBS).

1996.   *Loss Estimation Model.* Washington, D.C.: NIBS, in cooperation with the Federal Emergency Management Agency.

National Oceanic and Atmospheric Administration (NOAA).

1993.   *The Deadliest, Costliest, and Most Intense United States Hurricanes of This Century (and Other Frequently Requested Hurricane Facts).* NOAA Technical Memorandum NWS-NHC-31. Coral Gables, Fla.: National Hurricane Center.

National Research Council.

1994.   *Practical Lessons from the Loma Prieta Earthquake.* Washington, D.C.: National Academy Press.

Navaro, M.

1996.   Florida Facing Crisis in Insurance. *New York Times,* 25 April, p. A8.

News and Courier; Evening Post—Charleston, South Carolina.

1989.   *And Hugo Was His Name: Hurricane Hugo, a Diary of Destruction.* Sun City West, Ariz.: C. F. Boone Publishers.

NOVOSTI Press Agency.

1989.   *The Armenian Earthquake Disaster.* Translated by Elliott B. Urdang. Madison, Conn.: Sphinx Press.

Office of Inspector General.

1993.   *Public Assistance Program Administration in FEMA Region IX following the Loma Prieta Earthquake: Report of Inspection #92–9.* Washington, D.C.: Office of Inspector General, Office of Inspections, Federal Emergency Management Agency.

Office of Management and Budget (OMB). Executive Office of the President.

1996.   *Financing the Rebuilding: The Federal Financial Response to the Northridge Earthquake—July 30, 1996 Update.* Washington, D.C.: OMB.

Oliver-Smith, A.

1990.   Post Disaster Housing Reconstruction and Social Inequality: A Challenge to Policy and Practice. *Disasters* (London) 14 (1): 7–19.

1991.   Successes and Failures in Post Disaster Resettlement. *Disasters* (London) 15 (1): 12–23.

Pacheco, C., and G. Soto Curiel.

1986.   *Imagenes.* Mexico City: Renovacion Habitacion Popular.

Palm, R. I.

1990.   *Natural Hazards: An Integrative Framework for Research and Planning.* Baltimore: Johns Hopkins University Press.

Palm, R. I., and M. Hodgson.

1992.   *After a California Earthquake: Attitude and Behavior Change.* Chicago: University of Chicago Press.

Palm, R. I., et al.

1983.   *Home Mortgage Lenders, Real Property Appraisers, and Earthquake Hazards.* Program on Environment and Behavior, monograph no. 38. Boulder: Institute of Behavioral Science, University of Colorado.

Pantelic, J.

1989.   Post-Earthquake Housing Reconstruction in Mexico City: Making of a New Paradigm. In *Proceedings: Ninth World Conference on Earthquake Engineering (9 WCEE).* Vol. 8, Paper 13-2-9, pp. 655–60. Tokyo: Organizing Committee, Japan Association for Earthquake Disaster Prevention.

Perkins, J. B.

1992.   *Estimates of Uninhabitable Dwelling Units in Future Earthquakes Affecting the San Francisco Bay Region.* Report no. P92001EQK. Oakland, Calif.: Association of Bay Area Governments.

1996.   *Shaken Awake: Estimates of Uninhabitable Dwelling Units and Peak Shelter Populations in Future Earthquakes Affecting the San Francisco Bay Region.* Report no. P96002EQK. Oakland, Calif.: Association of Bay Area Governments.

Phillips, B. D.

1991.   *Post Disaster Shelter and Housing of Hispanics, the Elderly and the Homeless: National Science Foundation Report.* Dallas: Southern Methodist University.

1993.   Cultural Diversity in Disasters: Sheltering, Housing, and Long Term Recovery. *International Journal of Mass Emergencies and Disasters* (London) 11 (1): 99–110.

Phillips, B., and M. Ephraim.

1992.   *Living in the Aftermath: Blaming the Process in the Loma Prieta Earthquake.* Working Paper no. 80. Boulder: Natural Hazards Research and Applications Information Center, University of Colorado.

Phinney, D.

1989.   Small Towns Bear Brunt. *Northern California Real Estate Journal,* 6 November, p. 5.

Pomonis, A.

1990.   Economic Losses Inflicted by Major Recent Earthquakes. In *The Mission Report of the Earthquake Reconstruction Programme Formulation Mission to the Islamic Republic of Iran.* New York:

United Nations Development Programme, Office of the United Nations Disaster Relief Co-ordinator, United Nations.

Project CHART (Coordinated Hurricane Andrew Recovery Team).
1994.　　*Hurricane Andrew: Two Years in the Rebuilding.* Metropolitan Dade County, Miami: Project CHART.

Quint, M.
1995.　　A Storm over Housing Codes. *New York Times,* 1 December, pp. C1–17.

Rabinovitz, F. F., and M. C. Comerio.
1996.　　*The Impact of Housing Loss in the Northridge Earthquake on Low Income Tenants.* Los Angeles: Hamilton, Rabinovitz, and Alschuler, Inc.

Ramos-Reyes, A.
1986.　　*Programa de Revitalizacion del Centro Historico de la Cuidad de Mexico.* Mexico City: Departamento del Districto Federal DDF, Direccion General de Reordenacion Urbana y Proteccion Ecologica.

Riordan, R. J., Mayor of the City of Los Angeles, and the Ad Hoc Committee on Earthquake Recovery.
1995.　　*In the Wake of the Quake, a Prepared City Responds: A Report to the Los Angeles City Council.* Los Angeles: Mayor's Office.

Risk Management Solutions (RMS), Inc.
1995.　　*What If a Major Earthquake Strikes the Los Angeles Area?* Topical Issues Series. Menlo Park, Calif.: RMS.

Risk Management Solutions (RMS), Inc., and Failure Analysis Associates (FAA), Inc.
1995.　　*Japan—The Great Hanshin Earthquake: Event Report.* Menlo Park, Calif.: RMS and FAA.

Robinson, A.
1986.　　Mexico Beat. *Mexico City News,* 23 September, p. 20.

Rojahn, C., et al.
1993.　　*Preliminary Assessment of Damage to Engineered Structures Caused by Hurricane Andrew in Florida.* Report no. 55. Boulder: Natural Hazards Research and Applications Information Center, University of Colorado.

Rost, Y.
1990.　　*Armenian Tragedy.* Translated by Elizabeth Roberts. London: Weidenfeld and Nicholson.

Roth, R.
1996.　　Government and Private Sector Initiatives. In *Proceedings: Catastrophic Risk Conference.* Coral Gables, Fla.: Institute for International Research.

Rubin, C. B., M. D. Saperstein, and D. G. Barbee.
1985.　　*Community Recovery for a Major Natural Disaster.* Program on Environment and Behavior, monograph no. 41. Boulder: Institute of Behavioral Science, University of Colorado.

Russell, J., et al.

1994.   Findings and Recommendations of the Residential Buildings Cripple Wall Subcommittee of the City of Los Angeles Department of Building and Safety and the Structural Engineers Association of Southern California. Final Report. Los Angeles: Task Force on Evaluating Damage from the Northridge Earthquake.

Russell, T., and D. W. Jaffee.

1996.   Sharing the Risk: Northridge and the Financial Sector. In Proceedings: Analyzing Economic Impacts and Recovery from Urban Earthquakes: Issues for Policy Makers. Oakland, Calif.: Earthquake Engineering Research Institute.

Saffir, H. S.

1991.   Hurricane Hugo and Implications for Design Professionals and Code-Writing Authorities. Journal of Coastal Research. Charles W. Finkl and Orrin H. Pilkey, eds. Special Issue #8, Impact of Hurricane Hugo, Sept. 10–22. SI8 (spring): 13–24.

San Francisco City and County, Mayor's Office of Housing.

1989.   Earthquake Impact on Low and Moderate Income Housing. Report 4. San Francisco: Mayor's Office of Housing.

Schwartz, D. P.

1994.   New Knowledge of Northern California Earthquake Potential. In Proceedings of the Seminar on New Developments in Earthquake Ground Motion Estimation and Implications for Engineering Design and Practice. Publication no. 35. Redwood City, Calif.: Applied Technology Council.

Scientific Assessment and Strategy Team.

1994.   Science for Floodplain Management into the 21st Century. Washington, D.C.: GPO.

Secretaria de Educacion Publica.

1989.   Manual de Prodedimientos del Comite de Proteccion Civil. Mexico City: Secretaria de Educacion Publica.

Seismic Safety Commission, State of California.

1995.   Northridge Earthquake: Turning Loss into Gain. SSC Report 95–01. Sacramento: Seismic Safety Commission.

1996.   Significant California Earthquakes (Magnitude Greater Than 5.0). Sacramento: Seismic Safety Commission.

Shepard, R. C.

1994.   Floodplain Development: Lessons Learned from the Great Flood of 1993. Urban Land 53 (3): 19–24, 42, 44.

Shunsuke O., and T. Endo.

1987.   Damage Statistics of Reinforced Concrete and Masonry Buildings from the 1985 Mexico City Earthquake. In Research Progress Reports, 2nd US-Mexico Workshop on 1985 Mexico Earthquake Research, November 5–7, 1987. Mexico City: EERI, NSF, Instituto de Ingenieria UNAM.

Sidhu, K. I.

1993.   Disaster Management—Experiences from the Maharashtra

Earthquake. Maharashtra, India: Program Management Unit, Government of Maharashtra.

Sill, B. L., and P. Sparks, eds.

1990.   *Hurricane Hugo One Year Later. Proceedings of a Symposium and Public Forum Held in Charleston, S.C.* New York: American Society of Civil Engineers.

Singh, H., M. A. Thayer, and J. C. Murdoch.

1992.   *The Loma Prieta Earthquake: An Event Study of Changes in Risk Perceptions and the Housing Market.* San Diego: San Diego State University.

Smith, D. T., and D. B. Reed.

1990.   *A Centennial Survey of American Floods: Fifteen Significant Events in the United States, 1890–1990.* NOAA Technical Memorandum NWS SR 133. Fort Worth, Tex.: National Weather Service, Scientific Services Division, Southern Region.

Smith-Heimer, M. A.

1992.   Price Changes in Metropolitan Rental Submarkets, 1974–1985. Ph.D. diss., Department of City and Regional Planning, University of California at Berkeley.

Smolka, A., and G. Berz.

1989.   The Mexico Earthquake of September 19, 1985: An Analysis of Insured Loss and Implications for Risk Assessment. *Earthquake Spectra* 5 (1): 223–48.

Snarr, D. Neil, and E. L. Brown.

1994.   Post Disaster Housing Reconstruction: A Longitudinal Study of Resident Satisfaction. *Disasters* (London) 18 (1): 76–80.

Soberanis, P.

1990.   After the Quake: How Housing and Community Development Officials Responded to the San Francisco Disaster. *Journal of Housing* 47 (5): 276–79.

Solo, T. M.

1991.   Rebuilding the Tenements: Issues in El Salvador's Earthquake Reconstruction Program. *American Planning Association Journal* 57:300.

South Carolina Budget and Control Board.

1991.   *Economic Impact of Hurricane Hugo.* Columbia: South Carolina Budget and Control Board, Division of Research and Statistical Services, Office of Economic Research.

Spangle and Associates.

1991.   *Building after Earthquakes: Lessons for Planners.* Portola Valley, Calif.: William Spangle and Associates.

Sparks, P. R.

1991.   Wind Conditions in Hurricane Hugo and Their Effect on Buildings in Coastal South Carolina. *Journal of Coastal Research.* Charles W. Finkl and Orrin H. Pilkey, eds. Special Issue #8, Impact of Hurricane Hugo, Sept. 10–22. SI8 (spring): 13–24.

Stallings, R. A.
1995.   *Promoting Risk: Constructing the Earthquake Threat.* New York: Aldine de Gruyter.
Stanton, M.
1990.   Small Town Revitalization: Lessons from Watsonville, California. *Urban Land* 49 (11): 20–24.
Steinbrugge, K. V., and R. J. Roth Jr.
1994.   *Dwelling and Mobile Home Monetary Losses due to 1989 Loma Prieta, California, Earthquake, with an Emphasis on Loss Estimation.* U.S. Geological Survey Bulletin 1939. Washington, D.C.: GPO.
St. Louis Post-Dispatch.
1993.   Disaster before the Flood, 21 November, pp. 1–12.
Sylves, R. T.
1995.   *Renewing FEMA: Remaking Emergency Management.* Working paper no. 93. Boulder: Natural Hazards Research and Applications Information Center, University of Colorado.
Tavakoli, B., and S. Tavakoli.
1993.   Estimating the Vulnerability and Loss Functions of Residential Buildings. *Journal of Natural Hazards* 7 (2): 155–71.
Todd, D., et al.
1994.   *Northridge Earthquake Performance of Structures, Lifelines, and Fire Protection Systems.* Special Publication 862 (ICSSC TR14). Gaithersburg, Md.: National Institute of Standards Technology.
Tomioka, T.
1997.   Housing Reconstruction Measures from the Great Hanshin-Awaji Earthquake. In *Proceedings: 5th U.S.–Japan Workshop on Urban Earthquake Hazard Reduction.* Oakland, Calif.: Earthquake Engineering Research Institute.
Tranter, R. A. F.
1989.   Some Lessons from the October 17 Quake. *Public Management* (December): 2–4.
United Nations Center for Regional Development (UNCRD).
1990.   *Socioeconomic Impacts of Disasters.* UNCRD Meeting Report series, no. 45. Nagoya, Japan: UNCRD.
United Nations Centre for Human Settlements (U.N. Habitat).
1989.   *Human Settlements and Natural Disasters.* Nairobi, Kenya: United Nations.
1990.   *Technical Report on Luzon Earthquake of 16 July 1990, Republic of the Philippines, with Recommendations for Reconstruction and Development.* Project PHI/90/F01. Nairobi, Kenya: United Nations.
United Nations Centre for Regional Development (UNCRD).
1995.   *Comprehensive Study of the Great Hanshin Earthquake.* Research Report Series, no. 12. Nagoya, Japan: UNCRD.

United Nations Department of International Economic and Social Affairs (UNDIESA).
    1987.   *Prospects of World Urbanization.* New York: United Nations.
United Nations Economic Commission for Latin America and the Caribbean (UNECLAC).
    1986.   *1986 San Salvador Earthquake: Damage, Repercussions, and Assistance Required.* New York: United Nations, Economic Commission for Latin America and the Caribbean.
United Nations Population Fund (UNPF).
    1988.   *Cities: Statistical Administrative and Graphical Information on Major Urban Areas of the World.* Barcelona, Spain: Institut d'Estudia Metropolitans de Barcelona.
Upton, J.
    1986.   PSD Condemns Pre-quake Building Norms. *Mexico City News,* 19 September, p. 6.
    1986a.   Red Cross Plans to House 8000 Homeless by December. *Mexico City News,* 22 September, p. 4.
Urban Institute and Hamilton, Rabinovitz, and Alschuler, Inc.
    1996.   *Impacts of Disaster on Low Income Rental Housing: Lessons from the Northridge Earthquake.* Washington, D.C.: Urban Institute.
U.S. Congress.
    1950.   *Federal Disaster Act of 1950.* Pub. L. No. 81-875. 64 Stat. 1109.
U.S. Congress.
    1974.   *Disaster Relief Act of 1974.* Pub. L. No. 93-288. 88 Stat. 143.
U.S. Congress.
    1988.   *The Robert T. Stafford Disaster Relief and Emergency Assistance Amendments of 1988.* Pub. L. No. 101-707. 102 Stat. 4689.
U.S. Congress. House.
    1990.   Committee on Science, Space, and Technology. Subcommittee on Science, Research, and Technology. *Earthquake Insurance and Hazard Mitigation: Hearing before the Subcommittee on Science, Research, and Technology, Committee on Science, Space, and Technology.* 101st Cong., 2d sess. 26 July. [Report 141.]
    1993.   Committee on Public Works and Transportation. Subcommittee on Water Resources and Environment. *Natural Disaster Protection Act.* 100th Cong.
U.S. Congress. Senate.
    1993.   *Federal Disaster Policy and Future of Federal Emergency Management Agency: Hearing before a Subcommittee of the Committee on Appropriations.* 103d Cong., 1st sess. 27 January.
    1995.   Bipartisan Task Force on Funding Disaster Relief. *Report of the Senate Task Force on Funding Disaster Relief.* 104th Cong.
U.S. Geological Survey (USGS).
    1907.   *The San Francisco Earthquake and Fire of April 18, 1906 and Their Effects on Structures and Structural Materials.* Bulletin No. 324, Series R, Structural Materials 1, 60th Cong., Document 719. Washington, D.C.: GPO.

1990.   *The Next Big Earthquake in the San Francisco Bay Area May Come Sooner Than You Think.* Menlo Park, Calif.: USGS.

Valery, N.

1995.   Fear of Trembling. *Economist* (London), 22 April, pp. 3–12.

Wachs, M., and N. Kamel.

1996.   Decision Making after Disasters: Responding to the Northridge Earthquake. *ACCESS* (University of California at Berkeley Transportation Center) no. 8 (spring): 24–29.

West, C. T.

1996.   Indirect Economic Impacts of Natural Disasters: Policy Implications of Recent Research and Experience. In *Proceedings: Analyzing Economic Impacts and Recovery from Urban Earthquakes: Issues for Policy Makers.* Oakland, Calif.: Earthquake Engineering Research Institute.

West, C. T., and D. G. Lenze.

1994.   Modeling the Regional Impact of Natural Disaster and Recovery: A General Framework and an Application to Hurricane Andrew. *International Regional Science Review* 17 (2): 121–50.

Western States Seismic Policy Council.

1996.   *Western States Seismic Policy Council Newsletter* (spring): 2.

Wickham, J. C.

1997.   Residential Mobility Patterns of Households Displaced by the Northridge Earthquake. Master's thesis, Department of Geography, California State University at Northridge, Los Angeles.

Witt, J. L., and R. E. Rubin.

1995.   *Natural Disaster Insurance and Related Issues.* Administration policy paper, submitted to Vice President Al Gore, February 16. Washington, D.C.: Department of the Treasury.

Wong, K. M.

1993.   *High Seismic Economic Risk Buildings.* Oakland, Calif.: Vickerman, Zachary, and Miller.

Woodbridge, S. B.

1994.   Missed Chances in the Oakland Hills. *Progressive Architecture* 83 (7): 23–24.

Working Group on California Earthquake Probabilities (WGCEP).

1990.   *Probabilities of Large Earthquakes in the San Francisco Bay Region, California.* Circular no. 1053. Menlo Park, Calif.: U.S. Geological Survey.

Zaman, M. Q.

1991.   The Displaced Poor and Resettlement Policies in Bangladesh. *Disasters* (London) 15 (2): 117–25.

Index

Designer: Barbara Jellow
Compositor: Integrated Composition Systems
Text: 10/13 Sabon
Display: Sabon
Printer: Data Reproductions
Binder: John H. Dekker and Sons